Economics and Art Theory

Drawing on an interdisciplinary panel of contributors, this book presents a stimulating dialogue between economics and art theory and considers how this might aid our understanding of both areas of research.

The collection explores themes which both fields share, including rationality, abstraction and model building, the nature of social reality, representation and transformation. The contributions employ a broad range of methods to investigate the links between economics and art, and their coverage includes architecture, history of ideas, art theory, literature studies and beyond.

This innovative volume will be of interest to advanced students and scholars of economic theory, cultural economics, literary and art theory and it intends to be a starting point for new avenues of interdisciplinary research.

Stratos Myrogiannis is an Adjunct Lecturer in the School of Humanities at the Hellenic Open University, Greece.

Constantinos Repapis is Lecturer in Economics at Goldsmiths, University of London, UK.

Routledge Frontiers of Political Economy

The Failure of Markets
Energy, Housing and Health
Craig Allan Medlen

Marx's *Capital*, Capitalism and Limits to the State
Theoretical Considerations
Raju J Das

Behavioral Political Economy and Democratic Theory
Fortifying Democracy for the Digital Age
Petr Špecián

Economics, Social Science and Pluralism
A Real-World Approach
Victor A. Beker

Corporations, Accounting, Securities Laws, and the Extinction of Capitalism
Wm. Dennis Huber

Moral Discourse in the History of Economic Thought
Laurent Dobuzinskis

Economics and Art Theory
Edited by Stratos Myrogiannis and Constantinos Repapis

Capitalism and Agrarian Change
Production and Reproduction in Indonesia
Muchtar Habibi

For more information about this series, please visit: www.routledge.com/Routledge-Frontiers-of-Political-Economy/book-series/SE0345

Economics and Art Theory

Edited by
Stratos Myrogiannis and
Constantinos Repapis

Routledge
Taylor & Francis Group
LONDON AND NEW YORK

First published 2023
by Routledge
4 Park Square, Milton Park, Abingdon, Oxon OX14 4RN

and by Routledge
605 Third Avenue, New York, NY 10158

Routledge is an imprint of the Taylor & Francis Group, an informa business

British Library Cataloguing-in-Publication Data
A catalogue record for this book is available from the British Library

Library of Congress Cataloging-in-Publication Data
A catalog record has been requested for this book

ISBN: 978-0-367-61538-3 (hbk)
ISBN: 978-0-367-61541-3 (pbk)
ISBN: 978-1-003-10543-5 (ebk)

DOI: 10.4324/9781003105435

Typeset in Bembo
by codeMantra

Contents

Figures

Acknowledgements

The subject matter of this volume is the outcome of an exploratory project that started between Economists in Goldsmiths and the Independent Social Research Foundation (ISRF) that intends to open new avenues of interdisciplinary research between economics, the social sciences and the humanities. ISRF under the guidance of Louise Braddock awarded funding for a workshop on the 4th and 5th of July 2019 titled *Economics and the Plastic Arts*. It is this workshop that brought forth the volume both in its subject matter and in the specific contributions it covers. The workshop had a number of sessions by the following academics (in no particular order): John Latsis, Foteini Lika, C.D. Rose, Stratos Myrogiannis, Ragupathy Venkatachalam, Sarath Jakka, Astrid Van Der Bossche, Constantinos Repapis, Stavros Alifragkis, Ekaterina Svetlova, Ariane Hillig, Jill Gabbon, Leah Turner, Sara Stevano, Jorella Andrews, Louise Braddock, Sheila Dow, Jamie Morgan, Claire Pignol and Michael Uebel. There was also a very imaginative installation in the Richard Hoggart Building in Goldsmiths of works by artist Leah Durner that acted as visual anchors to the themes of the workshop. The workshop had a number of participants that contributed to the discussion, especially Victoria Chick, Christopher Newfield, Claudia Jefferies and Edgar Gutierrez. We would like to thank everyone, as this volume would not be possible without their contributions, comments, feedback and critical remarks.

The success of the workshop created the conditions for further work on the themes of the papers presented and those that emerged during the discussions. Therefore, it was decided that the findings of the workshop, augmented by further research by a number of the contributors, should be presented to a broader academic audience. This decision brought forth this volume, which explores anew the links discussed in the workshop and adds to the relevant research literature in, we hope, new and imaginative ways.

In preparation for the volume we benefited from the expert advice by ISRF during the various stages of the process, and we are grateful for the financial support. Christopher Newfield, Louise Braddock, Lars Cornelissen and Stuart Wilson have been constant friends during this journey. Finally, we would like to thank Routledge for the excellent support during the review and publication process and, specifically, Andy Hamphries, Emma Morley and Natalie Tomlinson.

We are very thankful to all that helped throughout this process, and we accept the sole rights to any errors found in the result.

Stratos Myrogiannis
Constantinos Repapis

Contributors

Dr Stavros Alifragkis

Adjunct Lecturer, Hellenic Open University

Stavros Alifragkis holds a diploma in architecture from the Department of Architecture, Aristotle University of Thessaloniki (2002). He attended MPhil courses on architecture and the moving image at the Department of Architecture, University of Cambridge (2003) and architectural theory, history and criticism at the School of Architecture, National Technical University of Athens (2004). He holds a PhD from the University of Cambridge (2010). His doctoral thesis focuses on the cinematic reconstruction of the socialist city of the future in Dziga Vertov's "Man with the Movie Camera" (USSR, 1929). His postdoctoral research on moving image databases about the city was conducted at the Department of Architecture, University of Thessaly (2015).

Stavros studies models of representation of the modern city and its architecture in different mediums (drawings, photography, cinema, literature) and the narrative mechanisms of space in late 19th- and 20th-century European cultures, with an emphasis on spatial database narratives. His research focuses on integral facets of modernity, such as tourism, and the creative interplay between built space and the moving image in the construction of an imagery of progress and prosperity. He has contributed to conferences with papers on cinematic cities and to film festivals with short, linear and interactive moving image projects.

Dr Louise Braddock

Director of Research (2011–2020), Independent Social Research Foundation

Louise Braddock researches and publishes on topics in philosophy and psychoanalysis. She trained as a psychiatrist before gaining her PhD in philosophy from the University of Reading in 2000. From 2006 to 2017, she was a Bye-Fellow at Girton College at the University of Cambridge where she taught philosophy. She lectured on philosophy of mind and the philosophy of psychoanalysis and also attended the long-standing Cambridge Psychoanalysis Reading Group. She is currently an Associate Member of the Philosophy Faculty at the University of Oxford, where she formerly taught and lectured on the philosophy of social science, and an academic associate of the British Psychoanalytical Society. In 2000, she co-founded the London Philosophy-Psychoanalysis Group, and since 2005 she has co-convened a regular interdisciplinary seminar in psychoanalysis at Oxford. Between 2011 and 2020, she was Director of Research for the Independent Social Research Foundation, funding social science research.

Professor Sheila Dow
ISRF Academic Advisor; Emeritus Professor, University of Stirling
Sheila Dow is Emeritus Professor of Economics at the University of Stirling, as well as Adjunct Professor at the University of Victoria in Canada. She has worked previously as an Economist with the Bank of England and the Government of Manitoba and as an Advisor on monetary policy to the UK Treasury Select Committee.

Sheila has published over 200 academic articles and book chapters and has written or co-edited 20 books in the areas of methodology, the history of economic thought (especially on Hume, Smith and Keynes), money and banking and regional finance. She has also worked on the teaching of economics from a pluralist perspective. Recent books include *Foundations for New Economic Thinking: a collection of essays*, Palgrave Macmillan, 2012, *A History of Scottish Economic Thought*, Routledge, 2006, co-edited, with Alexander Dow, and *Economic Methodology: An Inquiry*, Oxford University Press, 2002.

Dr Sarath Jakka
Postdoctoral Researcher, ICI Berlin (Institute for Cultural Inquiry)
Sarath Jakka is a Fellow at the ICI Berlin (Institute for Cultural Inquiry). As a part of ICI's research program on "Reduction", he is currently working on a project titled "Negative Capability: Reduction and the Politics of Attention in Mental Health Discourse". He completed his joint doctorate in early modern studies from the University of Kent, Canterbury and the University of Porto as an Erasmus Mundus Fellow at the TEEME (Text & Event in Early Modern Europe) programme. His PhD thesis explores the relations between utopian writing and 17th-century colonial efforts, focusing on the colonial promotional literature produced for a failed English colony in Madagascar.

Dr Foteini Lika
Independent scholar
Foteini Lika studied Modern Greek and Comparative Literature at the Aristotle University of Thessaloniki, Greece, and received her PhD in Modern and Medieval Languages from the University of Cambridge. She has taught Modern Greek and European Literature at the University of Cambridge, the Aristotle University of Thessaloniki and the Open University in Greece and Cyprus. She has published the monograph *Roidis and the Borrowed Muse: British Historiography, Fiction and Satire in Pope Joan*, as well as several articles on various Modern Greek and British writers. Her research interests include 19th- and 20th-century historiography and fiction, genre theories, poetics of satire, intertextuality and materiality.

Dr Stratos Myrogiannis

Adjunct Lecturer, School of Humanities, Hellenic Open University

Stratos Myrogiannis studied Modern Greek and Comparative Literature at the Aristotle University of Thessaloniki (MPhil) and Modern and Medieval Languages at the University of Cambridge (PhD). He has taught courses on Modern Greek Literature at the University of Cambridge. He currently teaches Literary Theory and Creative Writing at the Hellenic Open University. He has published papers on Modern Greek and European literature and history. His research interests include the history and theory of nationalism and national identity, crime fiction, literary theory and creative writing. He has published *The Emergence of a Greek Identity (1700–1821)*, Newcastle upon Tyne, Cambridge Scholars Publishing (2012) and *From Mystery Tales to the Detective Plot: the appearance of an enigmatic genre in the Greek 19th century*, Athens, Alexandria Publishing (2012).

Dr Claire Pignol

Associate Professor in Economics, University Paris I – Panthéon-Sorbonne

Claire Pignol is Associate Professor in Economics at University Paris I – Panthéon-Sorbonne, and a Member of PHARE (Philosophy, History and Analysis of Economic Representations). Her fields of research are the history of economic thought and economic philosophy. Her publications, in peer-reviewed journals and scholarly works, focus on the relationship between economic theory and moral and political philosophy and on representations of the economy in the novel, from the 18th to the 20th century. Her work studies economic notions (work, needs, money, interest) through a dialogue between, on the one hand, major representatives of economic thought (Smith, Walras, Robbins, Arrow) and, on the other hand, philosophers of politics and morality (Rousseau) or novelists (Defoe, Balzac, Perec, Alexievitch).

Dr Constantinos Repapis

Lecturer in Economics, Goldsmiths, University of London

Constantinos' research focuses on the history of economic thought, issues of economic methodology and interdisciplinary work. He has worked on the evolution of Hayek's business cycle theory and more generally on the development of economic theory during the 1930s. Furthermore, he is interested on how economic models influence government policy and the public discussion. He is also working on the conception of the common reader in economics and specifically reader reception as a tool on how economic theory gets standardised and disseminated.

Dr Michael Uebel

Research Affiliate, Office of the Associate Dean for Research, Steve Hicks School of Social Work, University of Texas at Austin

Michael Uebel has taught literature and theory at the University of Virginia, Georgetown University and the University of Kentucky. He has taught at the University of Texas at Austin in the School of Social Work where he was appointed Lecturer and is currently Affiliate of the Office for the Associate Dean for Research.

He has been a Candidate and Instructor at the Austin Center for Relational Psychoanalysis and Psychotherapy and is a Psychotherapist with the Veterans Health Administration, U.S. Department of Veterans Affairs, and maintains a private practice in Austin. Uebel was Fellow at the Houston-Galveston Psychoanalytic Institute (now The Center for Psychoanalytic Studies) in 2006–2007. He is the Author of a wide range of essays on cultural and intellectual history and on mental health practice and the Author and Editor of several books, including *Race and the Subject of Masculinities* (Duke University Press) and *Ecstatic Transformation: On the Uses of Alterity in the Middle Ages* (Palgrave).

Dr Ragupathy Venkatachalam

Senior Lecturer in Economics, Goldsmiths, University of London

Dr Ragupathy Venkatachalam is a Senior Lecturer in economics at the Institute of Management Studies, Goldsmiths, University of London. He has previously taught economics at the Centre for Development Studies, Trivandrum, India and worked as a Research Fellow at the Artificial Intelligence Economics Research Center at the National Chengchi University, Taiwan. He obtained his PhD from the University of Trento, Italy. His broad research areas include Endogenous Business Cycle Theory, Computable Economics, Behavioural Economics, Causal Inference and History of Economic Thought.

Foreword

Louise Braddock

The Independent Social Research Foundation was established in 2008 in the belief that economics as a discipline had become detached from a proper concern with human life. Academic and professional economists had come to preside over an institutionalised attrition of ethical thought for which economics research was itself responsible. It was foundational for the ISRF to mount a principled intellectual opposition to this state of affairs. In pursuit of this goal, the ISRF seeks and supports research across the social sciences which asserts the value of intellectual independence in going beyond the usual and the recognised and which critically challenges the boundaries of established approaches to the study of social life. Bringing a radically refashioned interdisciplinarity home to economics is, then, part of the ISRF's founding inspiration and the intention of the editors of this volume of essays is, as I understand it, to do just this.

In the Introduction to his celebrated book, *Painting as an Art*, the philosopher Richard Wollheim describes those who "in their scholarly work, make do with a psychology that, if they tried to live their lives by it, would leave them at the end of an ordinary day without lovers, friends or any insight into how this had come about". Wollheim was writing, in 1984, of art history and its practitioners and the remark itself is enigmatic, but the thought it compresses resonates more than nicely with the ISRF's reservations about the state of economics. Equally aptly, the philosophical thesis of the original workshop suggests a template for describing the thinking behind *Economics and the Plastic Arts* which is captured in its subtitle, *Understanding Economics through Art Theory*. The project of Wollheim's *Painting as an Art* is the writing of a critical form of art history "of a type not yet written", one that brings painting and philosophy together with an ethically adequate psychology. Such a psychology was in Wollheim's view psychoanalysis, and its explanatory contribution consisted not in "psychoanalysing" anything, but in drawing into play a sophisticated set of philosophically controlled and elaborated psychoanalytic concepts. For, writes Wollheim, it "must be absurd to bring to the understanding of art a conception of human nature less rich than what is required elsewhere".

While some scholarly attention directed to the links between economics and different types of psychology has included psychoanalysis, my purpose in this Foreword is to note the whole theme and to reference the thinking about the nature of art that *Painting as an Art* presents us with. For "painting", we may read "economics", bringing out the originality of the present collection by drawing on what Wollheim calls a substantive aesthetics. For painting or another activity to be an art or skill such that it produces a work with aesthetic value and meaning, the artist's intentional activity upon her materials must be understood in the most complete way open to the informed observer. To be informed is to place the artist's intention not only within her individual psychology; account must be taken of affect, relationality and depth in her character, of the history and context of both the artist and her work and of much more besides. Only in this way will the observer come to see how (in Sebastian Gardner's words) the artist has succeeded in "making a piece of the world over into a piece of the mind".

One way then to approach the papers collected together in *Economics and Art Theory* is to take up its editors' intention to think of the activities and reflections involving matters of economics themselves as forms of art. And, then, to go on to understand art in just the way Wollheim is proposing. The human world, the editors suggest, is itself plastic to the intentional activity, that is the meaning-making, of economic theorising. We may see economics as the *ars* or skill of moulding and modelling a plastic social world, on which the mind is leaving its imprint and exerting its dynamism to make that world over into a piece of the mind of the economic thinker as artist. And for our understanding of what economics is and does we should not settle for a "conception of human nature less rich than what is required elsewhere".

Introduction

Stratos Myrogiannis and Constantinos Repapis

The topic of Economics and Art Theory, that this volume intends to make a contribution to, appears at the same time to be both extremely wide in what it can encompass and quite narrow in what overlap may exist between these two distinct fields of thought and knowledge. The contribution of this volume is to instigate new avenues of dialogue and research between economics, the humanities and art by discussing fundamental questions on the nature of social reality and the ways we can go about investigating it.

Until now, the primary interest of economists in art has been to examine the valuation of artistic output, and a description of that market and labour processes.[1] As a consequence, there is a large literature on the economics of art, performance and other related products seen from the perspective of how these particular markets function. Related to this is the literature of Culture Economics that mediates the ground between the valuation of cultural goods and how cultural elements shape the nature of the economy. In this literature, culture is seen as a way to understand differences in economic outcomes. As Fernandes asks in the "Culture and Economics" entry of the *New Palgrave Dictionary of Economics*, "does culture matter, and if so, how much?" (Fernandes 2008: 1), a question that summarises in an efficient manner the viewpoint of this literature.[2]

Closer, however, to the subject matter of this volume is the interface of economics with literary theory. In this field, there have been substantial and innovative approaches that discuss various aspects of the interrelation of economics with literary forms, and more broadly the nature of narratives and how they are created. A landmark volume that investigates the intersection of literature and economics was edited by Woodmansee and Osteen (1999) that brought together contributions from economists, literary and cultural historians and showed how fertile the ground of this exchange can be.[3] A more recent contribution edited by Seybold and Chihara (2018) includes topics like rhetorics and economics; poetry in the great depression and economics in literature and novels. The focus on economics in novels is further explored by Akdere and Baron (2018) who investigate how economic ideas and metaphors shape literary texts. Furthermore, Morson and Schapiro (2017) make an impassioned argument for the use of literature to humanise, again, economics.

DOI: 10.4324/9781003105435-1

They note that Adam Smith merged historical and analytical understandings and was not only an analytical thinker but also a moralist. This is also a prescriptive statement on how economics should be re-oriented in the future. Finally, Richard Bronk's *The Romantic Economist* is an important milestone in the relation between economics and the romantic literature. He writes:

> Romanticism is a loose collection of philosophical beliefs and artistic creeds which celebrate the role of imagination, creativity and emotion, while being generally sceptical of the ability of scientific reason to provide a coherent set of universally applicable answers to human problems. Economics is a self-styled 'social science', proud of its mathematical modelling and dedicated to the analysis and prediction of market behaviour of rational agents seeking to optimize their wealth or utility. To many, Romanticism and economics seem to be quintessential polar opposites, perfect embodiments of C.P. Snow's 'two cultures', separated by a 'gulf of mutual incomprehension.'
>
> (Bronk 2009: 1)

Nevertheless, Bronk argues for a new approach in which romantic sensibilities are not an alien but a constituent feature of the economists' mindset.

This volume has similar considerations as its starting point but intends to broaden the discussion by opening up an interdisciplinary dialogue between economics and a variety of perspectives from the humanities that include art and architecture together with literary studies. The intention is not to see the output of these fields as commodities and explore, for instance, the particularities of art market process, but instead as methods and languages of thought and knowledge creation. Interpretations that can reveal novel insights about the economy and the way economists conceptualise their social reality. At the core of this dialogue is an understanding that these viewpoints share, to some degree, a common purpose, which is to shed light on the human condition and its social reality.

At a more reflective level, one of the aims of this edited volume is to explore how the humanities theorise about themselves and economics, and how this can relate and inform the way we understand both areas of study. In essence, what all contributors aim to illuminate is how the theoretical armoury of one discipline can inform the other and create categories that explore anew themes and concepts from a different vantagepoint. The novelty of this approach is the effort to tackle the relation of the humanities and arts with economics both from a theoretical and practical standpoint. In order to do so, all contributing chapters attempt to shed light on topics that appear disparate but share deep selective affinities. This attempt comes as a response to pressing needs, to view old problems in new frameworks that build interdisciplinary bridges.

It could be argued that the core considerations we are returning to in this volume are anything but new. Questions on the nature of art can be traced to the literature of Ancient Greece and Rome. In more recent eras, and more specifically, in modernity, we can trace part of these concerns to the Age of Reason. In his seminal Enlightenment work, *Laocoön*, Gotthold Lessing wrote about the strengths of the arts in representing different aspects of reality each with its own remit. He writes that "…Painting, in its imitations, makes use of entirely different means and signs from those which Poetry employs; the former employing figures and colours in space, the latter articulate sounds in time" (Lessing 1874: 149). For Lessing, this separation is essential as it sets limits to the ability of each art to imitate nature. He notes approvingly this distinction which he finds in the ancient writers noting that "Arts differed, as well in the object as the manner of their imitation" (Lessing 1874: 3). For Lessing, this is essential for the artist to convey naturally true sentiment to their audience. His whole treatise is about the distinction between conveying *Laocoön*'s suffering in poetical form or in sculptural depiction and the aesthetic criteria guiding each art. He notes that the screams a poet writes on paper the sculptor must "soften …. into signs" (Lessing 1874: 19). And thus, the same feeling is expressed through different forms if the artist intends (as they should according to Lessing) to capture the beauty of the natural world.

In this way, Lessing created the groundwork both for renewing the link between the perception of reality and representation and for distinguishing the domain of the different arts in what they can faithfully capture. The central core of this programmatic vision is the link between ancient and modern aesthetics in their interest in realistic representation through an improvement of the theory and practice of imitation. Implicit in this viewpoint is the belief that there is an optimum division between disciplines with remits that would achieve the best result in this singular quest for the representation of reality.

In contrast, the Romantics, and in particular the work of August Schlegel, distinguished between ancient and modern aesthetics, by both problematising the very nature of representation in art and, as a consequence, the distinct separation of fields of art. Schlegel is chiefly remembered today as a central figure of the German Romantic movement. He argued that modern art relates to the environment that arose within specific historical conditions and, as a result, requires a completely new framework of understanding. Art cannot be seen to mimic nature, an aspiration of ancient art that was re-affirmed during the Enlightenment and is the basis of neoclassical aesthetics. For Schlegel, art could not be a mere "imitation" or "representation" of nature; it is the product of a creative force and, therefore, of expression. Thus, he writes "but in the fine arts mere imitation is always fruitless; even what we borrow from others to assume a true poetical shape, must, as it were, be born again within us" (Schlegel 1861: 19).

At the core of this debate between Lessing and Schlegel are the contesting definitions of art. Lessing sees the different types of art as compartments, each with its strengths and limits in capturing and representing particular aspects of reality. For example, statues are good as capturing something at rest. Poetry is good at telling us of something in motion. Each can do specific things which determine it as a field, what it can represent and its limits.

In contrast, for Schlegel, art does not anymore mimic reality but, instead, is an expression of modern concerns, aspirations and thought patterns. In this respect, what fields of knowledge or expression fall within the label of "the arts" or "art" differs depending on how you define the term – Lessing and Schlegel would see it very differently. For Schlegel, it is not only sculpture, architecture and painting, but it also extends to encompass literature which is an act of expression.

Therefore, our initial interest in the subject emerged while examining the various methods the arts and economics use in their respective fields and the way they define their remit. If art essentially relates to the world as something that can be moulded, shaped and transformed, then it is nothing more than a mode of expression, a state of mind. Can, then, economics – with all its devices and other trappings – be itself considered an art? According to some of its practitioners, economics appears to be a rational, enlightenment-inspired machine to uncover our social and economic nature. Economic theory has been described as representing, predicting, abstracting, imagining, mimicking and simplifying reality in its effort to define its method of investigation. Also, economic theory is not monolithic and different traditions that emanate from different eras and strands within the discipline come up with a range of answers on the relation between economic theory and reality. Perhaps, one result of this plurality may be to see economic theory as a romantic reengineering of our society, its values and its processes. This leads us to the following question: How does art and economics mediate this difficult relation between reality, representation and expression?

What all contributions attempt to address is not only the way we see artistic production and economic analysis but also the very nature of reality and the reasons we ascribe to expression. These two different conceptions of art, by Schlegel and Lessing, define an important dialogue of beliefs on the view of reality. It is important to consider the questions that this fundamental dialogue unearths not only in relation to art and economics but also on the very nature of representation and understanding that are the subject matter of disciplines across the humanities and the social sciences. This kind of ontological and methodological questions constitute the point of investigation of this volume. The different chapters attempt to add to this discussion through diverse tools of investigation, that the contributors bring from their disciplinary backgrounds. To aid the reader, the volume is organised in three parts titled: Economics, Literature and Representation (Part I), Economics, Visual Arts and Abstractions (Part 2) and Reflections on Economics, Society and Art (Part 3).

The first part explores the intersection of economics and literary studies through the prism of representation. The idea that our world can be captured through simplified representations is one of the core recurring tropes of economic analysis. As Claire Pignol notes in the first chapter:

> To this end, we will explore the common background shared by economics and novels, as well as the specificity of each discipline. We will

> show, in particular, that, in spite of their diversity, economic thought has two objectives: on the one hand, to explain the social world through mechanisms, that is, to explain the efficient causes of wealth and welfare and, on the other, to advise "the statesman" how best to transform the social world and avoid disorder and misfortune.
>
> (Pignol 2023: 17)

Pignol points out that modern realist novels deal with economic problems that plague the common person and gives these pursuits and issues a dignity by placing the characters and their concerns at the centre of the narrative or discourse. As Pignol notes in this literature, the power by which the novel imitates reality as experienced by every day individuals makes us understand reality in ways that ancient literature and drama would have been incapable of doing.

A refreshing insight in Pignol's chapter is how economics and literature can work together in providing a complex picture of the individuals' behaviour and their psychological universe. As Pignol notes

> literary accounts of economics ... show, by construction, what escapes economic thought: the content of our representations of economic happiness and misfortune, and the opacity and contradictions of our desires, expectations and feelings. Literature is helpful by bringing into the light our singular experiences of economics.
>
> (Pignol 2023: 17-18).

Pignol uses as examples novels written by Georges Perec, Svetlana Alexievich and Édouard Louis to show the vapidity of consumer culture and also the desire behind acquiring new objects. The point of this conflicting depiction is to escape the urge to caricature reality through literature in order to criticise a simplistic representation of economic theorising. Instead, for Pignol, literature investigates where economics cannot go – the existentialist concerns which underlie our material universe and its consumerist pleasures.

This useful distinction between caricature and true representation in conjunction with the debate on the ancient vs modern literature and art finds its counterpoint in the next chapter by Foteini Lika. Her focus on men of feeling reaffirms the romantic vision by quoting Wordsworth "all good poetry is the spontaneous overflowing of powerful feelings" (Lika 2023: 33). Here, the dichotomy of rational vs sentimental man completely breaks down as Lika shows how ironic and even nonsensical it is when characters resort to mechanical felicific calculus to deal with extreme situations of life and death. She quotes Roidis' *Sensitive Man* where the character bemoans his kind heart as he has accepted to wake up early in the morning in order to stand as a second to a close friend who is to duel and possibly lose his life – in which case he may have to also pay the coachman's fare, an extra cost to consider. The sheer banality of these considerations, comically captured, achieves the opposite result to what Pignol outlined in the previous chapter – comic release through irony and the surrealism of the situation instead of deep realism through association with everyday characters and their concerns. As Lika argues, this critical viewpoint offers another perspective to the everyday and the extreme situations characters find themselves in. Irony, incompleteness, contradictions and the ability to imagine solutions that could not be arrived at through reason alone give characters a verisimilitude and at the same time give the reader tools for imaginative tropes and escapism so that they can also survive their own everyday reality.

In Likas' chapter, the link between economics and literature becomes a veritable tug-of-war. Malthus' population doctrine is seen as the epitome of an unfeeling view of reality that should be satirised and even ridiculed. Reading 19th century literature through the prism of the population debates instigated by Malthus' work gives it a depth that may be otherwise lost and shows the deep connection between literature and political economy at the time. At this juncture, it is hard not to remember the first lines of *Pride and Prejudice*, which famously are:

> It is a truth universally acknowledged, that a single man in possession of a good fortune, must be in want of a wife.
>
> However little known the feelings or views of such a man may be on his first entering a neighbourhood, this truth is so well fixed in the minds of the surrounding families, that he is considered the rightful property of someone or other of their daughters.
>
> (Austin 1853: 1)

One naturally assumes that the neighbours being well-bread and well-read had in mind Malthus' work, who noted "It is clearly the duty of each individual not to marry till he has a prospect of supporting his children" (Malthus 1996 [1803]: 492–93). But once this condition is fulfilled, an objective condition any neighbour versed in basic home economics could check out for themselves, the field is open and the marriage game begins. Here, again, in a sarcastic fashion, we see how the narratives of the romantic and the rational get intertwined in a literature that not only pokes fun but also essentially assimilates the logic of political economy.

This dichotomy of enlightenment vs romantic views of social reality that has occupied this introduction until now comes itself under implicit scrutiny in the third chapter by Stratos Myrogiannis. The focus is on the most prominent Modern Greek Enlightenment scholar, Adamantios Koraes, who played a crucial role in the creation of the Modern Greek language, identity and culture. Koraes, with his writings, had the double purpose of helping Modern Greeks gain their independence and form a new state on the enlightenment principles that he espoused and tried to transfer to the Greek-speaking population. His main weapon is his effort to create a Modern Greek language that has the philological gravitas befitting the legacy of Ancient Greek and, at the same time, is in tune with modern sensibilities. As Myrogiannis argues using the framework of Hayden White, historians create a version of their past that suits their purpose and interests of the past and about the past. The discourses that historians create not only define their narrative but also create their own reality. Koraes' efforts and achievements influenced not only his reading and writings of history but also the very evolution of the Modern Greek language and Modern Greek identity.

In Koraes' work, imitation or mimesis as a philosophical principle takes on another purpose – not only imitating nature in a proper fashion, as Lessing would argue, but also imitating the great nations of the West in order to become like them and one of them. He argues of a new Greek poetry across the lines of western literature so as to fashion a Modern Greek identity and language in the same way countries copy the economic organisation of the West. He writes revealingly: "Today, it is easy to transfer Enlightenment from one country to the other. As easily as transferring products and commercial goods" (Coray 1803: 62). And thus, the enlightenment project of representing faithfully reality through a refinement of technique and the separation of disciplines with clear and distinct remit undergoes a dramatic makeover as mimesis becomes the ultimate weapon of artistic expression in an effort to transform reality to meet the scholar's imagination and aspirations for the Greek nation.

With Myrogiannis' chapter, we transition out of the first part of the volume and into the next section that focuses directly on the interface of economics with architecture and figurative art. The fourth chapter written by Stavros Alifragkis focuses on the influence economic terms and their viewpoint of the world had on 20th century architecture. By discussing the aesthetic of the modern ocean liner, Alifragkis shows how perceptions of efficiency became central, not only for comfort and reducing production cost but also as an aesthetic principle. With efficiency and functionalism as the organising architectural principle, there is a clear break with the sensibilities of the past, a brake that, according to the proponents of the modernist movement, is based on logic and rationality for better living conditions and an environment uncluttered by unnecessary baggage.

The relation of this aesthetic viewpoint to economics is not merely incidental. As Alifragkis writes "In *Vers une Architecture*, Le Corbusier's investigations into modernity take the shape of a discussion on design optimisation as an experimental, evolutionary process towards perfected products" (Alifragkis 2023: 80). Le Corbusier's quest becomes a war with entrenched beliefs of the past and an emotional investment into the new aesthetic language that guides production from the time of the industrial revolution. Alifragkis writes that this new type of elegance and harmony in architecture "can be observed in the transformative evolution of production processes and performances that 'come from the workshop or the factory [...] a whole world working with perception, intelligence and precision [...]' (Le Corbusier 1986: 102)" (Alifragkis 2023: 85). It is hard not to parallel this view with Smith's opening pages of the *Wealth of Nations*, where the pin factory is not only seen as a harbinger of the industrial future but also as a moral and even aesthetic improvement over the past. The traditional small-scale producer, writes Smith

> when he first begins the new work he is seldom very keen and hearty; his mind, as they say, does not go to it, and for some time he rather trifles than applies to good purpose. The habit of sauntering and of indolent careless application, which is naturally, or rather necessarily acquired by every country workman who is obliged to change his work and his tools every half hour, [...] renders him almost always slothful and lazy, and incapable of any vigorous application even on the most pressing occasions. (Smith 1999: 114)

And, thus, the break between a sauntering and unproductive past and the promise of a logical, organised and efficient future based on rational decisions and a quest for efficiency binds (neo)classical economics and modernism into a common aesthetic journey.

Alifragkis' chapter ends with an assault on modernism in the form of a question. Is what we call efficient simply what we like and inefficient what we don't? Or to put the question in a more tangible form, is the whole new language of efficiency and economy towards a refined final product more of a rhetorical notion by the modernists and at best an indication of their sensibilities and interests rather than anything else? At a deeper level, this question is aimed at abstract theorising in general. What is its use? is it simply to put in formal terms the theorists' own beliefs and bias and little else?

This issue opens the next chapter by Ragupathy Venkatachalam that questions the very nature and point of system building that are pervasive in the social sciences and, in their own way, in the arts. Venkatachalam uses René Magritte and Escher to show that the point of art is anything but straightforward, and by analogy, the point of modelling should be viewed in the same complex manner. Venkatachalam's chapter introduces forcefully the concept of the absurd in quasi-realistic or superficially natural depictions. How can something both make sense and be absurd is a question that Escher's work brings dramatically to the forefront. What happens when what we see and what we are told are disjointed? The simplest (and even banal) answer is that it gives us pause. Venkatachalam perceptively writes that it does more than that: "Provocative artworks often shape perceptions to varying degrees by cleverly reorienting our attention, thereby stroking our imagination, creating a sense of wonder, appealing to our senses and even challenging our prevailing views of reality and the status quo" (Venkatachalam 2023: 103). It is in this space, opened by the disjunction that new ideas form, that theoretical investigation has its most dramatic breakthroughs. Venkatachalam argues that

> the fruitfulness of such an approach in economics is illustrated by drawing examples from the works of Kenneth Arrow, Piero Sraffa and Vela

> Velupillai. Each of them, in their own way, used formal frameworks to show impossibilities, indeterminacies and undecidabilities, thereby forging new ways to think about economic problems.
>
> (Venkatachalam 2023: 104)

In the chapter we see an entirely unexpected answer to the question of mimetic vs. artistic expression that has formed the organising centre of our investigation. It is not only that art is not intended to mimic nature but more that it becomes a philosophical tool through which nature is observed. Venkatachalam's analogy in the realm of economics makes a similar claim. The most robust abstract theories are there to make us sceptical, to make us question our understanding of reality not to resolve problems in a definite manner. The system builders he investigates – Arrow, Sraffa and Velupillai – have a large and diverse following because they have been able to create unique visions of the social world. But Venkatachalam argues that their success lies elsewhere. Not as theoretical edifices whose completeness and illuminating lustre acts as beacons across a sea of incomplete and chaotic thoughts but rather as refinements of everyday thought that have reached their terminus point, their point of disjunction. Their strength lies in showing the limits of theorising, in the most refined way. They are there not to display their massive ramparts and gleaming turrets but to expose the sand on which they are built.

This answer leads us to a nihilism that seems impossible to escape. If our most complex abstractions are neither the best attempts at realism nor unshakable totems to the power of the human mind, what else is there to hope for? Perhaps not much. The last chapter of the section eschews answers to such grand questions and intends only to offer quick fixes until we come up with something better. Repapis returns to architecture taking the opposite journey to Alifragkis' chapter, by trying to import ideas from architecture into economics. The chapter introduces the romantic notion of the fragment as a building block to broader understandings of social reality. The fragment is linked to a fractured view of reality – an attempt to mediate the ground between grand theory and complex reality. Repapis argues that fragments of theory and theoretical investigation, like architectural fragments, are really *spolia*, repossessed pieces from narratives (like buildings) that stood before and bring with them their own past and world view. This view of *spolia* as forming economics texts which now become new organisms that assimilate but are also shaped by them shows a dynamic element in theorising that can have no endpoint but can yield some insights in the interim. Repapis argues that this is a fruitful way to read complex texts in economics and especially Keynes' *General Theory*. However, this reaffirmation of the romantic viewpoint comes with a compromise. Without grand arches, there is no material to repossess. The romantic poets are proved right, but they are also scavengers.

This brings us to the three contributions of the last section that deals with reflections on the themes developed in this introduction and across the chapters of the first two sections. The first reflection by Sarath Jakka returns to the problem of the limits of abstraction by reviewing the work of E.F. Schumacher. In a way, Jakka's chapter returns to the considerations of Pignol's chapter, which is a question of the meta-economic concerns we have and the limits of the quantitative approach and language of economics. He points out that there are ways to think about the world outside the mechanistic mathematical constructs of economists, and in this, he agrees with Schumacher's belief that we need to place limits on individual and collective needs as a useful starting point. Problems like environmental sustainability cannot be solved within the calculative mode of modern economics. Mechanically accounting for the welfare of future generations and discounting through some heuristic their welfare to compare with the necessary environmental sacrifices of today will not lead to solutions but simply to more confusion.

Jakka's deeper point is that we should not gloss over uncertainty and ambiguity by presenting false certainties. A dose of scepticism is not to be avoided but necessary when dealing with complex issues which have no simple answers. One of the most revealing passages in this chapter is Schumacher's approach to maps. Jakka quotes the following passage:

> The first principle of the philosophical map-makers seemed to be 'If in doubt, leave it out,' or put it into a museum. It occurred to me, however, that the question of what constitutes proof was a very subtle and difficult one. Would it not be wiser to turn the principle into its opposite and say 'If in doubt, show it prominently'? After all, matters that are beyond doubt are, in a sense, dead; they do not constitute a challenge to the living.
>
> (Schumacher 1978: 11)

The point is that map makers and maps as objects of knowledge have a natural disposition to illuminate what they know and obscure what they do not. This reorienting towards the limits of knowledge rather than the certainties returns us to the themes explored in Venkatachalam's chapter.

In the next chapter, Uebel returns to the same problem when he writes "A single true description of a completely independent reality – of the kind, for example, the metaphysical realist posits – cannot exist since the world does not determine unitary answers to basic ontological questions independently of our mobile conceptual assumptions" (Uebel 2023: 175). His answer is to engage in equanimity, since "Perspectivism, like equanimity, is about nothing other than the accumulation of different points of view in pursuit of knowledge" (Uebel 2023: ibid). One interesting aspect of this reflective chapter is the return to mimesis as a way forward but through an entirely different path. Uebel writes extensively on the epistemology of Goethe's "delicate empiricism". Goethe's departure from Newton's conception of light and colour is an attempt to return to a morphology of light as a way to understand and organise nature. This may be an attempt to imitating nature in a very different light than the attempt to find abstract theories that build it up from an elemental understanding – the scientific project underlying Newton's conception. Uebel's perspectivism is partly an attempt to reconcile these ways of analysis as both useful and necessary – there are many ways to imitate nature. Like Jakka, the effort is to create a level playing field in a world in which scientific endeavours, narrowly defined, seem to be the only ones that command attention as truths.

Sheila Dow's concluding chapter discusses another angle of economic theorising – its internal pluralism. Dow notes the difference between mainstream and non-mainstream ways of doing economics and that they hold substantial differences not only in their methodology and ontology but also in the way they interact with other disciplines including the arts. Here, the distinction between certainty, a criterion of paramount importance for mainstream theory, and uncertainty, a feature of non-mainstream approaches is linked to the way one can do theorising. Open systems allow and need plurality of viewpoints, whereas closed ones focus on unidimensional analytical truths. But in both cases, persuasion is necessary to make their point to a diverse audience. Dow notes that Adam Smith was aware that "different systems of thought can arise, the success of each depending on powers of persuasion, with aesthetic appeal playing a powerful role" (Dow 2023: 199). This rounds up this volume on economics and art theory by noting that however much we may think artistic considerations are different and distinct to rational analysis, in the end, our choice of analytical framework is an aesthetic choice, and this makes the whole storytelling of economics, like that of art, an aesthetic as much as a rational experience.

In conclusion, the dialogue between economics and art theory or more broadly the humanities can be a fruitful one in ways that are unexpected. We can corral insights from the chapters in the following three categories:

A Several contributors point to how core concepts or theoretical insights in one field are viewed from outside that discipline, and through this exchange, these concepts gain a more complex meaning. For example, Lika's chapter shows the way rational men are satirised in 19th century literature and, also points to the fact that literature legitimises this new logic of political economy. Pignol's chapter sees how consumer wants are seen and problematised in literature, noting that literature can cover the ground that economics cannot extend into. Alifragkis's chapter problematises the complex meanings that efficiency takes as a production and an aesthetic imperative in architecture and, by implication in economics.

B Ontological questions can gain depth and be viewed from an entirely different light when pre-conceptions are questioned from the vantage point of a radically different field. For example, the insight that creative disjunction can be a way to see some of the constructs of abstract economic theorising is argued by Venkatachalam. Jakka's chapter asks us to not gloss over uncertainties but tries to be open and reflective about what we don't know. This is further strengthened in Uebel's chapter which at its core argues that we need to see beyond ontological clashes drawn along partisan disciplinary lines and embrace the possibility of complex truths.

C This naturally draws us to discuss methods and the way interdisciplinary dialogue may enhance methodological pluralism. For example, Repapis uses the framework developed for architectural *spolia* to analyse Keynes' *General Theory*. Dow discusses the importance of persuasion and aesthetic judgement when deciding between systems of thought and analysis. And Myrogiannis uses the framework of Hayden White to point to the fact that each narrative creates its own reality.

Thus, these contributions are not the end of the journey of interdisciplinary dialogue and exchange. Instead, we hope that they point to new avenues of research to be taken up in the future. This collection intends to show that insights can be found in the most unexpected of places – as long as researchers have an openness to see and an interest to engage with radically different forms of discourse and knowledge creation to what they are accustomed to.

Notes

1 See, e.g., the classic contribution of Baumol and Bawer (1966) or more recently Ginsburgh and Throsby (2006, 2013) for a survey of the literature.
2 Further introductions to this literature can be found in Towse and Hernández (2020) and Snowball (2007).
3 This was by no means the first investigation on the matter. Henderson (1995) had investigated economic texts of the past which had a more 'literary' form and McCloskey (1985, 1994) worked on key aspects of rhetoric in economics – to name only two celebrated contributions in a large field. The introduction by Woodmansee and Osteen (1999) offers an authoritative guide to this literature up to that point.

References

Akdere, Cinla, Christine Baron (2018), *Economics and Literature*, London: Routledge.
Austin, Jane (1853), *Pride and Prejudice*, London: RD Bentley.
Baumol, William J. and William G. Bowen (1966), *Performing Arts: The Economic Dilemma*, New York: The Twentieth Century Fund.
Bronk, Richard (2009), *The Romantic Economist. Imagination in Economics*, Cambridge: Cambridge University Press.
Coray, Adamante (1803), *Mémoire sur l'état actuel de la civilisation dans la Grèce: lu à la Société des observateurs de l'homme, le 16 Nivôse, an XI (6 janvier 1803)*, Paris, F. Didot.
Fernández Raquel (2008), "Culture and Economics", in *The New Palgrave Dictionary of Economics*, 2nd edition, Edited by Steven N. Durlauf and Lawrence E. Blume, London: Macmillan.
Ginsburgh, Victor A., David Throsby (2006), *Handbook of the Economics of Art and Culture*, Amsterdam: North Holland Publishing Company.

Ginsburgh, Victor A., David Throsby (2013), *Handbook of the Economics of Art and Culture, Volume 2,* Amsterdam: North Holland Publishing Company.
Henderson, Willie (1995), *Economics as Literature*, London: Routledge.
Lessing, G.E. (1874), *Laocoon*, translated by Robert Phillimore, London: Macmillan.
Malthus, Robert (1996), *An Essay on the Principle of Population: Second Edition [1803]* (The Six Editions 11 Volumes; London: Routledge/Thoemmes Press).
McCloskey, Donald N. (1985), *The Rhetoric of Economics*, Madison: University of Winsconsin Press.
McCloskey, Donald N. (1994), *Knowledge and Persuasion in Economics*, Cambridge: Cambridge University Press.
Morson, G. S., M. Schapiro (2017), *Cents and Sensibility*, Princeton: Princeton University Press.
Schlegel, Augustus Wilhelm (1861), *A Course of Lectures on Dramatic Art and Literature*, London: Henry G. Bohn.
Schumacher Ernst Friedrich (1978), *A Guide for the Perplexed,* London: Abacus, Sphere Books.
Seybold, Matt, Michelle Chihara (2018), *The Routledge Companion to Literature and Economics*, London: Routledge.
Smith, Adam (1999), *The Wealth of Nations* Books I-III, London: Penguin.
Snowball, Jeanette D. (2007), *Measuring the Value of Culture: Methods and Examples in Cultural Economics*, Berlin and Heidelberg: Springer-Verlag.
Towse, Ruth, Trilce Navarrete Hernández (2020), *Handbook of Cultural Economics, Third Edition*, Cheltenham: Edward Elgar.
Woodmansee M., M. Osteen (1999), *The New Economic Criticism*, London: Routledge.

Part I

Economics, literature and representation

1 Economic thought and novels

What can we expect from the economy?

Claire Pignol

Introduction

The question here raised concern the following: in their accounts of economic life – understood as that part of existence devoted to identifying and satisfying needs and striving to obtain wealth, whether material or not, that is likely to bring well-being or happiness – can novels, and especially those written since the 18th century, inform us where economic thought cannot? In other words, can novels elucidate our understanding of economics in a way that economic thought cannot? In exploring this issue, we do not aim to contradict economics or literature, or to substitute literary wisdom with the knowledge of economists. On the contrary, we wish to avoid two main pitfalls common in the use of literature in economics and by economists: first, the retreat into illustration, where literary accounts have the sole effect of making the general and abstract concepts of economic thought accessible and, second, the use of literature as a means of critiquing economic thought. We assume that literature, and especially the novel, can question economic phenomena and thought because of its proximity to economic thought. This proximity is illustrated by a striking simultaneity, in the 18th century, in the invention of economic thought and the birth of what Erich Auerbach calls the "modern" or "realistic novel".

Far from pitting against each other the knowledge obtained from economic and literary sources, this chapter aims at gathering up all the threads, by discovering what can be said about economic life by both disciplines. To this end, we will explore the common background shared by economics and novels, as well as the specificity of each discipline. We will show, in particular, that, in spite of their diversity, economic thought has two objectives: on the one hand, to explain the social world through mechanisms, that is, to explain the efficient causes of wealth and welfare and, on the other, to advise "the statesman" how best to transform the social world and avoid disorder and misfortune. From this, we will propose the following hypothesis: literary accounts of economics cannot and do not aim to elaborate on such mechanisms, but show, by construction, what escapes economic thought: the content of our representations of economic happiness and misfortune,

DOI: 10.4324/9781003105435-3

and the opacity and contradictions of our desires, expectations and feelings. Literature is helpful by bringing into the light our singular experiences of economics. The economic world calls not only for advice for statesmen but also for accounts or stories addressed to everyone.

This chapter is divided into five sections. The first three explore the relationships that can be established between economic thought and novel. The last two focus on the topics of self-interest and desire for wealth and compare what can or cannot be said about economics from novels of Georges Perec, Svetlana Alexievich and Édouard Louis.

The first section identifies two pitfalls in a comparison between literature and economics, met by Piketty (2014) and Maris (2014). The former makes the novel a living and pedagogical illustration of economic concepts and analysis, the latter, a critique of rational choice theory. We defend the idea that the use of the novel by the economist is really fruitful only beyond these functions of illustration or contestation, in bringing to light a complementarity that is based on both similarities and differences. The second section questions a striking simultaneity in the invention of the modern and realistic novel and economic though and shows what they have in common to grant a dignity hitherto denied to the ordinary individual, whose time is occupied by work and the spirit concerned with the satisfaction of his needs. The third section highlights the differences in forms, readers and purposes between novels and economic discourses and proposes the hypothesis that will be tested and exemplified in the last three sections: the novel explores the complexity, obscurity and contradictions of the desire for wealth.

The fourth section relies on Alexievitch's novel, *Second-Hand Times*, to show the contradictory feelings and conflicts of values lived by the characters with the development of a consumer society in Perestroika. The fifth section recalls debates, in Western Europe, about the same phenomena and questions, in the 18th century through Rousseau's and Smith's philosophies and in the 20th and 21st centuries through Perec's and Louis's novels.

Two pitfalls in a comparison between literature and economics

One way of using literature to explore economic issues would be to search novels for examples which illustrate phenomena, concepts or reasoning. Such literary examples can be historical or fictional facts that constraint decisions or the speeches of characters, which precede or accompany their economic decisions. This is the way in which Thomas Piketty made use of literature, when, in his *Capital in the Twenty-First Century* (2014), he uses Jane Austen's and Honoré de Balzac's novels to establish the historical relevance of his own economic analysis, for example, about return on capital. In Austen's *Mansfield Park* or in Balzac's *César Birotteau*, the return on capital apparently exceeds the rent coming from land ownership or public debt. However, in reality, one must take into account the wages for the work carried out by the owners of the capital, wages which reduce the apparent return on capital. Both Austen and Balzac carefully, and in great detail, inform the reader about such issues. Piketty uses this information, fictitious but consistent with the real data established by historians, to construct a concept of capital that includes all investments, whether real or financial. Then, in Chapter 7, he uses a scene from Balzac's *Le Père Goriot* in which Vautrin explains to Rastignac the benefits of a rich marriage, compared to those of a degree in law. The rich marriage provides a dowry, that is, a capital sum whose annual return will allow a lifestyle far superior to that based on the wage of a judge or even a prosecutor. The difference in the comparative returns of labour and capital, which is the basis of the trade-off between human and financial capital, is obvious. People become much richer by investing in capital than by spending their resources on education. Balzac, a witness of his time, has given us an account, in the words of his characters, of individual strategies for capital accumulation (Piketty 2014: 377–380).

The novel is here a pedagogical tool which makes theoretical ideas accessible and can confirm historical material. Piketty comments on Balzac's characters in the following way: "What is most frightening about Vautrin's lecture is that his brisk portrait of Restoration society contains such precise figures" (Piketty 2014: 240).

> The detailed income figures Vautrin gives are unimportant (although quite realistic): the key fact is that in nineteenth-century France and, for that matter, into the early twentieth century, *work and study alone were not enough to achieve the same level of comfort* afforded by inherited wealth and the income derived from it. This was so obvious to everyone that Balzac needed no statistics to prove it, no detailed figures concerning the deciles and centiles of the income hierarchy. Conditions were similar, moreover, in eighteenth- and nineteenth- century Britain. For Jane Austen's heroes, the question of work did not arise: all that mattered was the size of one's fortune, whether acquired through inheritance or marriage.
>
> (Piketty 2014: 240–241, our emphasis)

Novels, in this respect, can shed light on and illustrate the work of the economist and reinforce the historian's data by fleshing out the longstanding trends in income distribution. Fictitious examples of literature stress such "obvious" trends that the novelist needs "no statistics to prove it, no detailed figures" (Piketty 2014: 241). Literature also indicates the importance of economics through the concerns and calculations that precede the decisions made by the characters: Piketty takes for example the characters of César Birotteau, in Balzac's novel and Sir Thomas, in Austen's *Mansfield Park*, to show the arbitrage between "quiet capital or risky investments" (Piketty 2014: 184). Such a use of literature is convenient and meaningful but limited. It remains an illustration. It expresses, through its fictional language and artifices, the ideas to which the economist or historian can gain access by other means.

But fictions can hardly be read as proofs and both the novelist and economist would be helpless if the information within the novels was inconsistent with that established by historians of economics. This is why reading literature as an illustration of theoretical and historical knowledge in economics has its disadvantages.

The second pitfall, in comparing economics and literature, would be the opposite – to seek in literature a critique of economics. In *Houellebecq Économiste* (2014), Bernard Maris uses the author Michel Houellebecq in such a way: he calls him as a prosecution witness in a trial against economics. Maris's book is a pamphlet against economics, an "empty and boring" discipline, "an incredible ideological charlatanism which was also the morality of a time" (Maris 2014: 8). Why enlist Houellebecq in this denunciation? Because, says Maris, Houellebecq knows better than the economists how to speak regarding economic concepts – work, money, desire, consumption – and how to offer "a fragment of the truth of this world into which we are thrown and which anguishes us" (Maris 2014: 17) and to grasp "the economic malaise that is plaguing our era" (Maris 2014: 21). However, Maris does not aim to make Houellebecq an economist. On the contrary, according to him, Houellebecq "vaccinates us against the economy" (Maris 2014: 23). In *The Map and the Territory*, written by Houellebecq in 2014, the character of Hélène, a professor in economics scornful of her discipline, presents an opportunity for Maris to launch a full-scale attack on economic psychology, on which the foundations of the law of supply and demand, cost-benefit calculations and the theory of rational choice. Economic thinking is not a neutral description of observable behaviour. By describing "a world without ties, that is, without love and kindness", built for "cold and rational" beings (Maris 2014: 44–47), it actually states a moral of interest: "economics is more than a metaphysical elucubration: it is a moral of iron. You must act rationally in a cost-benefit calculation; you must be interested". This makes economics "a precise, vicious and deleterious ideology" (Maris 2014: 45). Here, Houellebecq refers to liberalism, which he defines as "the ideology of free individuals fighting against all", whose morality can be summed up as follows: "Be cruel and selfish. Dominate and kill your neighbour" (Maris 2014: 50).

Maris here assimilates economic theory to liberalism, and liberalism to managerial discourses, and, to these discourses, opposes "Houellebecq [who] hates liberalism, the ideology of free individuals fighting against all" (Maris 2014: 49), and enrols him in an indictment against the "employer's morality of risk, [...] the core of contemporary social and political consciousness" (Maris 2014: 64). He reads in his novels the perception of "the essence of capitalism, based on [the] uncertainty and anguish" of being eliminated in a society of generalised competition, on enslavement through consumption and suffocation at work. However, can we assimilate all economic thoughts and theories to managerial discourses which praise generalised competition? Does not economic thought express, using its own means, the very truth of capitalism? Maris believes the latter to be so, which leads Houellebecq, in the wake of Keynes, to identify with the consumer or saver, who accumulates a common pathology of infantilism (Maris 2014: 73–84).

If one should wish to read novels as a critique of economic thought, what kind of economic thought would be targeted? Is such a critique compatible with the pluralism of economic thought? Maris, rightly, gives a reading of Houellebecq as an anti-capitalist and anti-liberal critique of the economic world. Is such a reading formulated from within the discipline? What relationship can a "literary critique" of economics have with the controversies that arise from the objections of the humanities – history, sociology, social anthropology and political and moral philosophy? Do the accounts of economics offered by literature reveal something new and different? Reading novels as obvious critiques of economic thought may be a very unfair practice; unfair with regard to classical or neo-classical theories, which are nuanced and plastic and likely to give rise to very diverse interpretations;[1] unfair with regard to heterodox economists, who confront mainstream approaches in the field of economic analysis; even unfair with respect to the aim of the novel, which is not to build a critique of economic thought and to propose another theory. This is why reading literature as the means to a critique of economics is fraught with danger. Moreover, it neglects the fact that if literature, and especially the novel, can question economic phenomena and thought, it is, paradoxically, because of its proximity to economic thought. This proximity is illustrated by a striking simultaneity in the invention of economic thought and the birth of the modern or realistic novel.

Invention of the modern novel and economic thought: A striking simultaneity

The historical period, from the beginning of the 18th century onwards, saw the invention in western Europe of new literary forms and a hitherto unknown way of thinking with respect to the social world. In literature, myth and epic gave way to the novel, which allocated an important place to fundamental economic notions: work, need and wealth. Certainly, even before the 18th century, literature evoked these notions, for example in Petronius' *Satyricon* or in the Middle-age *Reynard the Fox*. But it is since the invention of the modern or realistic novel, in the words of Auerbach (2003 [1946]) or Rancière (2017), of which Defoe's *Robinson Crusoe* is an emblematic example, that literature has been bringing the ordinary individual concerned with economics to the status of the subject of serious fiction. Moreover, it was during the 18th century that economic discourse took the form of political economy, that is, of a positive science addressed to the legislator. Wealth became a political issue: states set themselves the objective of increasing, or maximising, the wealth of both the people and the sovereign.

The temporal coincidence between the birth of the novel and the invention of political economy is neither anecdotal nor accidental: if the modern or realistic novel is invented at the same time as political economy, this indicates that the novel and economic theory both express and produce a new conception of society. In very different ways, they both represent a society composed of human beings who live as ordinary individuals, separated from each other, that is, free to define their desires – in particular their desire for wealth and consumption – free to decide, autonomously, what can constitute their happiness.

Literary studies have revealed the importance of economics in the modern realistic novel. One such study is by Erich Auerbach who addresses

> the serious treatment of everyday reality, the rise of more extensive and socially inferior human groups to the position of subject matter for problematic-existential representation, on the one hand; on the other, the embedding of random persons and events in the general course of contemporary history, the fluid historical background. These, we believe, are the foundations of modem realism, and it is natural that the broad and elastic form of the novel should increasingly impose itself for a rendering comprising so many elements.
>
> (Auerbach 2003: 491)

What distinguishes modern realism from previous narrations is that its characters

> are not mere caricatures [...] but terrible realities which must be taken wholly seriously; they are involved in tragic complications, and notwithstanding their grotesqueness, are themselves tragic. In modem literature the technique of imitation can evolve a serious, problematic, and tragic conception of any character regardless of type and social standing, of any occurrence regardless of whether it be legendary, broadly political, or narrowly domestic; and in most cases it actually does so. Precisely that is completely impossible in antiquity.
>
> (Auerbach 2003: 31)

Similarly, Marthe Robert (2000) shows that Robinson Crusoe embodies a desire – the desire to escape one's social background – that might exist in every society, but that finds its legitimacy and the right political conditions in a bourgeois society:

> Robinson Crusoe [...] can only be described in a society in movement, where the man with neither birth right nor quality can have some hope to raise himself up by his own means, even if it means a hard fight against the legacy that prevented him from climbing. It is the genius of Daniel Defoe that foresaw just how much the narrative genre owes its existence to the ideologies of the free enterprise.
>
> (Robert 2000: 140)

The novel is modern and realistic, not so much because it deals with economics, but because it brings the most common economic issues out of comedy. Economic issues, plebeian issues par excellence, affect all individuals, first and foremost the poor, the serfs and the slaves, all occupied with subsistence and productive work. Giving importance in novels to these economic issues, making the characters deeply concerned with the rank of their heroes, means giving economic agents a dignity of which they were hitherto denied.

Economic thought is also plebeian thought, in relation to the political philosophy that precedes it. Such ideology bases the social bond not on reason and knowledge of the law, but on an experience of the economy common to every human being, experience that precedes and denies any prior social hierarchy. This is what is conveyed by Smith's idea that economic agents measure the exchange value of goods in terms of quantity of labour, that is, in terms of the hours of labour of which each agent has an intimate experience. Labour, in its modern conception, makes men equal. The novel, a literary form in which ordinary individuals, concerned with economy, attain the status of tragic characters, like economic thought expresses political modernity. The common desire of the novel and modern economic thought, to place the ordinary, possibly mediocre, individual at the centre of the narrative or discourse, gives rise to both the novel's character and the economic agent. Daniel Defoe's *Robinson Crusoe* is an exemplary illustration of this convergence. However, beyond this common characterisation of the novel and economic thought in the history of representations of man and society, it is necessary to reveal their differences, which lie in their form, the reader to whom they are addressed and their purpose.

Literary accounts or economic discourses: Forms, readers, purposes

The difference between novels and economic thought can be stated in the following way: what do, or can, Dickens or Balzac say because of their narrative art, that Ricardo or Keynes cannot because of the form of their science? This question concerns the limits of economic thought, as a "science" or as a philosophy, and the different, perhaps broader, power of the art of the novel. The question also addresses the kind of truth that literature can discover.

> Why do we need literature, in addition to science and philosophy, to help us solve some of our problems? And what exactly is the specificity of literature, considered as a path, which cannot be replaced by any other, to knowledge and truth?

asks Jacques Bouveresse in *La connaissance de l'écrivain* (2008: 29–30). It is this question, first asked concerning the relationship between literature and philosophy, which we again turn to in order to better understand the relationship between literature and economics. In both cases – literature and philosophy, or economic literature and economics – the texts are addressed to a reader. But Ricardo's reader is not the same as Dickens's. The novel, through the art of writing, affects its reader in a different way from the economic discourse.

The reader for whom the economist writes is of two types. He is, first of all, the social scientist (as well as the ordinary man desirous of scientific knowledge about the social world) who wants to understand the laws of economics. These laws are the mechanisms at work in the economic world. The notion of mechanism is the one that economic thought, since the 18th century, imported from the physical world to the social world. The order of the social world – the economic order – is conceived as a balance between forces, a balance that does not result from any individual or collective will. The mechanisms highlighted by economic theories determine the exchange values of goods, which vary without obeying any intention, in order to achieve a collectively desirable situation. This mechanism is called "harmony of interests" and is expressed by the notion of equilibrium. Understanding the mechanisms at work makes it possible to state the natural laws of economics that govern the economic world, that impose an economic order independent of will. These laws are certainly misleading because they do not impose themselves like physical laws. Their transgression is therefore possible. But the transgression of the natural laws of the social world can only produce disorder and unhappiness. This is why it is necessary to know these laws in order to respect them. This idea has characterised economic thought since the time of the Physiocrats and concerns both classical authors and neo-classical economists.

The second reader of political economy is "the statesman" or the legislator (as well as the citizen wishing to participate in public decisions), who will use his knowledge of the economic laws or mechanisms to promote public interest and avoid disorder or economic misfortune. The mechanisms described by economists may, or may not, lead to a desirable order. There may indeed be forces, or decisions, which prevent the realisation of a harmonious order. The legislator must, therefore, be aware of the mechanisms in order to respect them and correct their possible negative effects.

The novel is not primarily addressed to the legislator but to ordinary human beings who make economic decisions, i.e., decisions about the use of their time (between work and leisure) and their income (between consumption and saving), about the relations they establish with others (in production and exchange) and about the use of money (as a means of circulating wealth or as a store of value). Ordinary agents ask themselves whether their decisions are well-founded: their validity with regard to their own interest or desire – the questioning of individual rationality and its failings; and their validity with regard to the interests of others – the questioning of the socially or morally acceptable character of individual actions when they affect the situation of others. The latter is the most frequent case in economics, firstly, because most wealth is consumed privately and, therefore, the consumption of some necessarily affects that of others; second, because the organisation that results from the individual decisions of some not only affects the level of wealth consumed by others but also produces the framework within which others make their decisions. The ordinary reader will find in fictional stories representations of the effects of agents' behaviours on himself and others. These representations are singular, situated in time, space and in the personal history of the subject. The reader sees the characters confronted with choices similar to his or her own, who wonder about the relevance (with regard to their own interest) or the legitimacy (with regard to the interest of others) of their decisions. The reader observes the transformation of the characters in situations that are imposed on them as a result of their previous choices, those of others and random circumstances.

If the ordinary individual finds interest in reading novels that deal with economic issues, one must assume that she finds truths in them. Truths that, on the one hand, do not appear spontaneously to her and remain opaque in her ordinary relationship to the economy, truths that, on the other hand, are not expressed (or do not affect her in the same way) in the reasoning constructed by political economy. Let us hypothesise that these truths stated by the literature matter because agents do not have a clear awareness of what is at stake in their economic decisions and that economic reasoning is not sufficient to shed light on these issues. This myopic awareness concerns, in particular, the individual interest: novels offer a representation of the possible plurality of interests of the same agent and of its articulation with the interests of others. The economic actions that are effective (with regard to the interest of each individual) and legitimate (with regard to the interest of others) are not always identified with evidence and clarity, nor are they always revealed by economic reasoning. The notion of interest is certainly defined differently according to economic theories and the agents they study, but beyond these differences, a general and abstract notion, called interest, is supposed to be able to gather the agent's motives for action, i.e., what he expects from the economy. Conversely, novels describe how, in circumstances that depend on individual and collective history, the same subject is animated by a plurality of sometimes conflicting interests and passions and sees these contradictions appear in the course of the narrative.

It should not be assumed that the reader would look for and find in the novel a guide to action, a normative theory of decision whose illustration in characters and situations would allow the reader to apply it in their life. The novel is neither prescriptive nor theoretical. Beyond a representation aimed at giving the agent the means for an optimal decision, the question is whether the novel, by putting into text the conflicts experienced by the agents in their own passions and interests, and by making these conflicts appear not at the beginning of the story but as events and their subjective effects produced as these events unfold, can inform the agent about the causes or nature of an economic misfortune from which they suffer.

This question goes beyond inquiring what the ordinary man can discover in reading novels and also concerns the knowledge that the economist can derive from them. Do novels give the economist a view of what scientific or philosophical reasoning is not enough to reveal? If the answer is yes, it means that literature shows what is hidden by economic thought, perhaps because it does not mobilise the same faculties. Indeed, in science, philosophy or political economy, the text appeals to the understanding and aims at a proven truth, which is discovered at the moment and is, therefore, universal. Reasoning, be it deductive, hypothetico-deductive or inductive, is not based on singular examples. Certainly, there are examples, such as Adam Smith's pin factory, which give us food for thought, put us on the path of theoretical reasoning, attest to the correctness of a conjecture or, on the contrary, invalidate it. But they are not essential to reasoning. Once established, reasoning is valid even without an example. Of course, economists use rhetorical devices, fables and fiction. But economic reasoning claims to be logically established and to provide a framework for collective discussion and agreement on an agenda for action. Economic theory is addressed to the legislator to indicate the conditions under which political action can take care of the general interest: to satisfy needs efficiently and to distribute wealth fairly.

It is not the same in literature. Literature would be very embarrassed to demonstrate something by relying only on singular fictions and not on general propositions. It is not addressed to the reader's understanding but to his imagination. Through imagination, it reveals its multiple, sometimes contradictory, often opaque passions. Through the journey of a character that the reader discovers in the course of a story, she discovers truths that are not demonstrated or argued but, to use François Jullien's term, that are "decanted":

> truths that are not obtained through intelligence, but that are the result of a long journey of consciousness; truths that are not deduced but that are reached from the very unfolding of life; truths that are not of understanding but of discernment
>
> (Julien 2017: 33)

Literature, then, gives an account of what neither philosophy nor economics can account for: truths of experience, which can only be shown through the journey of a subject.

It is thus to the characters read as economic subjects that we will now turn, who appear in the romantic tales of Svetlana Alexievich, Georges Perec and Edouard Louis. All of them describe experiences linked to the desire for wealth and the suffering caused by the difficulties or impossibility to achieve satisfaction. Economic thought is well aware of the inadequacy of wealth to satisfy human needs. This is why it aims, from its very origins, to establish the means of increasing wealth and making optimal use of it. Novels question not the objective causes of wealth but the intimate upheavals produced by the desire for wealth in the periods in which such a desire is transformed and deployed.

Desire for wealth and conflicting values

In *Second-hand Time*, Svetlana Alexievich gives voice to ordinary people about the upheavals in their lives and their representation of happiness in the economy produced by Perestroika. She is "piecing together the history of 'domestic', 'interior' socialism. As it existed in a person's soul" (Alexievich 2016: 24), and as it was expressed in the soviet kitchens where, in the 1960s, dissident life and, later, Perestroika unfolded (Alexievich 2016: 40). She tells how these souls were overwhelmed by the changes in material life and in representations of the happiness expected from the use of wealth.

The profusion of consumer goods, the discovery of the purchasing power of money, says a character, "hit us like an atomic bomb" (Alexievich 2016: 43). The explosion is that of desires of which individuals had not been aware until then. The desirable life was no longer the adherence to a political ideal or the intellectual life in work or leisure but access to consumption:

> a Chekhovian life. Without any history. Without any values except for the value of human life–life in general. Now, we have new dreams: building a house, buying a decent car, planting gooseberries [...] Freedom turned out to be the rehabilitation of bourgeois existence, which has traditionally been suppressed in Russia. The freedom of Her Highness Consumption.
>
> (Alexievich 2016: 30)

The testimonies from which *Second-hand Time* was written express the conflicts of values experienced with astonishment and sometimes pain. The rise of consumerism was the promise of happiness but it also implied a renunciation of old desires, of what had previously been considered desirable and legitimate. The promise of happiness, partly kept, is described through the wonder at the transformation of daily life, invaded by colourful objects that come from a new inventiveness:

> Our country was suddenly covered in banks and billboards. A new breed of goods appeared. Instead of crummy boots and frumpy dresses, we finally got the stuff we'd always dreamed of: blue jeans, winter coats, lingerie, decent crockery [...] Everything bright and beautiful. Our old Soviet stuff was grey, ascetic, and looked like as if it had been manufactured in wartime. The libraries and theatres stood empty. Markets and shops had taken their place. Everyone decided that they wanted to be happy and they wanted it now. We were all like children discovering a new world.
>
> (Alexievich 2016: 54)

This happiness is thus accompanied by self-disappointment in renouncing the values on which Soviet society was based: culture, studious leisure.

Childlike – or childish – enthusiasm for riches is also derisory. A woman evokes the frenzy of consumerism:

> Those were the times… when people started changing everything… absolutely everything. Some left, changing homelands. Some changed their convictions and principles. Others changed their possessions, buying all new stuff for their homes. Throwing out everything old and soviet, and replacing it with everything new and imported. […] I ran into my neighbour: 'I'm embarrassed that I'm so excited because of a German coffee grinder … but I'm so happy!' And the character comments: It had only been moments ago–just a moment ago–that she had spent the night waiting in line to get her hands on a volume of Akhmatova. Now she was head over heels for a coffee grinder
>
> (Alexievich 2016: 109–110).

Happiness is parasitised by disappointment, either in oneself or in society as a whole, as the values attached to previously valued goods and activities, including literature, collapse:

> Out of habit, I would go into [a] bookshop […]. Mountains of books! The intelligentsia were selling off their libraries. People had grown poor, of course, but it wasn't just for the spare cash–it was because ultimately books had disappointed them. People were disillusioned. It became rude to ask: 'What are you reading?' Too much about our lives had changed, and these weren't things that you could read about in books.
>
> (Alexievich 2016: 57)

The genuine interest misunderstood

The abrupt introduction of the market economy in the Soviet Union at the beginning of the 1990s made visible conflicts of values that had also emerged in 18th-century Western Europe or in the period of economic reconstruction following the end of the Second World War. At the time of the rise of modern commercial society, two authors, Jean-Jacques Rousseau and Adam Smith, analysed the desire for wealth and the changes in the interest it generates. Rousseau expressed in the same movement the pleasure derived from the superfluous and the frustrations they bring with them as being the source of new needs.

The genesis of society in the *Discourse on the Origin and Foundations of Inequality among Men* (Rousseau 1913) shows how the new-born state of society "left [man] a great deal of leisure, which he employed to furnish himself with many conveniences unknown to his fathers". If the acquirement of these conveniences makes people at first happy,

> it lost with use almost all their power to please, and even degenerated into real needs, till the want of them became far more disagreeable than

> the possession of them had been pleasant. Men would have been unhappy at the loss of them, though the possession did not make them happy.
> (Rousseau 1913: 211)

As production and unequal appropriation of wealth develop, "the crowd grovels in want and obscurity" (Rousseau 1913: 234), and the rich themselves are unable to enjoy their wealth. In *Emile* or in *Julie ou La Nouvelle Héloïse*, (Rousseau 1961), Rousseau insists on the frustrations of wealth, which serves self-love, i.e., vanity, more than self-love, i.e., true enjoyment. In spite of the luxury that surrounds them, the rich are poorly served, poorly housed, poorly fed:

> The noise of the people in a house constantly disturbs the master's rest [...]. The crowd of his creditors makes him pay dearly for the crowd of his admirers. His apartments are so superb that he is forced to live in a small house to be comfortable, and his monkey is sometimes better housed than he is. If he wants to dine he depends on his cook and not on his hunger; if he wants to go out he is at the mercy of his horses.
> (Rousseau 1961: 546)

"These rich fools, martyrs to their own pomp", "these ostentatious voluptuaries, who spend their life in deadly dullness that they may seem to enjoy its pleasures" (Rousseau 1921: 206), use their wealth by sacrificing true voluptuousness and happiness. As Rousseau writes in *Julie*: "I defy any sensible man to contemplate for an hour in the palace of a prince and the splendour that shines there without falling into melancholy and lamenting the fate of mankind" (Rousseau 1961: 547). "Are the richest the happiest? What is the use of opulence for happiness?" (Rousseau 1961: 466)

Smith praises, albeit in a measured way, the wealth that comes from increased trade, market expansion and saving, resulting from the "desire of bettering our condition, a desire which, though generally calm and dispassionate, comes with us from the womb, and never leaves us till we go into the grave" (Smith 1776: 341), which is a form of self-love. The desire of bettering his condition amounts to a desire for wealth, through saving: "an augmentation of fortune is the means by which the greater part of men propose and wish to better their condition. It is the means the most vulgar and the most obvious" (Smith 1776: 341). This desire, like all the passions described by Smith, must be moderated or else leads to dissatisfaction. The poor man's son, described in the *Theory of Moral Sentiments* (Smith 1759: 181), because his desire for wealth is not contained within the bounds of prudence and justice, misjudges his interest:

> through the whole of his life he pursues the idea of a certain artificial and elegant repose which he may never arrive at for which he sacrifices a real tranquillity that is at all times in his power, and is, if in the extremity of old

> age he should at last attain to it, he will find to be in no respect preferable to that humble security and contentment which he had abandoned for it. (Smith 1759: 181)

Vanity of ostentatious consumption and "*l'esprit de système*" threaten the happiness derived from the use of wealth.

Rousseau's or Smith's analysis may partly coincide with Alexievich's narration but not entirely. Her characters express less an opposition between self-esteem and self-love, between vanity and true well-being, than between wonder at objects and disappointment in oneself through the invasion of the desire to consume. The feelings they express echo those described by Perec in his novel, published in 1965, *Things: A Story of the Sixties.* He tells the story of a young couple fascinated by wealth and by the profusion of new objects available in France in the sixties. His characters see in the possession and consumption of "things" a possibility of freedom and happiness, and Perec does not prove them wrong. In several interviews, he clearly states how much "those who thought that [he] condemned a society of consumption have misunderstood [his] book" (Perec 2003: 45), and how the happiness expected from the use of things is not, according to him, an illusion: "there is, I think, between the things of the modern word and happiness, an inevitable connection. A form of wealth of our civilization makes possible a type of happiness" (Ibid.). This happiness, however, escapes them: the acquisition of things leaves them frustrated, trapped "in a strange and shimmering world, the bedazzling universe of a market culture, in prisons of plenty, in the bewitching traps of comfort and happiness" (Perec 1990: 77). It is not insignificant that the universe of *Things* is "shimmering" and "bedazzling", just as, for Alexievich with Perestroika, "the world shattered into dozens of colourful little pieces. We were so terribly eager for the grey Soviet everyday to turn into an American film!" (Alexievich 2016: 54). What could be considered childish is essential: things are desirable less to satisfy a need, even if aesthetic, than because they are the image of a desirable life. Objects symbolise desirable life even more than they make it possible, and that is why they are precious.

In France, at the beginning of the 21st century, Édouard Louis (2018) states how much objects are desirable, less for their function of use, or to mark one's place in the social world through ostentatious consumption, than because they express a desire for life, for a life other than the one we have lived and are still living. He evokes his father's fascination with all technological innovations:

> You were fascinated by all technological innovations, as if, through the novelty they embodied, you could infuse your own life with a newness to which you were not entitled. You commented, in a voice part envy and part admiration, on ads for new phones, tablets, or computers. You didn't buy them, they cost too much. You made do with gadgets traveling salesmen hawked at the village market: a watch that went

> backwards, a machine for making Coke at home, a laser that could project the image of a naked woman on a wall a hundred yards away. In general, these memories are inhabited more by things than by people. You lived out your youth through the youth of these things.
>
> (Louis 2018: 45–46)

The desire for things is first of all a desire to reclaim a life that was stolen:

> A classic pattern: because you felt that you hadn't lived your youth to the fullest, you spent your whole life trying to be young. That's the trouble with stolen things, like you with your youth: we can never quite believe they are really ours, and so we have to keep stealing them forever. The theft never ends. You wanted to recapture your youth, to reclaim it, to resteal it. Only those who have always had everything given to them can truly feel what it is to possess. A sense of possession is not something one can acquire.
>
> (Louis 2018: 43)

We can read in the novels of Alexievich, Perec and Louis that the analysis of the origin and motive behind the desire for the things in which wealth consists is not limited to the alternative between the desire to enjoy things that bring utility and the desire for things to be paraded in ostentatious consumption. If things are desired, it is undoubtedly first of all because they carry much more than well-being or vanity. The separation between needs, the satisfaction of which are necessary for life, and desires, which are superfluous, is inoperative here. The things on which our desire is based are first of all symbols of a life that is obscurely imagined as possible and good. This is why deprivation is much more painful than that which would result only from the wounds of vanity or the absence of the superfluous. This is why fictional characters can voluntarily deprive themselves, like Édouard Louis's father, of riches that would outwardly seem more necessary but would not respond to a desire for life deeper than the enjoyment of well-being. Finally, this is why, in the voice of Svetlana Alexievich, suffering is also born of the suspicion that the possibility of a good life is not only in the happy dream of "planting gooseberries".

Conclusion

Economic science or political economy, as the science of wealth that feeds the state's action in order to enrich the sovereign and the people, wants to set out the conditions of the organisation of society in which agents, at best, satisfy their needs. In so doing, it has put a distance between, on the one hand, the political and social discourse and, on the other, the agents' representations of wealth, the happiness they expect from it, and the frustrations they encounter. Literary narratives take the reader inward and reveal what is at stake in the desire for wealth. In doing so, they open up a questioning that breaks up the abstract entities called "interest", "wealth", "desire" or "need" by plunging the reader into the singularity of his desires: their intermittency, their inconsistency, their darkness and their confusion. It is these truths of experience that François Jullien evokes, and which, the understanding of political economy remains blind to. However, it is this deeper insight that is necessary in order to understand the persistence of economic misfortune.

Note

1 One could think of the use made of David Ricardo by Piero Sraffa, *Production of Commodities by Means of Commodities* (1960), or the interpretation of the General Equilibrium Theory by market socialism.

References

Alexievich, Svetlana (2016), *Second-Hand Time. The Last of the Soviets*, trans. by Bela Shayevich, London: Fitzcarraldo Editions; originally published in Russian in 2013.

Auerbach, Erich (2003), *Mimesis: The Representation of Reality in Western Literature*, Fiftieth-Anniversary Edition, trans. by Willard Trask, Princeton: Princeton University Press; originally published in German in 1946.

Bouveresse, Jacques (2008), *La connaissance de l'écrivain. Sur la littérature, la vérité & la vie*, Éditions Agone.

Houellebecq, Michele (2014), *The Map and the Territory*, New York: Vintage Digital.

Jullien, François (2017), *Une seconde vie*, Éditions Grasset.

Louis, Édouard (2018), *Qui a tué mon père*, Paris: Éditions du Seuil.

Maris, Bernard (2014), *Houellebecq économiste*, Paris: Flammarion.

Perec, Georges (1990), *Things. A Story of the Sixties/A Man Asleep*, trans. by David Bellos, Boston, MA: David R. Godine; originally published in French in 1965 as *Les Choses*.

Perec, Georges (2003), *Entretiens et conférences*, vol. 1, Nantes: Éditions Joseph K.

Piketty, Thomas (2014), *Capital in the Twenty-First Century*, trans. by Arthur Goldhammer, Cambridge, MA & London: Harvard University Press.

Rancière, Jacques (2017), *Les Bords de la fiction*, Paris: Éditions du Seuil.

Robert, Marthe (2000), *Roman des origines et origines du roman*, Paris: Éditions Gallimard.

Rousseau, Jean-Jacques (1913), *Discourse on the Origin and Foundations of Inequality among Men*, in *The Discourses and Other Early Political Writings*, trans. by Victor Gourevitch, Cambridge: Cambridge University Press; originally published in French in 1755; available from http://oll.libertyfund.org/titles/rousseau-the-social-contract-and-discourses.

Rousseau, Jean-Jacques (1921), *Emile, or Education*, trans. by Barbara Foxley, London & Toronto: J. M. Dent & Sons; originally published in French in 1762; available from http://oll.libertyfund.org/titles/rousseau-emile-or-education.

Rousseau, Jean-Jacques (1961), *Julie ou La Nouvelle Héloïse*, in *Œuvres complètes*, vol. 2, edited by Bernard Guyon and Henri Coulet, Paris: Gallimard; originally published in 1761.

Smith, Adam (1759), *The Theory of Moral Sentiments*, edited by A. L. Macfie and D. D. Raphael, Indianapolis: Liberty Fund.

Smith, Adam (1776), *An Inquiry into the Nature and Causes of the Wealth of Nations*, edited by R. H. Campbell and A. Skinner, Indianapolis: Liberty Fund.

2 Men of feeling

Sympathy, imagination and the value of interdisciplinary exchange

Foteini Lika

Five of the main abilities and propensities at the core of Adam Smith's political theory will be discussed in this chapter. Specifically, sympathy, imagination, self-command,[1] reason and reflection[2] will be constant points of reference in this brief analysis of the works of eminent political theorists and celebrated literary men of the 18th and 19th centuries. In particular, basic precepts of Smith's *Theory of Moral Sentiments* (1759) and Malthus' *Essay on the Principle of Population* (1798) will become yardsticks against which a selection of fictional heroes will be judged: from Laurence Sterne's Yorick to Lord Byron's legendary Don Juan and Emmanuel Roidis' anonymous, yet notorious, "Sensitive Man".[3] Nonetheless, with the valuable aid of this ostensibly motley crew of theorists and novelists, I will try to fathom how fictional men of feeling employ sympathy and sex(uality) not only as a means of self-expression and gratification but also as a vehicle for self-subversion. At the same time, I will assess the aesthetic output of this international sentimental commerce, which has flourished with the increasing dissemination of economic ideas and the subsequent intellectual conversation between European nations. As a result, I will have the chance to show how key concepts of economic theory (sympathy, the impartial spectator, preventive population checks) are satirically embedded into emblematic literary texts, both in Britain and Greece, while further advancing the ongoing dialogue between Economics and the Humanities.

In the Preface of the *Lyrical Ballads* (1798), regarded by many as the utmost Romantic manifesto, Wordsworth rejected neoclassical tenets and declared that "*all good poetry is the spontaneous overflowing of powerful feelings*" (Wordsworth 2013, 98). And, while it is quite commonplace nowadays to acknowledge the early 19th century and Romanticism as an age of excessive feeling, it is also true that the 18th century was as much an age of sentiment.[4] I have chosen fictional men of feeling as the topic of my discussion because sentimentalism and its literary byproducts are, in the words of Terry Eagleton (2009, 19), a "luxurious ethics", thus pairing two conflicting aspects of Economics: exchange value and moral philosophy.

Eighteenth-century novelist Laurence Sterne, by both endorsing and satirizing sentimentality (Richetti 1999, 255), perpetuated this paradoxical rapport, thus tangibly demonstrating the surprising elasticity of moral sensibility

DOI: 10.4324/9781003105435-4

(Bell 1983, 52). How did he manage, though, to preserve the sentimental plasticity of his narrative matter? One likely answer to this question would be by conveying to his readers the creations of his main characters' sympathetic imagination. That Sterne's *A Sentimental Journey through France and Italy* (1768) made literary material for the concept of sympathy has long been noted by criticism (MacLean 1949, 399). Nevertheless, as keen readers of Adam Smith's moral philosophy know, sympathy cannot take place unless the powers of observation, imagination and reflection are involved. According to Smith,

> as we have no immediate experience of what other men feel, we can form no idea of the manner in which they are affected, but by conceiving what we ourselves should feel in the like situation [...] By the imagination we place ourselves in [their] situation.
>
> (Smith 1976a, 9)

Thus, an expression of sympathy for another person involves an act of reflection and imagination on the part of the observer or spectator, in the sense that we can only form a judgment with respect to the situation faced by another person by "changing places in the fancy with the sufferer" (Smith 1976a, 10).[5] In this respect, it is quite revealing that Smith chose to illustrate a discussion on how we enter into the sentiments and actions of others with an example inspired by a reader of historical writings:

> When we read in history concerning actions of proper and beneficent greatness of mind, how eagerly do we enter into such designs? [...] In imagination we become the very person whose actions are represented to us: we transport ourselves in fancy to the scenes of those distant and forgotten adventures, and imagine ourselves acting the part of a Scipio or a Camillus, a Timoleon or an Aristides.
>
> (Smith 1976a, 74–75)[6]

As a result, as Rae Greiner noted, Smith's representation of sympathy takes a self-consciously narrative form, thus making the pivotal argument of *The Theory of Moral Sentiments* "both ethical and aesthetic" and the book itself "a work of narrative theory" (Greiner 2009, 294).[7] What is more, in the following extract taken from the *Theory of Moral S*entiments, Smith not only acknowledges the novelists' pictorial capacities but also their instructive superiority over Stoic philosophers:

> The poets and romance-writers, who best paint the refinements and delicacies of love and friendship, and of all other private and domestic affections, Racine and Voltaire; Richardson, Marivaux, and Riccoboni; are, in such cases, much better instructors than Zeno, Chrysippus, or Epictetus.
>
> (Smith 1976a, 143)

Any reader of *A Sentimental Journey* will admit without hesitation that Sterne is a genius when it comes to the pictorial representation of moral experiences, real or imagined. In the next instance, Guido Reni's (1575–1642) artistry is invoked so as to sympathetically portray before our eyes the Franciscan Monk encountered by Yorick at Calais:

> It was one of those heads, which Guido has often painted—mild, pale—penetrating, free from all common-place ideas of fat contented ignorance looking downwards upon the earth—it look'd forwards; but look'd, as if it look'd at something beyond this world. How one of his order came by it, heaven above, who let it fall upon a monk's shoulders, best knows: but it would have suited a Bramin, and had I met it upon the plains of Indostan, I had reverenced it.
>
> (Sterne 2002, 8)

The work's perfect pictorial character and its delicate sense of the *tableau* are remarkable (MacLean 1949, 407). Nowhere is this more evident than in the mental projections of Yorick's sympathetic imagination:

> I began to figure to myself the miseries of confinement. I was in a right frame for it, and so I gave full scope to my imagination. I was going to begin with the millions of my fellow-creatures born to no inheritance but slavery; but finding, however affecting the picture was, that I could not bring it near me, and that the multitude of sad groups in it did but distract me— —I took a single captive, and having first shut him up in his dungeon, I then look'd through the twilight of his grated door to take his picture. [...] Upon looking nearer I saw him pale and feverish: in thirty years the western breeze had not once fann'd his blood—he had seen no sun, no moon in all that time—nor had the voice of friend or kinsman breathed though his lattice—his children— —But here my heart began to bleed [...]—I could not sustain the picture of confinement which my fancy had drawn [...].
>
> (Sterne 2002, 97–98)

Nonetheless, Sterne's pictorial vignettes, just like Smith's novelistic and illustrative cases in the *Theory of Moral Sentiments*, also anticipate Emmanuel Roidis' ability to produce characters that oscillate between general categories and particular types.[8] That the 19th-century Modern Greek writer was acquainted with Sterne's literary production, and *A Sentimental Journey* in particular, is known to criticism.[9] It would be worth looking though into his affinity with the sentimental tradition. One quasi-smithian type in Roidis' literary inventory is the case of the anonymous "Sensitive Man", whose self-indulgent monologue he conveyed to the public eye in the newspaper *Embros* (11.11.1896):

> It is rather unfortunate to have a very kind heart. I know this firsthand, since God made me a very sensitive man. [...] [O]nly the notion that my

> friend or his opponent can be hurt [in a duel] gives me the chills. This is all the more so, when I contemplate that, despite the bad weather, I have to wake up at seven on the day of the duel; I have to spend time running errands, meeting people and ratifying protocols; and I may even have to bear the risk of losing my money, in case, God forbid, my friend gets killed and I end up paying for the coachman.
>
> (Roidis 1978b, 172)

Here, the habits of economy, industry, attention and application of thought, which can be seen in the sensitive man's ironic reluctance to spend money, in his ability to rise early and multitask, in his careful completion of forms and in his contemplative mood, are cultivated from self-interested motives, as Smith suggested,[10] but in the end are praiseworthy, since they spring from an extremely sensitive heart. This dubious Roidian persona, however, could be no stranger to the Smithian universe, in view of the fact that the Scottish philosopher himself admitted: "how selfish soever man may be supposed, there are evidently some principles in his nature, which interest him in the fortune of others, and render their happiness necessary to him" (Smith 1976a, 9), even if that means, in the sensitive man's case, that he wishes for his friend's well-being only because he is unwilling to pay for his friend's last fare.

Consequently, it comes as no surprise that Smith's sympathy notion was also dubbed rather selfish by his contemporaries. In particular, the philosopher Thomas Reid, in a letter he sent to Lord Kames in 1778, admitted that "I have always thought Dr S[mith]'s system of sympathy wrong. It is indeed only a refinement of the selfish system" (Reid 1852, 92).[11] In addition, in "A Sketch of Dr Smith's Theory of Morals", he bitterly observed that Smith's system of sympathy "seems rather to account for mens put[t]ing on the Appearance of Virtue than for their being really virtuous" (Stewart-Robertson and Norton 1984, 315), a similarity they seem to share with Roidis' scandalous sensitive man. Elsewhere in the "Sketch", Reid argued damningly that:

> It is evident that the ultimate Measure & Standard of Right and Wrong in human Conduct according to this System of Sympathy, is not any fixed Judgment grounded upon Truth or upon the dictates of a well-informed Conscience but the variable opinions and passions of Men. So that we may apply to this system, what Cicero says of the Epicurean.
>
> (Stewart-Robertson and Norton 1984, 318)

Hence, in this neo-Epicurean respect, it is not so far-fetched to think of the sensitive man as a distant Smithian literary descendant.

Next follows one of the sensitive man's most representative ironic musings, in which he balances between other-regarding and self-regarding sentiments, his dread for the demise of his fellow man and for his own death while also showcasing extreme propriety ("I am not at all fond of selfish people"):

> I cannot see another man suffer and cry without upsetting my nerves. What is more, I cannot conceive how some people manage to attend distressing spectacles. If, by any chance, someone they know dies, they haste to the funeral, even if it snows. Whereas I cannot bear to see dead somebody I used to know, without being shaken by the idea that I, as well, will die someday. Furthermore, I would be bothered, if the dead man's relatives seemed to be reserved and consoled, because I am not at all fond of selfish people.
>
> (Roidis 1978b, 172)

As a result, he vacillates between excessive sensibility ("I cannot see another man suffer") and self-interest ("cry without upsetting my nerves"). This emphasis on seeing, conceiving and self-distancing, as well as on the theatricality of the spectator, is striking in the works of both authors.[12] Here, Roidis is both enacting Smith's notion of sympathetic imagination and the latter's views on the impartial spectator;[13] the "man within the breast" (Smith 1976a, 148, 153), the facilitator of self-command,[14] who regulates our judgments concerning our sentiments and conduct while also resonating one of Smith's most circulated credos that "Every man, as the Stoics used to say, is first and principally recommended to his own care" (Smith 1976a, 219).[15]

Even though, I do not suggest a direct influence coming to Roidis from Adam Smith's sympathy theory – after all Roidis does not mention him explicitly – I merely point to the likeness of thought between the Scottish moral philosopher and the Greek 19th-century novelist. Another such instance is the following extract, in which the sensitive man is not only trying to put himself in his friend's shoes but also in other less welcoming ones:

> Great must be the callousness of certain people who lend their friend money without reflecting that he might not be able to pay back his debts on time and as a result he might feel embarrassed and start avoiding them. Heartless people might dismiss this notion as trivial, but I would be heartbroken, if an old friend of mine encountered me in the street and passed me by, feigning he had not seen me.
>
> (Roidis 1978b, 172–173)

In this case, Roidis' protagonist is capable of demonstrating true Smithian sympathy, since he feels for his friend a passion (embarrassment) that arises from the imagination ("I would be") and is not in any way what his friend actually experiences,[16] thus becoming "the very person whose actions are represented to us" (Smith 1976a, 75). Furthermore, the sensitive man, making a momentary but "imaginary change of situations"[17] with the hypothetical sufferer – who is loaded with both psychological and actual debt – feels the latter's shame and then regains his own perspective, only to be overlooked by his friend. Consequently, he experiences first-hand the feeling of mortification which Smith so dramatically portrayed:

> to be overlooked, and to be disapproved of, are things entirely different, yet as obscurity covers us from the daylight of honour and approbation, to feel that we are taken no notice of, necessarily damps the most agreeable hope, and disappoints the most ardent desire, of human nature.
>
> (Smith 1976a, 51)

Similarly, the sensitive man's discretion-driven refusal to give financial aid to his friend is reminiscent of Yorick's self-conscious denial in *A Sentimental Journey* to give charity to a Franciscan monk:

> My heart smote me the moment he shut the door [...] every ungracious syllable I had utter'd, crowded back into my imagination: I reflected, I had no right over the poor Franciscan, but to deny him; and that the punishment of that was enough to the disappointed without the addition of unkind language—I consider'd his gray hairs—his courteous figure seem'd to re-enter and gently ask me what injury he had done me?—and why I could use him thus? [...] I have behaved very ill; said I within myself; but I have only just set out upon my travels; and shall learn better manners as I get along.
>
> (Sterne 2002, 11)

Both Yorick and the sensitive man, as genuine men of feeling, knowingly choose to reflect on the consequences of their actions and avoid becoming inauthentic representations of themselves.[18] Of course, in Roidis' case, the parody of sentimental feeling is achieved by overstretching sentimental vocabulary and argumentation, whereas in Sterne, the elasticity of moral feeling is ironically kept in check, when Yorick homeostatically contemplates the gulf between precept and practice and makes a narcissistic promise to himself that he will behave more charitably in the future.[19]

Furthermore, as Gillian Skinner astutely noted, *A Sentimental Journey* simulates charity as much as it simulates commerce, suggesting that "sensibility is a commercially useful quality", since Yorick's financial dealings "in certain cases become a replacement for the sexual transactions his sensibility might otherwise lead him to" (Skinner 1999, 115–116). One of the most memorable instances of this type of sentimental trade is the calculated give-and-take between Yorick and the beautiful Grisset in the Parisian glove shop:

> I was sensible the beautiful Grisset had not ask'd a single livre above the price—I wish'd she had ask'd a livre more, and was puzzling my brains how to bring the matter about—Do you think, my dear Sir, said

> she, mistaking my embarrassment, that I could ask a *sous* too much of a stranger—and of a stranger whose politeness, more than his want of gloves, has done me the honour to lay himself at my mercy?
>
> (Sterne 2002, 75)

Therefore, from the previous incident, we can see that societies, and especially commercial ones, are not only based on interactions among strangers, but they "place individuals at the most appropriate distance to facilitate moral development" (Paganelli 2010, 427) and self-command. What is more, Yorick's ephemeral passions keep the wheels of commerce moving, simultaneously benefiting societal cohesiveness and intercultural exchange between different, or even hostile, nations.

In a similar manner, in Roidis' short story, the sensitive man's sexual and risky proclivities provide prostitutes and carriage owners with a steady income, thus inextricably linking his insatiable wants with the whole process of economic development[20] and further advancing the societal prosperity through this form of sentimental commerce:[21]

> My wife's spell of sickness forced me to spend a lot on cars, theatrical plays, dinners at "Grande Bretagne" and short trips with friends to Kifissia and Penteli. My biggest expense though, during those days that my wife seemed unwell and my worry and unhappiness were so great, was the fact that I was compelled to find consolation in the arms of a French lady in Faliro.
>
> (Roidis 1978b, 174)

Consequently, both Sterne's Yorick and Roidis' sensitive man, apart from having a soft spot for French ladies, are also the fictional embodiments of Smith's, and Dr. Mandeville's, assessment that "private vices [are] public benefits, since without them no society could prosper or flourish" (Smith 1976a, 313).

Having seen how Adam Smith's theory on sympathy can be applied on 18- and 19th-century fictional men of feeling, I will examine the long shadow that Thomas Robert Malthus' work cast on literary authors and their fictions. As Robert Mayhew (2014, 5) observed, it is hard to imagine two more conflicting characters than those of Malthus and his most famous 18th-century predecessor at Jesus College, Cambridge, Laurence Sterne, because "where Malthus is the great progenitor of 'dismal science' of classical economics, Sterne possesses irreverent Rabelaisian wit; sex is a realm of production for the one, of double entendre for the other".[22] Sterne, however, will not be the point of reference this time. The focus will rather be on the late Romantic poets, and specifically Lord Byron.

As R. Mayhew pithily remarked, "the thirty years from the publication of the *Lyrical Ballads* had seen the Lake poets mine an extraordinary rich vein of social, poetic, and moral criticism in their attacks on Malthus, who had truly been their malign muse" (Mayhew 2014, 94).[23] However, in order to fully grasp Byron's scathing critique, it is imperative to review some of Malthus' seminal beliefs.

Foremost, Malthus was adamant that natural rates of human reproduction, when unchecked, would lead to geometric increases in population:

> In a state therefore of great equality and virtue, where pure and simple manners prevailed, and where the means of subsistence were so abundant, that no part of the society could have any fears about providing amply for a family, the power of population being left to exert itself unchecked, the increase of the human species would evidently be much greater than any increase that has been hitherto known. [...] That population, when unchecked, goes on doubling itself every twenty five years, or increases in a geometrical ratio.
>
> (Malthus 1966 [1798], 20–21)

Therefore, it seemed quite obvious to him that something had to be done to keep the population in check and to prevent wholesale starvation. He distinguished between two broad kinds of checks that limited population growth: "These checks to population, which [...] keep down the number to the level of the means of subsistence, may be classed under two general heads—the preventive, and the positive checks" (Malthus 1996a [1803], 9). Positive checks, such as famine, disease and warfare, were natural forces that adjusted the population downward:

> But should [the vices of mankind] fail in this war of extermination, sickly seasons, epidemics, pestilence, and plague, advance in terrific array and sweep off their thousands and ten thousands. Should success still be incomplete; gigantic inevitable famine stalks in the rear, and with one mighty blow, levels the population with the food of the world.
>
> (Malthus 1966 [1798], 139–140)[24]

Whereas preventive checks, such as moral restraint, were human or social forces that achieved the same balancing act by less violent means:

> On examining these obstacles to the increase of population which I have classed under the heads of preventive and positive checks it will appear that they are all resolvable into moral restraint, vice and misery. Of the preventive checks, the restraint from marriage which is not followed by irregular gratifications may be properly termed moral restraint.
>
> (Malthus 1996a [1803], 11)[25]

Malthus – when discussing what assistance might be given to the distressed, lower classes – observed that the English Poor Laws tended to create the poor they maintained, because they encouraged them to marry and reproduce without means of support. For this reason, he advocated fewer marriages and stressed that "It is clearly the duty of each individual not to marry till he has a prospect of supporting his children" (Malthus 1996a [1803], 492–493).[26] Malthus, however, was sufficiently propertied and therefore exempt from his own censures. Furthermore, he notoriously prophesied that if the poor obeyed their passions instead of their reason, or were not industrious and frugal, while they were single, so as "to save a sum for the common contingencies of the married state", they should expect "to suffer the natural evils which Providence has prepared for those who disobey the repeated admonitions" (Malthus 1996b [1817, vol. 3], 117). This is only one of Malthus' arguments which helped cement his notorious reputation among the Romantics.

Undoubtedly, Byron must have read Malthus' *Essay on the Principle of Population* before writing on 21st August 1811 to his half-sister Augusta in reply to her condolences for his mother's death, for he there admitted that:

> Notwithstanding Malthus tells us that, were it not for Battle, Murder, and Sudden death, we should be overstocked, I think we have latterly had a redundancy of theses national benefits, and therefore I give you all credit for your matronly behaviour.
>
> (Byron 1973, 74)[27]

Scarcely three weeks later (13th September 1811), he reiterated Malthus' views on positive checks in a letter to Francis Hodgson: "Did you ever read 'Malthus on Population'? If he be right, war and pestilence are our best friends, to save us from being eaten alive, in this 'best of all possible Worlds'" (Byron 1973, 98).[28]

Furthermore, having as his starting point the amorous exploits of an iconic man of feeling,[29] the infamous Don Juan, Byron not only utilized Malthusian doctrines in his narratorial digressions,[30] but also, in what is undeniably the most gleamingly witty of all the Romantic assaults, vilified Malthus for the same vices he was reproaching his contemporaries. That is the reason why, he neatly satirized Malthus not for his financial standing: "While sages write against all procreation, / Unless a man calculate his means" (Canto XII, 21, 166–167/ Byron 1996, 425), but rather for his double standards[31] and his lack of prudential restraint: "And Malthus does the thing 'gainst which he writes" (Canto XII, 20, 160/ Byron 1996, 425).[32] Hence, after having unsympathetically exposed Malthus to his readers, Byron's temperamental narrator ironically declares "I say, methinks that philo-genitiveness / Might meet from men a little more forgiveness" (Canto XII, 20, 175–176/ Byron 1996, 425).

Moreover, Byron packed down much of the romantic critique of Malthus' *Essay* into one brilliantly ironic stanza in Canto XV of *Don Juan*, in which the political philosopher is faulted for being a hard-hearting enemy of the poor ("thou shalt not marry") and a wily apostle of the rich ("unless well"):

> Had Adeline read Malthus? I can't tell.
> I wish she had; his book's the eleventh commandment,

Which says, "thou shalt not marry", unless well.
This he (as far as I can understand) meant.
Tis not my purpose on his views to dwell
No canvass what "so eminent a hand" meant,
But certes it conducts to lives ascetic,
Or turning marriage into arithmetic.
(Canto XV, 38/ Byron 1996, 506)

Nonetheless, it is interesting to see that for Malthus, marriage was not mere numerals, his approach was foremost a moral one.[33] After all, as he admitted in the *Principles of Political Economy* (1820), the science of political economy "bears a nearer resemblance to the science of morals and politics than that of mathematics" (Malthus 1989, 2). This, however, was not the only time that Byron capitalized on economic tropes. This unseemly connection between morality and calculation is further explored in the following extract from *Don Juan*, in which immorality and corn prices are figuratively yoked while also making explicit the interdisciplinary alignment between political economy and moral philosophy. In this case, Byron is alluding to the vastly unpopular 1815 Corn Law, which was designed to keep the price of bread artificially inflated by banning the import of foreign grain, thus serving the interests of the powerful, Whig and Tory, landowners:

But now I'm going to be immoral, now
I mean to show things really as they are,
Not as they ought to be, for I avow,
That till we see what's what in fact, we're far
From much improvement with that virtuous plough
Which skims the surface, leaving scarce a scar
Upon the black loam long manured by vice,
Only to keep its corn at the old price.
(Canto XII, 40, 313–320/ Byron 1996, 430)

Apart from the population checks that Malthus addressed in his works, his name was also linked with the highly charged issue of the Corn Laws,[34] on which he wrote two pamphlets, *Observations on the Effects of the Corn Laws* (1814) and *The Grounds of an Opinion on the Policy of Restricting the Importation of Foreign Corn* (1815). The Corn Laws were a system of state intervention in the operation of the market, and Malthus' *Observations*, written at a critical juncture when the revision of the Corn Laws was about to be debated in Parliament, indicate that Malthus was eager to influence the course of political events. However, he did not wish in this pamphlet to take sides either for or against agricultural protection. Rather, his main object was

to state, with the strictest impartiality, what appear to me to be the advantages and disadvantages of each system, in the actual circumstances of

> our present situation, and [...] to assist in affording the materials for a just and enlightened decision.
>
> (Malthus 1970, 97)

Malthus' fascination with corn and its price can be explained if we take into account his opinions regarding the riches of different countries and the quantity of food which they produce:

> Corn countries are more populous than pasture countries; and rice countries more populous than corn countries. The lands in England are not suited to rice, but they would all bear potatoes: and Dr. Adam Smith observes, that if potatoes were to become the favourite vegetable food of the common people, and if the same quantity of land was employed in their culture, as is now employed in the culture of corn, the country would be able to support a much greater population.
>
> (Malthus 1966 [1798], 136–137)

Given that the English of Malthus' time had not become potato eaters but invested on their own home-growth of corn and wheat, the issue of corn price arose, since, with the continued importation of corn, a fall of prices took place, which

> had not only checked all progress of improvement, but had already occasioned a considerable loss of agricultural advances; and [...] a continuation of low prices would, in spite of a diminution of rents, unquestionably destroy a great mass of farming capital all over the country, and essentially diminish its cultivation and produce.
>
> (Malthus 1970, 140).

For all these reasons, Malthus was of the opinion in the *Grounds* (1815) that calculated restrictions should be imposed on the importation of corn so that England could become nearly independent of foreign, particularly French, supplies of corn (Malthus 1970, 151). Hence, his support of the Corn Bill made it even easier to regard him as "an ogre who wanted large families of little children to be starved into extinction" (James 1979, 269).

Byron was also aware of this divisive situation when he made the following contemplative remarks in Canto IX, 32 about the discontented landed gentry, who tried to protect their own interests at the poor farmers' expense:

> At least he pays no rent and has best right
> To be the first of what we used to call
> "Gentlemen Farmers", a race worn out quite,
> Since lately there have been no rents at all,
> And "Gentlemen" are in a piteous plight,
> And "farmers" can't raise Ceres from her fall.

She fell with Buonaparte. What strange thoughts
Arise, when we see Emperors fall with oats!

(Byron 1996, 361)

The last lines, as Peter Cochran (Byron 2009, 18) succinctly stated, are "a semi-facetious meditation on the post-Waterloo economic depression, which hit England as the price of corn – kept artificially high by the war – fell".[35] The Napoleonic Wars is the field where numerals abound in Byron's narrative account, either in the form of falling prices or fallen men. After all, as Markovits (2018, 646) explained: "love and war both resonate numerically in *Don Juan*: the reproductive promise of sex stands in opposition to the poem's discourse of death", thus providing Byron's seemingly sober counter-argument to Malthus' grim estimations.

As it is easy for the modern reader to surmise from the previous extracts, Romantic literature not only talked back at the market (Ittensohn 2017, 39) but also emphasized the natural processes that bring humans and their environments into reciprocal relationships and so did the British political economy of the time.[36] Political economy was a developing discipline in Byron's time and, since "politics" not only meant economics but also the whole intellectual concern tagged as "moral philosophy" (Heinzelman 1981, 373), it is in this wide-ranging sense that Byron's philosophical reflections in Canto XII of *Don Juan* become a matter pertaining to political economy: "But my best canto, save one on astronomy, / will turn upon political economy" (Canto XII, 88, 7–8 / Byron 1996, 442). Therefore, as we had the chance to see, not only Malthus became a constant subject of derision, an ill-disposed Muse for the English Romantics, and particularly Byron, but also political economy began to be viewed and labelled as a dismal science.[37] In particular, when Thomas Carlyle coined the term "dismal science", he juxtaposed it to the "gay science" of poetry (Levy 2002, 158); and nowhere is this contrast more evident than in Byron's jocoserious verses.

Nonetheless, Romantic and "moral" England did not have the monopoly of taunting Malthus. This 19th-century literary fad spread like wildfire and reached, albeit belatedly, peripheral Greece. Specifically, Emmanuel Roidis (1978c, 134–137) paid a rather charming tribute to the political economist in a letter he penned on 1.6.1875 for the satirical newspaper he was also editing ("Asmodeus"). Roidis, assuming the satiric persona of Annah Merrilies, aired his views on the plastic arts and especially on the works of two sculptors of his time: Ioannis Vitsaris (1843–1892) and Georgios Vroutos (1843–1909). It is quite revealing though that the Greek writer invoked Malthus' authority in order to assess the aesthetic value of the work of his two contemporary sculptors, since it is redolent of the fact that "the practice of judging works of art need not make reference at all to the concept of value before the emergence of political economy" (Guillory 1993, 303).

Annah, Roidis' fictional "heteronym", loosely resembles Scott's heroine in *Guy Mannering*, the mysterious gypsy Meg Merrilies, since the rationalist genius of her creator shines forth in every word she utters.[38] From the letter she supposedly mailed to "Asmodeus", we learn that she is Scottish, she has a PhD and her main occupation is the circulation of Malthus' ideas on population. Having read Pindar and ardently loving ancient Greece, she came to Athens to witness the "resurrection" of the 12 Olympian gods by the sculptor Georgios Vroutos. Furthermore, possessing ample common sense and superior reasoning faculties, she is not fond of nebulous conversations but priggishly prefers to examine things in terms of their possible utility:[39]

> Dear editor, the fact that you are a Modern Greek and a journalist, grants you the bliss of ignorance. Yet you might have heard that wise Malthus has calculated that, while earth's population is constantly growing, our planet cannot expand or multiply. As a result, after not so many and not so distant Olympiads, its inhabitants, unable to find any food and housing, will end up eating each other like spiders in a bottle.
>
> (Roidis 1978c, 135)

She then explains how in order to save mankind from this scourge, her mentor and his followers proposed many remedies, among which the suggestions "to thwart marriage between the destitute, to allow no one to get married before completing the age of thirty, medical prescriptions for infertility and many more" (Roidis 1978c, 135–136). She soberly realizes, however, that "the former of these, infringe on constitutional freedoms, while the latter on morality" (Roidis 1978c, 136).[40] Hence, the problem of overpopulation remains unsolved, while "the danger of cannibalism is still looming" (Roidis 1978c, 136).[41]

Thus, she racks her brains as to how to profitably utilize Vroutos' and Vitsaris' statues, along with other Modern Greek sculptures, with the aim of simultaneously promoting Malthus' practicality and his preventive checks on population so as to reduce the passion between the sexes, "this natural propensity [which] exists still in undiminished vigour" (Malthus 1966 [1798], 62). For this reason, she devises a practical yet aesthetically-oriented scheme in order to instigate sexual and marital aversion to young British pupils and orphans. She proposes to place copies of these statues in the latters' dining halls and dormitories (Roidis 1978c, 136)[42] so as to create the impression to the youngsters that equally hideous things are hidden under all women's silky dresses:

> Knowing how indelible the impressions of childhood are I thought that my mentor's system would be more efficiently disseminated [...] if one could instill extreme sexual and marital aversion to young children, even with deceit; to this end, I thought I could utilize the products of Modern Greek art. Therefore, upon my return to England, I will ask the Malthusian Society to raise funds, so that we can buy at least five hundred

> copies of the statue of Aphrodite by Mr. Vroutos Esq. These statues will be placed in school dining halls and dormitories, as well as in English orphanages.
>
> (Roidis 1978c, 136)

As we have already seen, Malthus accepted the proposition that sexuality can be controlled by reason, after all in the 1803 edition of his *Essay on Population* he conceded that: "The preventive check, is peculiar to man, and arises from that distinctive superiority in his reasoning faculties, which enables him to calculate distant consequences" (Malthus 1996a [1803], 9) and in the 1817 edition of the same work he included "moral restraint" into his "preventive checks":

> By moral restraint I would be understood to mean a restraint from marriage, from prudential motives, with a conduct strictly moral during the period of this restraint; and I have never intentionally deviated from this sense. When I have wished to consider the restraint from marriage unconnected with its consequences, I have either called it prudential restraint, or a part of the preventive check, of which indeed it forms the principal branch.
>
> (Malthus 1996b [1817, vol. 1], 22)[43]

Whereas the English economist explicitly expressed his preference for reason, Emmanuel Roidis, in the guise of an unassuming Scottish lady,[44] proposed an alternative population check to inculcate sexual moderation. In lieu of the improper arts,[45] which Malthus so vehemently abhorred:

> I should always particularly reprobate any artificial and unnatural modes of checking population, both on account of their immorality and their tendency to remove a necessary stimulus to industry.[46]
>
> (Malthus 1996b [1817, vol. 3], 393)

Roidis introduced the use of plastic arts as a form of "aesthetic restraint", thus favouring artistic instead of artificial checks on population.

His choice was not random, since he had been exposed to more than his fair share of Georgios Vroutos' artistry. As Kleon Paraschos admitted, "Around 1875, here in Greece, wherever Roidis would turn his eyes to, it would be difficult for him to find something to please him" (Paraschos 1942, 118). By 1875, Roidis was still stationed in Philellinon Street.[47] Therefore, among the things he would probably find particularly displeasing, or even distasteful, would be the "archaeolatry"[48] emanating from Vroutos' nearby neoclassical, pink-walled workshop (Markianos 1950, 157): "Opposite the Anglican Church in Philellinon Street there stands [...] a small building with a classicizing relief pediment decorated with plaster busts of ancient gods and heroes, among which Zeus' somber bearded face figures prominently" (Xenopoulos 1894, 40). Consequently, the products of Vroutos' craftsmanship were more than familiar to Roidis, since they were of close everyday proximity to him. Accordingly, it is quite expected that he wished that others could also have the pleasure of savouring them on a daily basis as household items. After all, the management of domestic resources and the juxtaposition of the public with the private sphere has always been a matter of "oeconomy",[49] and here lies the connection with Malthus' work.

Furthermore, Roidis, instead of reason, privileged imagination as the driving force behind the self-correcting check he proposed, thus showcasing the superiority of reflection over calculation as a distinct human faculty, given that students would certainly abstain from procreation by envisaging their future misfortunes through the apotropaic properties of Vitsaris' and Vroutos' statues. Therefore, where the political economist stressed the capacity to calculate distant consequences as a fundamental part for the formation of moral character, the novelist favoured aesthetic foresight and ideation as the ultimate preventive and prudential checks and transformed the said students into beings who, in Malthus' words, "look before and after" (Malthus 1989, 251). In this way, Roidis not only humorously advanced Malthus' argument that prudential habits among the lower classes of society are enhanced by civil and political liberty and education (Malthus 1989, 251) but also implicitly acknowledged the supreme role of aesthetic literacy as well. Consequently, by inextricably binding plastic arts to political economy, he self-reflexively suggested that economics is not monolithic but can greatly benefit even from the most disputed or unappealing artistic endeavours.

To conclude this brief analysis, so far we have seen that during the 18th- and 19th-century political writers and novelists not only shared common concerns but also a common vocabulary regarding morality and sensibility. Therefore, by focusing on Smithian sympathy and on Malthus' population principles, we had the chance to follow the fictional afterlives of these concepts both in Britain (with Sterne's and Byron's work) and in Greece (with Roidis' literary output). And while it might initially seem that the economic texts were cut off from their contemporary audiences, there was a significant dialogue between economics and literature of the time, since all the authors discussed manifested, in Keynes' terms, "an extraordinary continuity of feeling" (Keynes 1972, 86) and actual matter.[50] The political theorists have done so by writing in a lucid and disinterested fashion while approaching Economics as a humane, moral science and not as a form of mathematical speculation;[51] and the literary authors by self-consciously writing about feelings with a prosaic sanity free from sentimentalism,[52] but not lacking in imagination. Hence, it is this enlightened – and post-enlightened – sense that Smith, Malthus, Sterne, Byron and Roidis are real men of feeling belonging in the same free-thinking company (Figure 2.1).

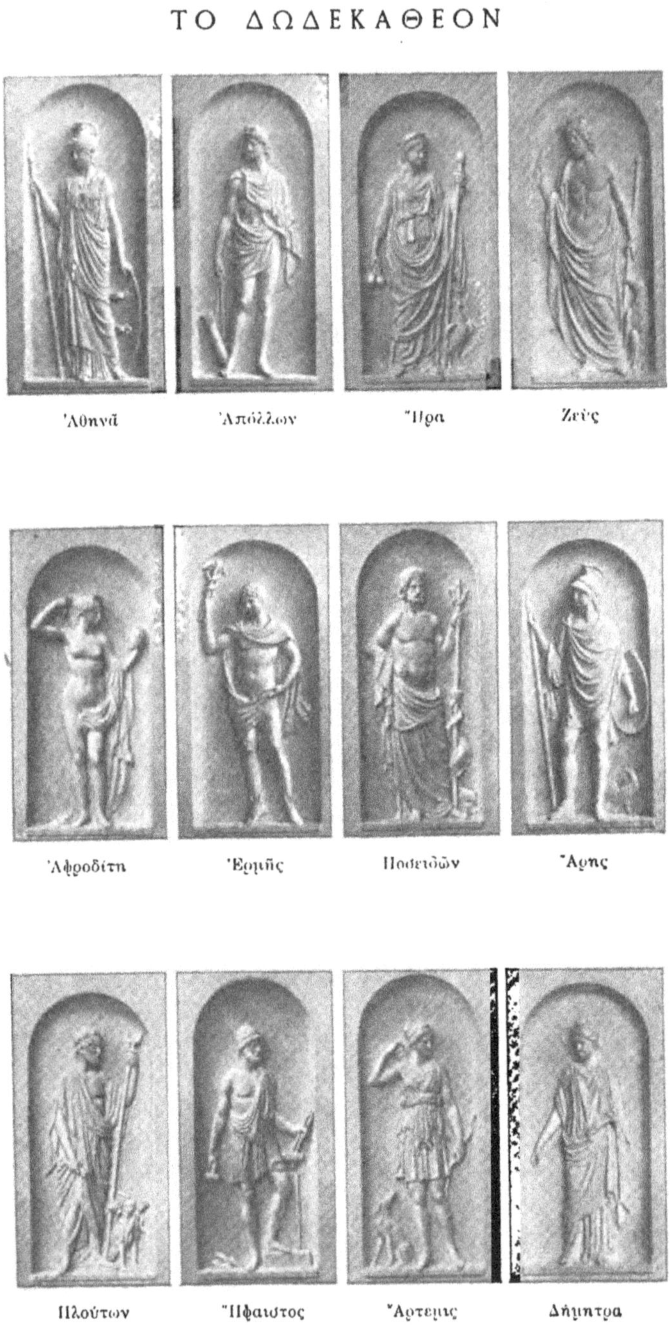

Figure 2.1 "The Twelve Olympians" by Georgios Vroutos, as they were depicted in the *Eikonografimeni Estia* [Illustrated Hestia] (Xenopoulos 1894, 41).

Notes

1 Cf. Smith (1976a, 25):

> As taste and good judgment, when are considered as qualities which deserve praise and admiration, are supposed to imply a delicacy of sentiment and an acuteness of understanding not commonly to be met with; so the virtues of sensibility and self-command are not apprehended to consist in the ordinary, but in the uncommon degrees of those faculties.

2 See also Skinner (1992, 144).
3 Emmanuel Roidis (1836–1904) was an influential Modern Greek critic, short-story writer, essayist and translator. Today, he is mostly known for his only novel, the irreverent and witty *Pope Joan* (1866), which "is as much a send-up of the contemporary Greek vogue for romantic historical novels [...] as a satire on the medieval (and contemporary Greek) church" (Beaton 2017a, 409). *Pope Joan's* most recent English translation is by David Connolly (Roïdes 2019).
4 Eagleton (2009, 12): "Sensibility, that key term of the age, represents a kind of rhetoric of the body, a social semiotics of blushing, palpitating, weeping, fainting and the like" and cf. Eagleton (2003, 155).
5 Cf. Skinner (1992, 145) and see also Knud Haakonssen's "Introduction" in the *Theory of Moral Sentiments*: "The act of sympathetic understanding is a creation of order in the observer's perceptions by means of an imagined rationale for the observed behavior" (Haakonssen 2002, xiv).
6 Cf. Amrozowicz (2013, 148):

> By imagining himself in the place of an historical agent who is selected by the author as to one to whom the reader is probably not emotionally indifferent – such as a Cato or a Scipio– the reader, via the sympathetic process, cannot fail to come to a moral judgment about himself and how he would act in a similar situation.

7 Greiner is not the only theorist to think so, since, according to Stephanie DeGooyer, we might refer to Smith's theory of sympathy as "novelistic" (DeGooyer 2018, 683).
8 Cf. also Greiner (2009, 299).
9 See Lika (2018, 170–172) and cf. Roidis (1978a, 308): "No one could believe that one lifetime would suffice to write twenty volumes, such as Goethe's *Werther*, Rousseau's *Heloise*, Chateaubriand's *Atala*, Sterne's *Sentimental Journey*; or to confine ourselves to contemporary writers, Flaubert's *Madame Bovary* and Mérimée's *Colomba*." All translations of Greek texts not taken from an English edition are mine, unless otherwise stated.
10 Smith acknowledged in the *Theory of Moral Sentiments* the double-edged quality of economic prudence and self-preservation:

> The habits of oeconomy, industry, discretion, attention, and application of thought, are generally supposed to be cultivated from self-interested motives, and at the same time are apprehended to be very praise-worthy qualities, which deserve the esteem and approbation of everybody
>
> (Smith 1976a, 304).

11 Thomas Robert Malthus was 10 years old when Smith published *The Wealth of Nations*, yet unlike Smith's contemporaries, he was not at all against Smith's "self-love principle":

> It is to the established administration of property, and to the apparently narrow principle of self-love, that we are indebted for all the noblest exertions

> of human genius, all the finer and more delicate emotions of the soul, for everything, indeed, that distinguishes the civilized, from the savage state.
> (Malthus 1966 [1798], 286–287)

12 On Smith's theatricality, see David Marshall 1984.

13 Smith 1976a, 110:

> We can never survey our own sentiments and motives, we can never form any judgment concerning them; unless we remove ourselves, as it were, from our own natural station, and endeavour to view them as at a certain distance from us. [...] We endeavour to examine our own conduct as we imagine any other fair and impartial spectator would examine it.

For the concept of the impartial spectator in Smith's theory, see also Raphael (2007, 32–42).

14 As Istvan Hont (2015, 37) noted: "The impartial spectator was a device for the inner regulation of one's own self – in other words, a facilitator of self-command."

15 It is worth noting that, despite Smith's own admission, Istvan Hont deems his theory as more Epicurean than Stoic (2015, 37):

> It is often claimed that self-command was a Stoic virtue; it was not so for Smith. His was no heroic virtue based on a tough theory of the government of the soul. If anything, it was an Epicurean theory of self-command.

16 Cf. Smith (1976a, 12):

> Sympathy, therefore, does not arise so much from the view of the passion, as from that of the situation which excites it. We sometimes feel for another, a passion of which he himself seems to be altogether incapable; because, when we put ourselves in his case, that passion arises in our breast from the imagination, though it does not in his from the reality.

17 Cf. Smith (1976a, 317):

> But though sympathy is very properly said to arise from an imaginary change of situations with the person principally concerned, yet this imaginary change is not supposed to happen to me in my own person and character, but in that of the person with whom I sympathize.

18 Cf. DeGooyer (2016, 208): "He is not an ignorant unreflective man of feeling, [...] he reflects in order to avoid or delay an unrepresentative representation of himself."

19 Critics have been puzzled by Sterne's portraiture of sentimentality, deeming him as a rather tricky case: "Sterne, however, is an ambiguous case, as a satirist of sentimentalism as well as a probable champion of it" (Eagleton 2009, 25 fn34).

20 See also Skinner (1992, 163).

21 See Smith (1976b, 477–478): "By pursuing his own interest he frequently promotes that of the society more effectually than when he really intends to promote it" and cf. also Smith (1976b, 477): "he intends only his own gain, and he is in this, as in many other cases, led by an invisible hand to promote an end which was no part of his intention."

22 Regarding the terminological origins of "dismal science", see Milgate (2008, 697): "Thomas Carlyle is chiefly remembered in economics as the originator of the epithet the 'dismal' science ('The Nigger Question', 1849; in Miscellaneous Essays, vol. 7, p. 84)" and cf. Levy (2002, 19): "The term dismal science did not originate in Carlyle's 1853 booklet Occasional Discourse on the Nigger Question, it originated in 1849 essay in Fraser's entitled 'Occasional Discourse on the Nigger Question'" and Carlyle (2010, 354).

23 For Malthus' demonization, see Heilbroner (1986, 83); and for the abuse of his work, see Bonar (1880, 5).

24 See also Malthus (1966 [1798], 99–100):

> To these two great checks to population, [...] which I have called the preventive and the positive checks, may be added, vicious customs with respect to women, great cities, unwholesome manufactures, luxury, pestilence and war. All these checks may be fairly resolved into misery and vice;

and cf. Reisman (2018, 54), who includes abortion and infanticide among the positives checks: "Pestilence, famine, miscarriage, abortion and infanticide are all positive checks that sweep away the excess".

25 See also Jensen (2003, 130–131):

> The only controls on population were the positive checks, primarily death (hunger, illness, war) and the preventive checks (vice and misery – and later, moral constraint). [...] Preventive checks are all limitations on the birth rate, while positive are all limitations after birth.

26 This Malthusian concern is also mirrored in Byron's musings in Canto XII, 14,105–108 that: "But if Love don't, cash does, and cash alone. / Cash rules the grove, and fells it, too, besides. / Without cash, camps were thin, and courts were none. / Without Cash, Malthus tells, you, 'take no brides'" (Byron 1996, 423 and cf. Mayhew 2014, 100).

27 See also Beaty (1969, 18).

28 Cf. Beaty (1969, 19).

29 For more on Byron's authorial plans for "Donny Johnny", see Byron (1978, 78):

> I meant to have made him a *Cavalier Servente* [an official lover of a married woman] in Italy, and a cause for a divorce in England, and a Sentimental 'Werther-faced man' in Germany, so as to show the different ridicules of the society in each of those countries.

30 Cf. Beaton (2017b, 251): "Malthus first appears by name in *Don Juan*, and indeed in Byron's poetry, in canto 11, written that same autumn of 1822, but comes into his own in canto 12, where he is named no fewer than three times."

31 As Karl Marx rather matter-of-factly observed, Malthus was forced to keep his celibacy for some time, not out of virtue but out of necessity: "Although Malthus was a parson of the English State Church, he had taken the monastic vow of celibacy – one of the conditions of holding a Fellowship in Protestant Cambridge University" (Marx 1953, 83).

32 Ernest Hartley Coleridge, an editor of Byron's works, suggested that the poet might be referring to an apocryphal story that Malthus had 11 daughters (Byron 1903, vol. 6, 461). The originator of these controversial rumours, which plagued Malthus' reputation, was Antoine-Elisée Cherbuliez, who in 1850 reported what happened at Sismondi's Geneva residence on the occasion of Malthus' visit in Switzerland: "Finally the Reverent Malthus and his family are announced. His family! This was an unexpected novelty. Then, one saw a lovely girl entering, and a second, and a third, a fourth... Well, they were no less than eleven!" (Faccarello 2020, 130). For another contemporary context for the interpretation of this line, see also Hazlitt (1807, 307):

> I am happy to learn that Mr. Malthus has been able to reconcile the sense of duty and interest with the gratification of his favourite passion. By preaching the virtue of celibacy with such success to others, he found it no longer necessary to practise it himself.

33 Cf. McLane (2017, 131): "Malthus's essay is as much a theory of moral sentiments as a quantitative analytic."

34 Thomas Love Peacock also satirized Malthus as "Mr Fax" in his spoof novel *Melincourt* (1817) and laid bare some of the reasons why he disliked him. Among Mr Fax's most memorable caricatured utterances is the following: "More men than corn is a fearful pre-eminence, the sole and fruitful cause of penury, disease, and war, plague, pestilence, and famine" (Peacock 1817, 101).

35 Peter Cochran's online edition of *Don Juan* can be accessed on his personal website https://petercochran.wordpress.com.

36 Cf. Gallagher (2009, 71).

37 See Milgate and Stimson (2009, 122): "the *Essay on Population* was seen as opposing Smith's political economy with a 'dismal science' – and as functioning as a 'de-moralizer' of an existing 'moral economy'" and cf. Mallarmé's later reflection on literature, which testifies to the competitive situation in which poetry is placed in relation to the economic sphere: "Tout se résume dans l'Esthétique et l'Économie politique" (Mallarmé 1895, 79).

38 Cf. Jackson-Houlston (2017, 60).

39 Cf. Thomas Robert Malthus (1996a [1803], 504):

> I do not see how it is possible for any person, who acknowledges the principle of utility as the great foundation of morals, to escape the conclusion that moral restraint, till we are in a condition to support a family, is the strict line of duty.

Roidis was also familiar with Bentham's ideas on utilitarianism (Roidis 1978d, 413).

40 Malthus himself, in his *Summary View of the Principle of Population* (1830), acknowledged that preventive checks such as prudential restraint on marriage cannot be enforced but are a free-willed choice: "Prudence cannot be enforced by laws, without a great violation of natural liberty, and a great risk of producing more evil than good" (Malthus 1830, 45). Furthermore, he went to great lengths to explain how abstinence from marriage is a win-win form of moral restraint:

> Moral restraint, in application to the present subject, may be defined to be, abstinence from marriage, either for a time or permanently, from prudential considerations, with a strictly moral conduct towards the sex in the interval. And this is the only mode of keeping population on a level with the means of subsistence, which is perfectly consistent with virtue and happiness.
>
> (Malthus 1830, 43)

41 In the first edition of the *Essay* (1798), Malthus does not mention cannibalism, and it is not until the edition of 1803 that he refers to anthropophagy in the context of the checks of population:

> The Abbé Raynal, speaking of the ancient state of the British isles, and of islanders in general; says of them: 'It is among these people that we trace the origin of that multitude of singular institutions that retard the progress of population. Anthropophagy, the castration of males, the infibulation of females, late marriages, the consecration of virginity, the approbation of celibacy, the punishments exercised against girls who become mothers at too early an age,' etc. These customs, caused by a superabundance of population in islands, have been carried, he says, to the continents, where philosophers of our days are still employed to investigate the reason of them.
>
> (Malthus 1996a [1803], 46).

42 Apart from the 500 copies of Vroutos' statue of Aphrodite that Roidis suggested to utilize as a preventive check (Roidis 1978c, 136), he then satirically proposed

to "erect 'Vroutian Aphrodites' in high-schools and 'Vitsarian Arabs' in girls' schools to expel temptation" (Roidis 1978c, 137). Cf. also Fotos Yiofyllis (1956, 443): "Roidis used to write [...] erect Vitsarian Arab statues in girls' schools to expel temptation." For the record, Vitsaris presented the said statue at the Olympia exhibition in 1875 and he was honoured with the bronze award. For more information on Christos, the Black Guy, see Vatopoulos (2007).

43 For the prevalence of moral restraint as a check on population, see Malthus (1996a [1803], 483) and cf. Petersen (1979, 472), who, nonetheless, quotes moral restraint as a positive check.

44 This is not the first time that Roidis assumes a satiric persona and employs plastic arts and particularly sculpture in order to make his point palpable. One of the most memorable instances that springs up to mind is the character of the quick-witted yet physically-impaired Dionysios Sourlis, the imaginary author of the "Agriniot Letters" Roidis penned to defend his *Pope Joan*. As for the use of the plastic arts as a preventive means of racial amelioration, see Roidis (1866, 203).

45 See Jensen (2003, 124): "Some experts on Malthus interpret these as abortion (such as A. Flew, in the introduction to the 1985-reprint of the first *Essay*); others interpret this to include all forms of birth control."

46 Malthus expressed his condemnation of artificial checks, the Appendix to the 1817 edition of the *Essay* (Malthus 1996b [1817, vol. 3], 393) and cf. Malthus' *Summary View of the Principle of Population*, in which he reiterated his arguments against contraception (Malthus 1830, 43):

> The remaining checks of the preventive kind, are the sort of intercourse which renders some of the women of large towns unprolific; a general corruption of morals with regard to the sex, which has a similar effect; unnatural passions and improper arts to prevent the consequences of irregular connections. These evidently come under the head of vice.

47 "The years 1866–1875 did not 'go to waste'. [...]. His house in Philellinon Street was the meeting place of scholars and the *jeunesse dorée*. Receptions, excursions, and above all sword fights were on the everyday agenda" (Andreadis 1911, μ').

48 Cf. Michailidis 1909, 235:

> [Vroutos] was so attached to the ancient art that many of his works (the Twelve Olympians [Dodekatheon], Nike etc.) were inspired or copied from ancient marbles. He was so committed to this cult of antiquity [...] that he did not dare to try anything new.

The making of copies and variants of ancient sculptures was common practice throughout the 19th century, see Pavlopoulos (2001, 135).

49 Derived from the classic Aristotelian model of *oikos*, 'oeconomy' was the practice of managing the economic and moral resources of the household (Harvey 2012, 24). The meaning of economy, however, changed over the 17th, 18th, and early 19th centuries: "In the OED, examples of 'economical' which concern specifically material resources and their development, or political economy, date only from 1781" (Harvey 2012, 59).

50 Cf. Keynes (1972, 86):

> It is profoundly in the English tradition of humane science in that tradition of Scotch and English thought, in which there has been, I think, an extraordinary continuity of feeling, if I may so express it, from the eighteenth century to the present time the tradition which is suggested by the names of Locke, Hume, Adam Smith, Paley, Bentham, Darwin, and Mill, a tradition marked by a love of truth and a most noble lucidity, by a prosaic sanity free from

sentiment or metaphysic, and by an immense disinterestedness and public spirit. There is a continuity in these writings, not only of feeling, but of actual matter. It is in this company that Malthus belongs.

51 See also Keynes' view on Economics as a science: "In economics that is not the case, and to convert a model into a quantitative formula is to destroy its usefulness as an instrument of thought" (Keynes 1989, 299). For the subsequent narrowing of economic thought, see Frazer (1937, 373).

52 See Purton's analogous musings about Sterne: "Sterne is ultimately motivated, not by benevolence, but by curiosity. He is less a sentimentalist than a scientific – or Lockean – observer of emotions" (Purton 2012, 35).

References

Amrozowicz, Michael C. (2013), 'Adam Smith: History and Poetics', in Christopher J. Berry, Maria Pia Paganelli, and Craig Smith (eds.), *The Oxford Handbook of Adam Smith* (Oxford: Oxford University Press), 143–158.

Andreadis, Andreas Michael (1911), *Εμμανουήλ Ροΐδης: Βιογραφικόν Σημείωμα* [Emmanuel Roidis: Curriculum Vitae] (Athens: Nikolaos Chiotis).

Beaton, Roderick (2017a), 'Afterword', in Margaret Alexiou and Douglas Cairns (eds.), *Greek Laughter and Tears: Antiquity and After* (Edinburgh: Edinburgh University Press), 403–412.

——— (2017b), 'Byron and Greece: Lessons in "Political Economy"', in Roderick Beaton and Christine Kenyon Jones (eds.), *Byron: The Poetry of Politics and the Politics of Poetry* (Abingdon: Routledge), 249–261.

Beaty, Frederick L. (1969), 'Byron on Malthus and the Population Problem', *Keats-Shelley Journal*, 18, 17–26.

Bell, Michael (1983), *The Sentiment of Reality: Truth of Feeling in the European Novel* (London: Allen & Unwin).

Bonar, James (1880), *Parson Malthus* (Edinburgh: Lorimer and Gillies).

Byron, George Gordon (1903), *The Works of Lord Byron: Poetry Vol. VI*, ed. Ernest Hartley Coleridge, 7 vols. (6; London: John Murray).

——— (1973), *Byron's Letters and Journals, Volume II: 'Famous in My Time,' 1810–1812*, ed. Leslie A. Marchand (London: John Murray).

——— (1978), *Byron's Letters and Journals, Volume VIII: 'Born for Opposition,' 1821*, ed. Leslie A. Marchand (London: John Murray).

——— (1996), *Don Juan*, ed. T. G. Steffan, E. Steffan, and W. W. Pratt (London: Penguin).

——— (2009), *Don Juan* [online text], ed. Peter Cochran <https://petercochran.files.wordpress.com/2009/03/don_juan_canto_9.pdf>

Carlyle, Thomas (2010), 'The Nigger Question', in Henry Duff Traill (ed.), *The Works of Thomas Carlyle* (6; Cambridge: Cambridge University Press), 348–383.

DeGooyer, Stephanie (2016), 'The Poetics of the Passport in A Sentimental Journey', in Peter de Voogd, Judith Hawley, and Melvyn New (eds.), *Sterne, Tristram, Yorick: Tercentenary Essays on Laurence Sterne* (Newark: University of Delaware Press), 201–218.

——— (2018), '"The Eyes of Other People": Adam Smith's Triangular Sympathy and the Sentimental Novel', *ELH*, 85 (3), 669–690.

Eagleton, Terry (2003), *After Theory* (New York: Basic Books).

——— (2009), *Trouble with Strangers: A Study of Ethics* (Oxford: Wiley-Blackwell).

Faccarello, Gilbert (2020), '"Enlightened Saint Malthus" or the "Gloomy Protestant of Dismal England"? The Reception of Malthus in the French Language', in Gilbert Faccarello, Masashi Izumo, and Hiromi Morishita (eds.), *Malthus across Nations: The Reception of Thomas Robert Malthus in Europe, America and Japan* (Cheltenham, UK: Edward Elgar Publishing), 83–173.

Frazer, Lindley M. (1937), *Economic Thought and Language: A Critique of Some Fundamental Economic Concepts* (London: Adam & Charles Black).

Gallagher, Catherine (2009), 'The Romantics and the Political Economists', in James Chandler (ed.), *The Cambridge History of English Romantic Literature* (Cambridge: Cambridge University Press), 71–100.

Greiner, Rae (2009), 'Sympathy Time: Adam Smith, George Eliot, and the Realist Novel', *Narrative*, 17 (3), 291–311.

Guillory, John (1993), *Cultural Capital: The Problem of Literary Canon Formation* (Chicago and London: University of Chicago Press).

Haakonssen, Knud (2002), 'Introduction', *Adam Smith, Theory of Moral Sentiments* (Cambridge: Cambridge University Press), vii–xxiv.

Harvey, Karen (2012), *The Little Republic: Masculinity and Domestic Authority in Eighteenth-Century Britain* (Oxford: Oxford University Press).

Hazlitt, William (1807), *A Reply to the Essay on Population by the Rev. T. R. Malthus. In a Series of Letters, to Which Are Added Extracts from the Essay; With Notes* (London: Longman, Hurst, Rees, and Orme).

Heilbroner, Robert L. (1986), 'The Gloomy Presentiments of Parson Malthus and David Ricardo', in *The Worldly Philosophers: The Lives, Times and Ideas of the Great Economic Thinkers* (New York: Simon & Schuster), 75–104.

Heinzelman, Kurt (1981), 'Byron's Poetry of Politics: The Economic Basis of the "Poetical Character"', *Texas Studies in Literature and Language*, 23 (3, An Issue Devoted to Romanticism and Criticism), 361–388.

Hont, Istvan (2015), *Politics in Commercial Society: Jean-Jacques Rousseau and Adam Smith*, ed. Béla Kapossy and Michael Sonenscher (Cambridge, MA: Harvard University Press).

Ittensohn, Mark (2017), 'Fictionalising the Romantic Marketplace: Self-reflexivity in the Early-Nineteenth-Century Frame Tale', *Victoriographies*, 7 (1), 25–41.

Jackson-Houlston, Caroline M. (2017), *Gendering Walter Scott: Sex, Violence and Romantic Period Writing* (Abingdon: Routledge).

James, Patricia (1979), *Population Malthus: His Life and Times* (London: Routledge and Kegan Paul).

Jensen, An-Magritt (2003), 'The Power of Passion and the Improper Acts: A Gendered Malthus', in An-Magritt Jensen, Torbjørn Knutsen, and Anders Skonhoft (eds.), *Visiting Malthus: The Man, His Times, the Issues* (Oslo: Abstract Forlag As), 124–141.

Keynes, John Maynard (1972), 'Thomas Robert Malthus', in *Essays in Biography* (The Collected Writings of John Maynard Keynes, X; London: Macmillan), 71–108.

——— (1989), *The General Theory and After, Part II Defence and Development* (The Collected Writings of John Maynard Keynes, XIV; London: Macmillan).

Levy, David M. (2002), *How the Dismal Science Got Its Name: Classical Economics and the Ur-text of Racial Politics* (Ann Arbor: University of Michigan Press).

Lika, Foteini (2018), *Roidis and the Borrowed Muse: British Historiography Fiction and Satire in Pope Joan* (Newcastle upon Tyne: Cambridge Scholars Publishing).

MacLean, Kenneth (1949), 'Imagination and Sympathy: Sterne and Adam Smith', *Journal of the History of Ideas*, 10 (3), 399–410.

Mallarmé, Stéphane (1895), *La Musique et les Lettres* (Paris: Librairie Académique Didier, Perrin et Cie).
Malthus, Thomas Robert (1830), *A Summary View of the Principle of Population* (London: John Murray).
——— (1966), *First Essay on Population: A Reprint in Facsimile of an Essay on the Principle of Population, as It Affects the Future Improvement of Society, 1798* (London: Macmillan).
——— (1970), *The Pamphlets of Thomas Robert Malthus* (New York: Augustus M. Kelley).
——— (1989), *Principles of Political Economy: Variorum* Edition, ed. John Pullen (1; Cambridge: Cambridge University Press).
——— (1996a), *An Essay on the Principle of Population: Second Edition [1803]* (The Six Editions 11 Volumes; London: Routledge/Thoemmes Press).
——— (1996b), *An Essay on the Principle of Population: Fifth Edition [1817]*, 3 vols. (The Six Editions 11 Volumes, 1; London: Routledge/Thoemmes Press).
Markianos, D. I. (1950), 'Καλλιτεχνικά Μνημόσυνα. Γεώργιος Βρούτος, ο Αθηναίος Γλύπτης [Artistic Memorials. Georgios Vroutos, the Athenian Sculptor]', *Elliniki Dimiourgia*, (47), 156–158.
Markovits, Stephanie (2018), 'Don Juan's Numerals', *European Romantic Review*, 29 (5), 639–655.
Marshall, David (1984), 'Adam Smith and the Theatricality of Moral Sentiments', *Critical Inquiry*, 10 (4), 592–613.
Marx, Karl (1953), 'Parson Malthus', in Ronald L. Meek (ed.), *Marx and Engels on Malthus* (London: Lawrence and Wishart), 83–84.
Mayhew, Robert J. (2014), *Malthus: The Life and Legacies of an Untimely Prophet* (Cambridge: Belknap Press of Harvard University Press).
McLane, Maureen N. (2017), 'Malthus Our Contemporary? Toward a Political Economy of Sex', in Joel Faflak (ed.), *Marking Time: Romanticism and Evolution* (Toronto: University of Toronto Press), 122–144.
Michailidis, Kimon (1909), 'Ζωγραφική και Γλυπτική [Painting and Sculpture]', *Panathinaia*, 17 (200), 235.
Milgate, Murray (2008), 'Carlyle, Thomas (1795–1881)', in Steven N. Durlauf and Lawrence E. Blume (eds.), *The New Palgrave Dictionary of Economics* (2nd edn.; New York: Palgrave Macmillan), 697–698.
Milgate, Murray and Stimson, Shannon C. (2009), *After Adam Smith: A Century of Transformation in Politics and Political Economy* (Princeton: Princeton University Press).
Paganelli, Maria Pia (2010), 'The Moralizing Role of Distance in Adam Smith: The *Theory of Moral Sentiments* as Possible Praise of Commerce', *History of Political Economy*, 42 (3), 425–441.
Paraschos, Kleon (1942), *Εμμανουήλ Ροΐδης: Η Ζωή, το Έργο, η Εποχή του* [Emmanuel Roidis: His Life, His Work, His Times] (1; Athens: Aetos).
Pavlopoulos, Dimitris (2001), 'Ένα Κλασικιστικό Ανάγλυφο του 19ου αιώνα [A 19th Century Classicising Relief]', *Mouseio Benaki-Periodiko*, 1, 127–136.
Peacock, Thomas Love (1817), *Melincourt* (1; London: S. Gosnell).
Petersen, William (1979), 'Malthus and the Intellectuals', *Population and Development Review*, 5 (3), 469–478.
Purton, Valerie (2012), *Dickens and the Sentimental Tradition: Fielding, Richardson, Sterne, Goldsmith, Sheridan, Lamb* (London: Anthem Press).

Raphael, D. D. (2007), *The Impartial Spectator: Adam Smith's Moral Philosophy* (Oxford: Clarendon Press).
Reid, Thomas (1852), *The Works of Thomas Reid, D.D.; Now Fully Collected, with Selections from His Unpublished Letters*, ed. William Hamilton and Dugald Stewart (Edinburgh: Maclachlan and Stewart).
Reisman, David (2018), *Thomas Robert Malthus* (Great Thinkers in Economics; Cham, Switzerland: Palgrave Macmillan).
Richetti, John (1999), *The English Novel in History 1700–1780* (London: Routledge).
Roïdes, Emmanuel (2019), *Pope Joan*, trans. David Connolly (Athens: Aiora Press).
Roidis, Emmanuel (1866), *Η Πάπισσα Ιωάννα: Μεσαιωνική Μελέτη* [Pope Joan: Medieval Study] (Athens: I. Kassandreos).
——— (1978a), 'Ρίχτερ ο Μοναδικός [Richter, the One and Only]', in Alkis Angelou (ed.), *Άπαντα: Πέμπτος Τόμος 1894–1904* (5; Athens: Ermis), 306–317.
——— (1978b), 'Μονόλογος Ευαισθήτου [Monologue of a Sensitive Man]', in Alkis Angelou (ed.), *Άπαντα: Πέμπτος Τόμος 1894–1904* (5; Athens: Ermis), 172–175.
——— (1978c), 'Ασμοδαίος, Επιστολή 1-6-1875 [Asmodeus, Letter 1-6-1875]', in Alkis Angelou (ed.), *Άπαντα: Δεύτερος Τόμος 1868–1879* (2; Athens: Ermis), 134–137.
——— (1978d), 'Αριστοτέλης Βαλαωρίτης [Aristotle Valaoritis]', in Alkis Angelou (ed.), *Άπαντα: Δεύτερος Τόμος 1868–1879* (2; Athens: Ermis), 405–420.
Skinner, Andrew S. (1992), "Adam Smith: Ethics and Self-love", in P. Jones and A. S. Skinner (eds.), *Adam Smith Reviewed* (Edinburgh: Edinburgh University Press), 142–167.
Skinner, Gillian (1999), "Above Oeconomy': The History of Lady Barton, The Man of Feeling and A Sentimental Journey', *Sensibility and Economics in the Novel, 1740–1800: The Price of a Tear* (London: Macmillan), 91–116.
Smith, Adam (1976a), *The Theory of Moral Sentiments*, ed. D. D. Raphael and A. L. Macfie (Oxford: Oxford University Press).
——— (1976b), *An Inquiry into the Nature and Causes of the Wealth of Nations*, ed. Edwin Cannan (Chicago: University of Chicago Press).
Sterne, Laurence (2002), *A Sentimental Journey through France and Italy and Continuation of the Bramine's Journal: The Text and Notes*, ed. Melvyn New and W. G. Day (The Florida Edition of the Works of Laurence Sterne, Vol. 6; Florida: University Press of Florida).
Stewart-Robertson, J. C. and Norton, David Fate (1984), 'Thomas Reid on Adam Smith's Theory of Morals', *Journal of the History of Ideas*, 45 (2), 309–321.
Vatopoulos, Nikos (2007), 'Ο Άραβας των Αθηνών διά χειρός Ν. Γύζη [The Athenian Arab by N. Gyzis]', *Kathimerini*, 03.01.2007.
Wordsworth, William and Coleridge, Samuel Taylor (2013), *Lyrical Ballads: 1798 and 1802* (Oxford: Oxford University Press).
Xenopoulos, Grigorios (1894), ''Ελληνες Καλλιτέχναι: Γεώργιος Βρούτος [Greek Artists: Georgios Vroutos]', *Eikonografimeni Estia*, (3), 40–43.
Yiofyllis, Fotos (1956), 'Νεοέλληνες Ζωγράφοι και Γλύπτες: Ιωάννης Βιτσάρης [Modern Greek Painters and Sculptors: Ioannis Vitsaris]', *Nea Estia* 690, 442–443.

3 Adamantios Koraes and his tropics of discourse

Art, science and economics as therapeutic debts

Stratos Myrogiannis

Introduction

The interplay between art, science and economics has always been a challenging issue. In this chapter, we set out to examine how these three concepts shaped the thought of Adamantios Koraes, one of the most prominent representatives of the Modern Greek Enlightenment. We will focus not only on Koraes comments on these three topics but also on how he invoked concepts within his writings in order to comment on crucial issues of his time and, mainly, on the role of Enlightenment ideas on the awakening and the emancipation of people living under foreign rule. What's interesting about Koraes's discussions on art, science and economics is that he had spent several years as a merchant in Amsterdam but he also professionally trained as a doctor before dedicating his life to the study of Ancient Greek and Roman thought, by preparing new editions of ancient philosophers and writers alike. In addition, we will focus on how he used language, relevant vocabulary and, how he linguistically styled his discourse. Since this topic has not been extensively studied until now, it is difficult to do full justice in a few pages. This chapter is more exploratory in nature, mapping some of the basic contours of Koraes's thought and charting possible avenues for future research.

Theoretical framework: tropics of discourse

When dealing with works that is hard to categorize, as is Koraes's works, which are mostly lengthy introductions to his editions of Ancient Greek and Roman writers, and editions of his personal correspondence, it is equally hard to find the appropriate methodological tools. In our case, we will take into account the theoretical work of Hayden White since most of Koraes's writings to be examined can be registered as (a) essays of historical, literary, political and sociological interest and (b) letters on various topics showing a historical interest or scope. Consequently, given that Koraes was particularly interested in the historical dimension of his preferred topics, so much so that he adopted a role resembling that of an amateur historian, we believe that White's theoretical scheme fits well with the scope of the suggested discourse

DOI: 10.4324/9781003105435-5

analysis. In analysing historical works, White persuasively showed that the same methodological and theoretical tools should be used when interpreting literary or historical narratives, since, in all these types of discourse, language is used in the same way for the representation of reality. More specifically, he argued that historians always construct a specific version of the past, by relating it to their own prejudices that shapes a preferred reality of past events and about past events. This is why they remind us of writers of fiction (Paul 2011: 5). We will also deploy the concept of implied author, as it was used by Booth (Booth 1961: 70–71) and Eco (1979: 7). In addition, since we are especially interested in examining how Koraes represents reality, we will adopt White's assumption (White 1972: 5–20), i.e., that, in essence, every type of discourse deploys tropics and/or figurative language despite its fictional or realistic intentions. In this sense, we accept the premise that figurative language is present in both historical and fictional works in order to endow any story with a plot (Paul 2011: 88). We also accept that tropics are constitutive elements of every discourse since through them every discourse defines its narrative (White 1985: 2) but also, as in our case, every discourse defines its own reality. This latter hypothesis will prove itself useful when we will examine the particularities of Koraes's discourse on art, science and economics and their interplay.

In what follows, we will focus on Koraes's stylistic and linguistic choices, i.e., his rhetoric and the poetics of his texts. We use tropics and/or figurative language as deviations from what is considered normal or literal use of language. These deviations create figures of speech and modes of thought that diverge from a predictable and standard linguistic use. In this way, tropics are capable of revealing qualities of texts that appear to be inaccessible at first glance. Closely related to this is the issue of representation of reality but due to space and time limitations, we cannot afford to deal in depth neither with the concept of representation or with what is real in history and/or literature. In short, we accept the premise that all efforts to represent reality "as it is" are mere illusions. Moreover, any effort to represent reality is, in essence, also an effort to interpret it. In other words, whatever we say about reality is closely related to the specific language we use to say it. Hence, we are interested in analysing and reviewing how texts make sense and produce meaning both on the level of the authorial intention and on the level of the reader's response. From this point of view, the concept of mimesis seems rather important since it shows that every attempt on the part of the author to represent things ends up distorting to some degree, the object to be represented.

In this chapter, we are going to focus on the stylistic choices made by Koraes, meaning the kind of words and terms he used in order to refer to his social environment and the particular social and political issues of his time. At a second level, we are also interested in the variety of ways his linguistic choices can be interpreted in specific contexts. Consequently, along with Hayden White, we accept that realistic and fictional discourses appear to be no different from each other since they are both regarded as semiological apparatuses that produce meanings through a process of representation and interpretation with the help of signifieds and extralinguistic elements (White 1987: x). There is always the case that readers will understand different things to what an author wanted them to understand. In this case, there is no objectively safe way for us to evaluate an argument. What we can do is to evaluate it in terms of its internal validity or its correspondence to a specific reality. Unfortunately, this latter process takes us back to the problem of representation. What we are left with is that in order to evaluate a discourse, we have to examine how convincing it is based on the ways it is used to represent a specific historical reality. So, the cogency of discourse depends on human agents both on the level of production and interpretation. Nevertheless, we shouldn't forget that human agents are themselves sensitive and vulnerable to tropics and figurative language, which makes the issue of cogency even harder for readers to comprehend.

What all these theoretic clarifications amount to is an effort on our part to explain that we face two kinds of difficulties when dealing with Koraes's work. The first one is that it is quite hard to categorize Koraes's works. This makes the choice of a suitable theoretical tool even harder. We believe that White's methodology, along with its related concepts, suits well the needs of this chapter. The second difficulty is that very often, Koraes changed his views on a number of issues. His flexibility makes our effort to examine his thought a real challenge in terms of validity and consistency. Koraes was a skilful writer who did not hesitate to adjust his opinions according to taste or to distance himself from what he had written elsewhere. If a new context or a new condition allowed for a slightly changed point of view or a slightly changed argument – compared to what he had previously written – he was not averse to change. Nevertheless, it is important to point out that he also remained quite consistent in a variety of subjects throughout his life. The complexity of his position and of his thought today creates problems to any researcher trying to fit his work into a simple classification rubric. Instead, we will concentrate to show how he linked the different topics in an overarching narrative.

Koraes's views on art and science

A Modern Greek *emigré* and an avid student of Ancient Greek and Roman heritage, Adamantios Koraes spent most of his life in Paris. He arrived in the cultural capital of Europe in 1788 and he never saw again the land of his beloved Greek island. We should have in mind that a number of intellectuals from other countries, for example David Hume, Ferdinando Galiani, Adam Smith and others, also spent some time in Paris, since it was one of the most prestigious centres of the Enlightenment intellectual movement in the long 18th century (Roncaglia 2017: 52). Koraes's views on art were influenced by the thinkers of the Enlightenment. The analysis of his views and also his linguistic choices on a number of issues related to art will help us understand his aesthetics. Also, we will examine how his theoretical position manifests itself in his writings.

First, we have to look into the aesthetic theories of the time in order to examine how Koraes's views fit within the intellectual and artistic *milieu* of the age of Enlightenment. Even if someone agreed with what Peter Gay stated about the art of the Enlightenment, i.e., that "there was no distinctive Enlightenment style in the arts" (Gay 1969: 216), it would be difficult not to see that at the same time, there was a variety of well-defined styles. It is well-known that the 18th century witnessed the rise of the Rococo style and Neoclassicism. Apart from other more prominent characteristics of neoclassical art, such as the highlighting of the virtues of antiquity and the belief that ancient societies had achieved ways of life more attuned to the demands of rationality, it is worth mentioning a certain tendency, especially in painting, and more specifically in the paintings of J. L. David to narrate ancient themes as a commentary on the problems of contemporary everyday life (Soergel 2005: 462, 507–508). In a twisted form, this trend also appears in Koraes's writings. Another concept that Koraes was preoccupied with – and featured in the 18th-century discourse on aesthetics – was a genuine willingness to revive perceived antiquity virtues like clarity, harmony and rationality in aspects of everyday life. Finally, it should be noted that Enlightenment aesthetics was a premium field for philosophical contemplation on numerous issues (Mücke 2015: 73–75) – art, science and economics included.

We should also keep in mind that more often than one might think, the *philosophes* and artists dealt with philosophy and art as a moralizing and civilizing force (Gay 1969: 219). Before continuing with the examination of Koraes's writings, we have to highlight two more aspects of the thought of Enlightenment thinkers that we will revisit in the relevant sections. The first one is the study of history and the historical way of thinking as a methodological tool. We know that this subject preoccupied Koraes in his writings. It seems that a similar thing, i.e., the employment of historical materials also concerned Hume since for him, as in Koraes's case, the study of history was an "invention" which "extends our experience to all past ages, and to the most distant nations" (Miller 1985: 556). Secondly, other philosophers like Sir James Steuart, influenced by Hume, believed that "what the recent revolutions in the politics of Europe had indicated was the regular progress of mankind, from great simplicity to complicated refinement" (Skinner 2003: 185). This approach, from simpler to complicated forms of social existence, had an impact not only on numerous disciplines, such as politics and economics, but also on many Enlightenment *philosophes* and, among them, on Koraes.

In this intellectual and artistic milieu and, influenced by the doctrines of French Enlightenment, Koraes vividly expressed his views on art in a number of instances within his work. We will start our analysis from the comments he made about art in general and then we move on to more detailed comments on a variety of subjects. In the introduction to his Isocrates edition (1807), he mentioned that

> the art of rhetoric – and all other arts – has been born out of observation and becomes perfect and complete with experience, while the aim of philosophy is to make up general rules; thus, philosophy is the source of all the arts.
>
> (Koraes 1984: 263–264)[1]

So, when discussing art, the starting point for Koraes is the illuminating hypothesis that observation and experience is essential for all the arts, which all stem from philosophy. This premise is not new in the era of the Enlightenment when one of the most prominent representatives of Enlightenment science, Isaac Newton dominated the field with his scientific method: experiment and observation (Gay 1969: 129). So, for Koraes, philosophy is the mother of all the arts and all the arts reach perfection through experience and observation, two of the most celebrated concepts of Enlightenment science. In the same introduction, Koraes repeated the same argument, slightly changed this time: "I was saying that neither science nor art can be easily taught or come to perfection without the aid of philosophy" (Koraes 1984: 223). Nevertheless, for Koraes, philosophy is mainly a hunt for truth as can be seen in his introduction of the 1821 edition of Aristotle's *Politics*: "I can't recall who among the Ancients said that philosophy is a hunt for truth" (Koraes 1988: 659). In this extract, we can detect how he invoked Ancient Greek thought in order to comment on contemporary philosophy, a rhetorical device which reveals how Koraes understood the reality of his time.

As we mentioned at the beginning, when it comes to philosophical reasoning, consistency is not Koraes's strong point. A few years earlier, the Modern Greek *philosophe* had accepted that the real goal of philosophy is to know one's self, as he commented in the introduction of the fourth volume of Plutarch (1812):

> The first objective of philosophy is to help people to get to know themselves, that is, to find out who they are, where and when were they born, to know the conditions of their lives and how to deal with them, and what kind of help they can provide for their country. In short, as the philosopher Ariston from Chios used to say, a philosopher has to imitate the art of an actor.
>
> (Koraes 1984: 491)

Leaving aside Koraes's flexibility on academic and philosophical issues, a trait that we have already mentioned, it is quite interesting to analyse the connection he drew between philosophy and art in general, and also philosophy and the art of acting in particular. For him, philosophy is a protean and multi-faceted concept, a doctrine with many functions, a prerequisite for dealing with art. To venture an interpretation on Koraes's comments on philosophy, we could point out the analogy he drew between a philosopher and an actor, which discloses, according to Koraes, the complexity of both arts, philosophy and acting.

In another introductory volume on Plutarch (1810), he also argued that the aim of philosophy is to help people achieve progress without hurting their mind while elsewhere in the same volume, he accepted that philosophy refines human nature (Koraes 1984: 398, 405). Human nature, and its relation to philosophy or science, was a common theme during the Enlightenment. Many thinkers tried to analyse the role of human nature on the development of science, e.g., for Hume 'all the sciences have a relation, greater or less, to human nature, and that however wide any of them may seem to run from it, they still return back by one passage or another' (Skinner 2003: 180). The study of human nature was thus to be based upon empirical evidence. So, for Koraes, all arts stemmed from philosophy, which refines human nature through experiment and observation. Last but not least, in another introduction, this time on Marcus Aurelius's *Meditations* (or *To Himself*, 1816), he claimed that philosophy is the most appropriate "treatment" for the newly-emerged nations that still need to be developed to reach perfection (Koraes 1988: 403–404). What Koraes added in this clarification on philosophy is the concept of "therapy", which he probably borrowed from the intellectual milieu of the late 18th century in Germany, where Ancient Greece was seen by artists and authors as a remedy to the excesses of the Enlightenment (Güthenke 2008: 5). The analogy or metaphor of therapy is quite significant in Koraes's thought and we will return to it in the course of this chapter since it is one of the most powerful figurative uses of language in his work.

Another concept which Koraes was also particularly preoccupied with was the concept of education. In his autobiography (1829), he accepted that "only education perfects the gifts of nature" (Koraes 1984: θ'). Education played a crucial role in Koraes's thought since he did not only highlight the link between education and human nature (as he did with philosophy and human nature) but also the link between art and education since he accepted that art could help Modern Greeks to educate themselves in order to make Greece an independent and free country (Koraes 1984: 313). In addition, let's not forget that Koraes began his series of translations of Ancient Greek and Roman authors with Theophrastos's *Characters*, a work which easily falls within the category of fictional allegory with philosophical connotations. So, in Koraes's mind, education along with art and philosophy were some of the cultural prerequisites for a free and independent Modern Greek state. This assumption also reveals crucial ideological and political threads of his thought. These qualities were also present in his volume on Aristotle's *Nicomachean Ethics* where he commented on the relation between ethics and politics and also on philosophy and science: "While different in name, ethics and politics are the same science, namely practical philosophy, which is called the art of life by Cicero and Plutarch" (Koraes 1990: 16). As it can be easily seen, in the span of one sentence, Koraes mentioned ethics, politics, philosophy and science as belonging to one concept: the art of life while borrowing his terminology from Cicero and Plutarch. This rhetorical device on his part is not new within his work. Nevertheless, with this phrase, the complexity of his thought and more specifically the way he reflected on art and science becomes clearer as he considered all these concepts as one art, the art of life. To make things even more complicated, he added economics (along with ethics and politics) as integral part of philosophy: "Ethics, politics and economics are rightfully considered parts of philosophy" (Koraes 1984: 178).[2]

Apart from the concepts of art, philosophy, science, economics, education and their interrelation, in his writings, and more specifically when he described how Modern Greeks could benefit from other more advanced nations, the concept of mimesis emerges. More specifically, in 1814, he mentioned something which he read or heard somewhere – he is vague about his sources in this occasion – that the development of the language of Modern Greeks should begin with the cultivation of poetry since poetry was the starting point for other nations too. So, according to Koraes, Modern Greeks should imitate the art of poetry of other more advanced nations in order to develop their own national poetry (Koraes 1984: 566–567). The concept of imitation or, in other words, the concept of "mimesis" had also preoccupied the Modern Greek *philosophe*, who offered his comments on Batteux's definition of literature (Tabaki 1998: 91 and Dimaras 1979: 115). To be more specific, for Koraes, the history of literature is a history of *mimeses* on all levels. In order to support his argument, i.e., that, in essence, the history of literature is nothing but a history of literary mimeses since all authors imitate other authors, Koraes took as an example Heliodoros's work. He argued that Heliodorus's initial idea was much later imitated by Torquatto Tasso, who fashioned his characters after Heliodorus's fictional heroes (Koraes 1984: 28–29). So, in Koraes's mind, literature (and art for that matter) was all about imitating the best of antiquity in a convincing way but also adapting characters and elements into a contemporary setting. This assumption, in essence, makes mimesis, in Koraes's terms, an integral part of art.

Among his numerous comments on a variety of topics, Koraes (*Atakta*, B′, 1829) found an original way to comment on how language works by mentioning the art of painting:

> [Language] is created within the premature minds of uncivilised people and, next, by people in a barbarous state [...] these people portrayed the meanings of words to their friends with such poor colours (no better colours were available back then). Next, more intelligent people appeared, who were thinking better than the latter, and managed to express themselves correctly and to portray their thoughts into words way better than before.
>
> (Koraes 1995: 226–227)

In this phrase, he invoked the art of painting in order to explain how languages evolved from the dawn of time until his days. Leaving aside the implications of this phrase in relation to Koraes's theory of language, it is worth mentioning that he often used figurative language, and in this case, the metaphor of painting in order to express his thought. In addition, this extract also shows that he deployed a historical approach to investigate his preferred subjects, examining the origins of things or earlier manifestations of different phenomena.

Thus, influenced by the most widely accepted ideas of his time, Koraes reflected on art, science and economics with no obvious originality. He repeated common themes and motives of the Enlightenment. In a way, he confirmed that, in essence, "historical interpretation is limited to the repertoire of available forms" (Paul 2011: 97). His innovation, if, in fact, there is an innovative way of thinking in Koraes's writings regarding art, science and economics, is yet to be revealed and revolves around two poles: on the one hand, he linked the development of art and science to the national cause of the Modern Greeks of his time. If Modern Greeks wanted to have a free and independent state, first they had to develop their culture through art, science and economic activity, as we will see below, in order to prepare themselves to claim a free and independent state. On the other hand, he talked about art, science and economics mostly in medical terms, and more specifically, in terms of the therapeutical influence of art, science and economics on Modern Greeks since in such a way they would perfect themselves both as individuals and collectively as a nation. We will return to this theme in the last part of this chapter.

Koraes's entrepreneurship experience in Amsterdam and his views on economics

In the early Enlightenment, modern commercial society was a concept that preoccupied the minds of intellectuals (Porter 2001: 384). Today, we accept that the intellectual basis for almost all classical economics is to be found in Adam Smith's work and, especially, in the *Wealth of Nations* (1776) (O' Brien 2003: 112). The Enlightenment piloted a transition from *homo civilis* to *homo economicus*, which involved the rationalization of selfishness and self-interest as enlightened ideology (Porter 2001: 396). More specifically, the morality of economy was self-defeating, whereas the new political economy prided itself upon being grounded on natural science, in particular Newtonian physics (Porter 2001: 387). A very popular conceptual categorization that also kept Koraes's mind busy was the idea of distinct sectors of economic activity. The model which Quesnay and Mirabeau developed provided a 'picture' of an economic system with distinct sectors of activity (agriculture, manufacture, trade) and the appropriate socio-economic classes (Broadie 2003: 193). We should also keep in mind that for the enlightenment *philosophes*, economics was related to philosophy and also to state building and morality. In addition, during the Enlightenment, most classical economists had intellectual interests besides economics (O' Brien 2003: 113). Koraes, like Francois Quesnay, was a doctor by profession and an intellectual who showed an active and profound interest in economics, seen both as a theoretical discipline and as a practical business, vital for state building.

In the course of the Modern Greek Enlightenment, some intellectuals showed an early interest in economics and economic thought. We know that one of the most prominent figures of the early Modern Greek Enlightenment, Evgenios Voulgaris translated and taught Genovesi's *Elements of Metaphysics* (Angelou 1999: 63–64) while Dimitrios Katartzis studied political economy (Angelou 1999: 91–92). As for Koraes, we know that in his mid-20s (1771), he arrived to Amsterdam to become a commercial representative of the family business (Iliou 1976: ς'). At first, during the first ten months, he led his life as a man of tradition, meaning the Eastern Christian-Orthodox tradition (Iliou 1976: κζ'). However, in Amsterdam, Koraes found what he always wanted: the ideal of civilized Europe. After the first few months, he let himself be carried away by all the things he found interesting, thus seeking to open up himself to new experiences. He adopted to a new western European way of life; he went to the opera house and learned to play the guitar. Most important of all, he threw away his old clothes and started to wear new western European-style attire because only in this way he could gain acceptability in western polite society. In addition, he followed the European trends of the time in collecting, and he attempted to buy a skeleton in order to start building his own cabinet of curiosities (Iliou 1976: λα'–λδ').

Unfortunately, his skills in commerce were not good enough and financial downfall did not take long to occur. To his defence, he did try to introduce some new ideas in order to increase the margin of profit while he was studying the role of gold in economics (Iliou 1976: με'–μζ' and Angelou 1999: 92–93). Due to his failure as a merchant, his opponents often used to call him "the bankrupt philosophe" while his bankruptcy forced him to leave Amsterdam in 1778 (Iliou 1976: ξγ'–ξη'). In essence, he tried hard to set the family business free from the old working model by dismissing the middlemen in order to proceed to a more profitable scheme (Iliou 1976: μζ'–μη'). This attempt has already been interpreted as an attempt on the part of Koraes to make the family business adjust to the emerging European commercial and financial reality (Iliou 1976: νε'). Before getting bankrupt and in order to respond to the new economic reality of his time, he made investments and founded his own small factory where he intended to process the raw materials he used to trade in order to increase profits and shorten process times. Despite his failure, he continued to show an interest in commerce throughout his life (Iliou 1976: νζ'– νθ').

The experience Koraes gained from his commercial activities brought him closer to the developments of economic thought in Europe. He was aware of the latest economic ideas within Europe since he read books about political economy that circulated in his time. We know from his correspondence that he had read all the famous economists of his time, i.e., Adam Smith, Malthus and Ricardo. We also know that he read Adam Smith's *The Wealth of Nations* in its French translation, i.e., *Richesse de Nations* (Damalas 1885, vol 3: 217) and he sent a copy of it to his homeland (Damalas 1885, vol 3: 217 and Dimaras 1983: 149). He also wanted to have Malthus's work translated (Angelou 1999: 97–98).[3] He sent to Rotas the book *Traite del' Economie Politique* commenting (the letter to Rotas dates 28.8.1815):

> I recommend that you read carefully this last one and if there is a way, you can teach it to others because the content of this book is useful to the happiness of nations. This discipline is new, it began forty or fifty years ago but now it has become clearer.
>
> (Dimaras 1979: 426)

He sent the same book to Petros Skilitzes-Omirides, as we know from a letter to the recipient which dates 28.8.1815 (Dimaras 1979: 424). As for Ricardo, we are not quite sure when and if he read his work, although Iliou believed that he had read something relevant (Iliou 1976: ξ'). Nevertheless, in a letter to Prevost (2 April 1817), Koraes mentioned a book of political economy entitled *Conversations sur l'Economie Politique* (1817, by Madame [Jane] Marcet). Although the names of Say, Sismondi and Tracy appear in this book, the name of Ricardo is not listed in the contents. He also aligned himself with the majority of the classical economists who favoured education (O'Brien 2003: 127). Along with his interest in education, Koraes commented on the wealth of a nation in connection to the Enlightenment and the improvement of manners: "The rise in the number of printed books is attributed to the spread of the Enlightenment. As more and more books will circulate among people, they will contribute to the advancement of education and the improvement of manners" (*Mémoire* 1803: 57).

Koraes's theoretical knowledge of economics and also the experience he gained as a merchant in Amsterdam helped him to sharpen his thought on a number of topics relating to economic issues. In his writings, we find comments on more specialized areas of economic thought. These comments are related, once more, to philosophy (Introduction to Aristotle's *Politics*, 1821) and also to religion and wealth, meaning richness in financial terms: "see that philosophy and religion accuse wealth, not because wealth is bad *pe se*, but because it is a sharp weapon that a few men can successfully handle without hurting themselves or their country" (Koraes 1988: 740). What draws our attention is that he discussed wealth not only in financial terms but also in its relation to philosophy and religion. Also, he was concerned with more practical issues of economics such as taxes. As he mentioned in his introduction to Aristotle's *Nicomachean Ethics* (1822), he believed that each citizen should pay taxes according to their financial capacity (Koraes 1990: 81). Another interesting conceptual combination within Koraes's thought is when he relates, in a single argument, such phenomenally disparate things such as agriculture, art and commerce:

> [T]he benefits of agriculture are many and of great importance. When there is progress in agriculture, there is also progress in the arts and in commerce. Agriculture not only makes citizens rich, due to the pleasure of all the goods, but also develops good manners in their hearts.
>
> (Koraes 1990: 78–79)

Thus, in his mind influenced, as it seems, by the physiocrats, art, commercial activity and agriculture are all intricately connected, and together constitute evidence of social progress. Quite early in his life, he did not hesitate to bring together commercial activity and wealth along with the concepts of mimesis and lifestyle:

> [I]n this barren island everyone, according to their taste, imitates or tries to imitate the way of life of people they met during their travels across the world. A luxurious way of life has become more and more popular and as long as it is fuelled by commerce, it will help people become more and more civilized and enlightened.
>
> (*Mémoire* 1803: 32)

As we can see, Koraes kept bringing together the concepts of art, science, economics along with philosophy, commercial activity, mimesis and therapy (among others) in order to reinforce his arguments depending each time on the specific topic and context he wrote about. What is more important in his thought is that he often considered the practical implications of some or all of these concepts as necessary cultural prerequisites if the national cause of Modern Greeks was to be successful.

In what follows, we are going to see how he managed to fruitfully bring together all these concepts and whether his intellectual and professional background played a role in the shaping of his thought. In other words, we will focus on the stylistic and figurative ways Koraes invoked the concepts he was preoccupied with throughout his life. In this way, we will examine how he handled these concepts which also preoccupied the minds of other Enlightenment thinkers at that time. Koraes managed to reflect on these significant ideas in a rather individual and original way. In this sense, the "bankrupt philosophe" should be acknowledged as a thinker who managed to find new ways to speak about art, science and economics within the intellectual milieu of the Enlightenment.

Stylistic choices

So far, we have seen Koraes's views on art, economics and science and their interrelation within Koraes's own writings. His views are quite compatible with the intellectual milieu of the age of Enlightenment. In what follows, we set out to examine in depth the specific stylistic choices Koraes made when commenting on the aforementioned concepts and, at a second level, we intend to see whether his professional activities or his training, namely his medical training and his engagement with commercial activities, had any impact on the vocabulary he used on specific topics. Through a detailed discourse analysis of specific extracts, we aim to show that his dual professional background had an impact on the way he conceived reality and also on the way he understood art, science and economics. In essence, what we are investigating is a research hypothesis based on specific stylistic choices Koraes used in his work – either intentionally or not – while taking into account the theoretical concepts of the model or implied author (Eco 1979: 7 and Booth 1961: 70–71). Since, though, the model or implied author is nothing but a reader-created construct (Rimmon-Kenan 1983: 87), we attempt, as empirical readers, to imagine and bring to light perspectives of the text that reflect what the model or implied author in Koraes's work might have thought when writing what he did. In this way, our findings might suggest an attempt, on the part of the empirical reader, to unearth hidden or well-disguised attributes of Koraes's stylistic choices.

As we have already seen, quite often in his works, we come across the concept of "therapy" in its many forms: therapy, cure, treatment, etc. It is worth mentioning that in the original, he always used the same word, i.e., "therapy", while in translation, there were different terms used depending on the occasion. It is hardly a surprise when we read sentences like the following about philosophy (Introduction to Claudius Aelianus's *Varia Historia*, 1805): "The woes of Modern Greeks towards philosophy had finally been heard, hence the compassionate philosophy returned to its old homeland in order to cure the open wounds of Greece" (Koraes 1984: 181). This is one of many instances that Koraes invoked the concept of philosophy as a panacea to cure the problems of Modern Greeks. As can be easily seen, he used figurative language, i.e., the use of the word "cure" metaphorically in order to comment on a contemporary problem of the Greek nation by invoking (Ancient Greek) philosophy. Most importantly, the political or ideological implications of his phrase cannot be ignored, especially given the specific context of his time. On this matter, we agree with White that every narrative can't be deprived of intentions or choices and discourse analysis can reveal stylistic choices that hide ideological or political implications beneath the surface of the text (White 1987: ix).

The same term is also used when he talked about the improvement of the morals of the peoples – a very popular theme within Koraes's writings (Introduction to Aesop's *Fables*, 1810):

> As I have said before, the degeneration of language led to the degeneration of the morals, thus our nation was deprived of its virtues. In order to deal with this depravation, two means of treatment were available: to recall and follow the rational and moral lessons of philosophy and to

> rekindle the love of reading and getting to know the glorious poets and writers of Ancient Greece.
>
> (Koraes 1988: 52)

As in the previous example, Koraes again invoked Ancient Greek philosophy and culture as the only available cure (in the original Greek he used the term "therapy") for the perceived "degenerate" condition of Modern Greek language and of the Modern Greeks as a people. Apart from the use of figurative language that relates philosophy as a treatment for the wounds of Modern Greece, we can also see the terms Koraes used to describe the reality of his time. In a (figurative) way, he saw the reality of his time through his vision of Greek antiquity. Such an interpretation leads us to conceive that the tropics of discourse or figurative language always relates more meaning than what the author wanted us to understand or to what an author himself understood since, by its very nature, discourse is a code or a medium between us and reality (White 1985: 4). On this note, and speaking of morals, when commenting upon the importance of ethics (Introduction to Hippocrates and Galen, 1816), Koraes combined medicine (meaning therapy) and ethics:

> You still need a great amount of virtue (which some of you might not even be aware of) because medicine needs to be combined with ethics in order to be done in the right way [...] the body rarely suffers without a suffering soul [...] so, be doctors not only of bodies but, also, of souls which you cannot cure if you do not cure your own soul first.
>
> (Koraes 1988: 365–366)

The truth is that he had already united in his thought and in his writings (Introduction to Beccaria, 1802) the concepts of wealth, profit, education, medicine, science with the value of precious metals and the concept of therapy. So, when he talked about the newly acquired wealth of the rich Modern Greeks, he noted:

> The Modern Greeks of our time are aware that there is no other cure for them but the light of the sciences [...] the rich among our nation are aware that in our time gold and silver are nothing but noble metals and they cannot simply be turned into real money unless by someone who knows how to use them. They are also aware that wealth without education and virtue cannot make someone look better than they really are [...] they are aware that the money they intend to offer in order to cover the nudity of our homeland will return way bigger profits upon their heads.
>
> (Valetas 1964: 92)

On a slightly different note, he did not fail to acknowledge that the Enlightenment, as a historical context, was an excellent framework for the circulation both of ideas and goods. So, in his thought, he managed to metaphorically link commercial activity to science: "Today, it is easy to transfer Enlightenment from one country to the other, as easily as transferring products and commercial goods" (*Mémoire* 1803: 62). On the same page, commercial activity was mentioned in relation to science and the Enlightenment:

> The last decades among all the things Modern Greeks trade, they have also added the commerce of the sciences from all over Europe and especially from France, by trading books and enlightenment ideas in the same way they trade textiles, metals and other industrial products from Europe.
>
> (*Mémoire* 1803: 62)

It is quite clear in his thought that goods as well as ideas, art, science and ideology (the Modern Greek national cause that he so fiercely advocated) could well be transferred from one country to the other so that the not so advanced people could cure themselves of their own cultural, ideological and political inadequacies.

He finally put all the concepts together when he interpreted – in economic terms – the efforts of the Modern Greeks of his time to educate themselves in order to claim their independence. He spoke metaphorically when he pointed out:

> Despite their poor condition and without closing their eyes to the lights of Europe, the Modern Greeks of our time saw the Europeans as fellow debtors who paid back their debts, which were raised by extra taxes, a capital that the Europeans had taken from Ancient Greeks.
>
> (*Mémoire* 1803: 12)

The metaphor of the cultural debt which Europeans have to return to Modern Greeks because the former are indebted to Ancient Greeks was an idea that roughly emerged at the end of the 18th and the beginning of the 19th century (Hanink 2017: 106–107). It was essentially linked to the philhellenic movement of the same era and it went hand by hand with the idea that Ancient Hellas is the origin of civilization (Leontis 1995: 4). In addition, as we have already seen, the idea of the "cultural debt" was also used by Koraes in his works. Indeed, it was actually one of Koraes's most common metaphors within his work. One of his most used and beloved phrases, i.e., "the lights of Europe" signifies all the concepts Koraes was preoccupied with, i.e., art, science, economics, philosophy, education, manners, culture and others, which were to be returned by western Europeans to Modern Greeks as a debt to be paid back because time has come for Modern Greeks to rise to the occasion and claim their cultural emancipation but also their independence and freedom. This narrative, forged mainly by Koraes and also by others during this period, merged political, economic, philosophical and artistic considerations into a unified national ideology to support a national cause, that is, the Greek independence.

Reflections on Koraes's thought on art and economics

In this chapter, what we tried to show is that apart from the specific views Koraes had on art, science and economics, he developed a specific vocabulary and terminology, drawn from his professional background as a merchant and as a doctor. The figurative language he used reveals the quite unique way he developed during his life in order to talk about all the aforementioned concepts and many more, as we have seen, but also about a variety of issues and, mostly, about the independence of his homeland. To be more specific, two significant metaphors prevail in his thought when commenting upon art and science, economics and philosophy. First is the concept of "therapy", which was derived from his medical studies and it was used with increasing frequency as the most efficient metaphor when he talked about the enlightenment of Modern Greeks. Second is the concept of the "cultural debt", which was to be paid back by Europeans to Modern Greeks since Europeans were indebted to Ancient Greeks. Both these concepts functioned as powerful metaphors within Koraes's work and both were linked to the Modern Greek national cause. In addition, these two significant metaphors reveal the ways in which Koraes perceived the political and social situation of his time, that is, the advancement of Modern Greek culture with the help of the already "enlightened" western Europe. Also, these metaphors reveal the terms in which he expected the, according to him, long overdue help from western Europeans to Modern Greece in the form of a cultural therapeutic debt which would "cure" all the wounds of the suffering Modern Greek nation under Ottoman yoke.

We have left for last Koraes's self-image. As previously mentioned, he encouraged young Modern Greeks to: "be doctors not only of bodies, but, also, of souls" (Koraes 1988: 365–366). This is exactly what he fought for during his life; he had already studied medicine and managed to become a doctor; thus, he had already paid his debts to his homeland. What he had also been trying to do for the most part of his life was to become doctor of his fellow compatriots' souls. And he managed to do so, if at all, not with his degree in medicine but with his editions of Ancient Greek and Roman texts, through his essays on what Modern Greeks should do in order to cure their ignorance and become enlightened enough to claim their independence. So, when Koraes commented on art, science and economics, he saw himself as a doctor of the soul for those in need.

In conclusion, one might ask how did Koraes relate art and economics with science? The answer is through his stylistic and linguistic choices, i.e., the terminology he used to comment on social and political issues of his time. When writing about art, science and economics, Koraes was heavily influenced by the thinkers and the intellectual milieu of the Enlightenment. For him, philosophy is the mother of the arts, while the arts perfect themselves through science and experience. In addition, economics, according to Koraes, is an integral part of philosophy. He might have come to this conclusion from his experience as a merchant in Amsterdam. In short, in his work, Koraes combined in novel ways art, science and economics. In addition to this, the Modern Greek *philosophe* developed the concept of "therapy", which was probably borrowed both from the intellectual environment of the Enlightenment and also from his medical training as a doctor. All these concepts were for Koraes a way to approach the ancient Greek and Roman literature and its internal perceived virtues. For this, he spoke of mimesis, which had the double purpose of emulating the Ancients and the enlightened Moderns.

Where did Koraes find inspiration to relate art, science and economics in the specific ways he did? Our research hypothesis is that he drew inspiration from his professional background as a doctor (in Montpelier) and also as merchant (in Amsterdam). In addition, this juxtaposition of ancient and modern cultures and ideas received in Koraes's work a particular twist as it was weaponized to argue in favour of the Greek independence. In his thought and also in his work, he linked art to science and economics through a very indicative metaphor: it was the "cultural debt" the Europeans had to pay back to Modern Greeks in order to return what they had taken in cultural terms from Ancient Greeks. This inventive metaphor contained art and science (cultural element) seen in economic terms (debt). If the Modern Greeks of the time managed to acquire the cultural debt the Europeans had to return to them, they could successfully claim their independence from Ottoman yoke.

Notes

1 All translations of Koraes's extracts are mine and only for the needs of this chapter.
2 Also, in a letter to his friend, Alexandros Vasileiou, dated 20 March 1806 when referring to Kant, he states that the only way to make a mistake when dealing with philosophy is to be vague about something: "Being vague creates vagueness in Philosophy and Religion alike" (Dimaras 1966: 314).
3 We know that Koraes read some of Malthus's work from one of his letters, dated 28 October 1809, sent to his friend Alexandros Vasileiou where he mentioned:

> A few days ago Prevost sent me from Geneva a copy of Malthus's *Essai sur le principe de population*. It's an excellent book and worthy to be translated into Modern Greek [...] I am reading it with the utmost delight.
>
> (Dimaras 1966: 547)

References

Angelou, Alkis (1999), *Των Φώτων Β'. Όψεις του Νεοελληνικού Διαφωτισμού*, Athens, MIET.
Booth, Wayne C. (1961), *The Rhetoric of Fiction*, Chicago, Chicago University Press.
Coray, Adamante (1803), *Mémoire sur l'état actuel de la civilisation dans la Grèce: lu à la Société des observateurs de l'homme, le 16 Nivôse, an XI (6 janvier 1803)*, Paris, F. Didot.

Damalas, Nikolaos (ed.) (1885), *Επιστολαί Αδαμαντίου Κοραή, τ. Α'- Γ'*, Athens, Perri Brothers Printing House.

Dimaras, K. Th. et al. (eds) (1966), *Αδαμάντιος Κοραής, Αλληλογραφία, τ. Β' 1799–1809*, Athens, Bibliopoleion tis Estias.

——— (1979), *Αδαμάντιος Κοραής, Αλληλογραφία, τ. Γ' 1810–1816*, Athens, Bibliopoleion tis Estias.

——— (1983), *Αδαμάντιος Κοραής, Αλληλογραφία, τ. Ε' 1823–1826*, Athens, Bibliopoleion tis Estias.

Eco, Umberto (1979), *The Role of the Reader: Explorations in the Semiotics of Texts*, Bloomington, Indiana University Press.

Gay, Peter (1969), *The Enlightenment: An Interpretation. The Science of Freedom*, New York, W. W. Norton & Company.

Güthenke, Constanze (2008), *Placing Modern Greece: The Dynamics of Romantic Hellenism, 1770–1840*, Oxford, OUP.

Hanink, Johanna (2017), *The Classical Debt. Greek Antiquity in an Era of Austerity*, Cambridge, MA, The Belknap Press of Harvard University Press.

Iliou, Filippos (ed.) (1976), *Σταμάτης Πέτρου, Γράμματα από το Άμστερνταμ*, Athens, Ermis.

——— (1984), *Αδαμάντιου Κοραή. Προλεγόμενα στους Αρχαίους Έλληνες Συγγραφείς και η αυτοβιογραφία του* (preface by K. Th. Dimaras), Athens, MIET.

——— (1988), *Αδαμάντιου Κοραή. Προλεγόμενα στους Αρχαίους Έλληνες Συγγραφείς. Τόμος Β'* (preface by Em. Fragkiskos), Athens, MIET.

——— (1990), *Αδαμάντιου Κοραή. Προλεγόμενα στους Αρχαίους Έλληνες Συγγραφείς. Τόμος Γ'* (preface by L. Droulia), Athens, MIET.

——— (1995), *Αδαμάντιου Κοραή. Προλεγόμενα στους Αρχαίους Έλληνες Συγγραφείς. Τόμος Δ'*, Athens, MIET.

Leontis, Artemis (1995), *Topographies of Hellenism. Mapping the Homeland*, Ithaca, NY, Cornell University Press.

Miller, Eugene F. (ed.) (1985), *David Hume, Essays Moral, Political and Literary*, Indianapolis, Liberty Fund.

Mücke, Dorothea E. von (2015), *The Practices of the Enlightenment: Aesthetics, Authorship, and the Public*, New York, Columbia University Press.

Myrogiannis, Stratos (2012), *The Emergence of a Greek Identity (1700–1821)*, Newcastle upon Tyne, Cambridge Scholars Publishing.

O'Brien, Dennis P. (2003), "Classical Economics" in Warren J. Samuels, Jeff E. Biddle, and John B. Davis (eds), *A Companion to the History of Economic Thought*, Oxford, Blackwell Publishing, pp. 112–129.

Paul, Herman (2011), *Hayden White. The Historical Imagination*, Cambridge, Polity Press.

Porter, Roy (2001), *Enlightenment. Britain and the Creation of the Modern World*, London, Penguin Books.

Rimmon-Kenan, Shlomith (1983), *Narrative Fiction. Contemporary Poetics*, London, Methuen.

Roncaglia, Alessandro (2017), *A Brief History of Economic Thought*, Cambridge, CUP.

Skinner, Andrew S. (2003), "Economic Theory" in Alexander Broadie (ed.), *The Cambridge Companion to the Scottish Enlightenment*, Cambridge, CUP, pp. 178–204.

Soergel, Philip M. (2005), "Visual Arts" in Philip M. Soergel (ed), *Arts and Humanities Through the Eras: The Age of the Baroque and Enlightenment (1600–1800)*, London, Thomson Gale, pp. 456–520.

Tabaki, Anna (1998), «Η οπτική του Κοραή για τη λογοτεχνία και το θέατρο», *Παράβασις/Pa.raba.sis*, v. 2, pp. 81–101.
Valetas, Giorgos (ed.) (1964), *Κοραής. Άπαντα τα Πρωτότυπα Έργα*. vols. A1–A2, Athens, Dorikos.
White, Hayden (1972), "The Structure of Historical Narrative," *Clio*, 1, 3 (1972), pp. 5–20.
——— (1985), *Tropics of Discourse: Essays in Cultural Criticism*, Baltimore, The Johns Hopkins University Press.
——— (1987), *The Content of the Form. Narrative Discourse and Historical Interpretation*, Baltimore, The Johns Hopkins University Press.

Part II

Economics, visual arts and abstractions

4 Economy, efficiency and the promenade deck

Thoughts on the history of architectural theory

Stavros Alifragkis

Introduction

This chapter charts an eclectic and somewhat idiosyncratic itinerary across 19th and early 20th century history of architectural theory with a view to reappraise the relevance of such heavily debated notions as efficiency and optimisation in relation to two popular metaphors: nature and the machine. Furthermore, it sets out to explore the various, direct or – most commonly – indirect ways economic efficiency, in its modern manifestation, shaped by such paradigmatic case studies as the pin factory from Adam Smith's (1723–1790) *Wealth of Nations* (1776), has infused fresh rigour into the formal discussion of architectural functionalism. In particular, this chapter delves into early 20th century fascination with shipbuilding, captured in the precursory writings of modernism's champion, Le Corbusier (1887–1965), as a source of inspiration for an architecture that is both elegant and practical. Furthermore, it describes an architecture that keeps in tune with the proliferation of the machine and the standardisation of production as effective remedies for underperformance and inefficiency. However, the aesthetic paradigm of the interwar ocean liner, as will become evident in the ensuing pages, sends out mixed messages about its symbolic and ideological functions. The ambiguity of the example of the liner corresponds mutatis mutandis to the inherent ambivalence of modernity, 'a language-specific disorder,' whose sociological attributes have been studied by Zygmunt Bauman in his powerful critique *Modernity and Ambivalence* (1993: 1). Aspects of efficiency that arise from this conflict are contrasted against the competing analogy with nature and, in particular, a specific take on nature that was forged in the intellectual background of 19th century American transcendentalism, and the writings of Horatio Greenough (1805–1852) and Henry D. Thoreau (1817–1862). These provide a broader understanding of efficiency as a lifestyle and offer valuable insights into its components that are worth re-examining in the light of postmodern criticism of functionalism.

This chapter discusses efficiency as an operative factor in architectural design, setting out from the premise that ships have functioned, over the course of time, as emblematic concentrations of form-making meaning that

DOI: 10.4324/9781003105435-7

uniquely combine questions of aesthetic and functional nature. In *Vers une Architecture* (1923), shipbuilding registers as one of the special foci, along other potent manifestations of technological advancement, of Le Corbusier's investigations into optimal performance as an integral component of early 20th century architectural modernity. The first section of this chapter discusses Le Corbusier's manipulation of relevant imagery, in specific ocean liners, that heightens the communicative power of his aphorisms, thus resulting in a singular, image-text fugal argumentation. In *Vers une Architecture*, Le Corbusier's investigations into modernity take the shape of a discussion on design optimisation as an experimental, evolutionary process towards perfected products. Establishing standards and design standardisation are discussed in the second section of this chapter as the result of logical reasoning and the application of laws of 'penetration' and 'selection' according to Le Corbusier. RMS *Aquitania* functions here as a telling example of the rhetorical use of the machine metaphor and its highly selective application to functional design. The ocean liner, as a metaphor for practicality and elegance, becomes the initiator – the cognitive mould – of such prominent traits of the modernist architectural vocabulary as the elongated window or the linear corridor. At the same time, the liner has been associated with the semantically rich notion of 'architectural promenade,' a potent agent for producing meaningful spaces and an acute tool for retrospective spatial analyses, that goes beyond aspects of function, in the realms of embodied cognition, kinesthetic experience and the aesthetic appreciation of the natural and humanmade environment. These are also discussed in the second section of this chapter. The apparent inconsistencies of this metaphor are discussed in the following section, where proto-modern conceptions of functionalism, put forward by Greenough in particular, involve both the machine and nature in the construction of a model for efficiency, as distinct but compatible instances of an evolutionary progress towards optimal design. In the last section of this chapter, this investigation into functional and efficient design foregrounds the simplicity, frugality and prudence of asceticism, described by Thoreau as the essential facets of 'economy.' Thoreau, drawing upon his experiences with life in nature, in a single-room, self-built cabin at the shores of Walden Pond near Concord, Massachusetts, calls attention to the ethical underpinnings of modern functional minimalism or, more precisely, the lack of virtue or a strong sense of righteousness that have enslaved the majority of his fellow Americans in a futile and eventually disastrous pursuit of superfluous luxury. Thoreau illustrates his case for 'simplicity and nakedness' by harshly criticising mid-19th century home decoration trends. However, his reproach to ornament epitomises a wider concern with consumerism. Furthermore, Thoreau's personal involvement in the family pencil business as pencil-making engineer could be said to have nurtured a taste for practicality and efficiency (Petrovski 1990) and laid the formal framework – not unlike Smith's pin factory example – for his later philosophical pursuits, thus rendering Thoreau a proponent of early 20th century ascetic modernism *avant la lettre*.

Shipbuilding and architectural design

Swiss-French architect, city planner and theoretician Le Corbusier's seminal publication *Vers une Architecture* (1923) signalled the dawn of a 'brave new world' – both in the Shakespearean[1] and the Huxleyan sense – for architectural design and thinking. In his pivotal modernist manifesto, Le Corbusier urges his colleagues to embark upon a cognitive adventure into the uncharted waters of the machine age, one that will eventually enable them to *see* the breaking light of a novel and glorious epoch. What better way to contemplate this new era than the Foucauldian heterotopia of the deck of an ocean liner putting out to the open sea (Foucault 1984: 46–49). The aptly illustrated chapter 'Des Yeux qui ne Voient pas… Les Paquebots' (Le Corbusier 1958: 65–80)[2] provides ample proof of the structural relevance between shipbuilding and nascent modern architecture. RMS *Aquitania*,[3] for instance, which features prominently in the chapter and on the cover of *Vers une Architecture*, teaches architects:

> [t]he value of a long promenade, a volume that's satisfying and interesting; unity of materials, beautiful arrangement of the structural elements, soundly set out and combined into a unity.[4]

This passage serves as the didactic caption to a picture by Bedford Lemere & Co, a British architectural photography firm, of the first class promenade on the port side of the Bridge Deck (B Deck) of RMS *Aquitania*, looking towards the sheltered part of the deck (Figure 4.1).[5] Despite its unintended classical resonances, where the aesthetic appreciation of architectural composition has departed very little from Vitruvius' (80/70–15 BC) order [ordination], arrangement [disposition] and eurythmy [eurythmia] (1997: book I, ch. II, 48–55) or Leon Battista Alberti's (1404–1472) number [numerus], proportion [finitio] and distribution [collocatio] (1986: book IX, ch. V, 194–197), the caption proposes a forward way of thinking about architectural design, mainly by virtue of its intended image-text juxtaposition. The overall layout of *Vers une Architecture*, its spreads in particular, elicit, according to Panayotis Tournikiotis (Τουρνικιώτης 2004: 255; 2010: 103–109), a twofold reasoning with its provocative content: one that adheres to the text and one that follows the relatively autonomous rhetoric of the images and the visual intensity of their juxtapositions (e.g. the Parthenon and the Delage Grand-Sport placed side by side). Their combined reading and appreciation trigger mental correlations of immense communicative potential about the future of architectural design. In this respect, ocean liners, both functional and aesthetically pleasing, constitute floating machines of grandeur, whose rationalism and efficiency are propounded by means of suggestive imagery that sets their sleek design against less perfected objects, such as a Renaissance tailpiece by French painter and interior designer Paul Vera[6] (1882–1957) (Le Corbusier 1958: 70).

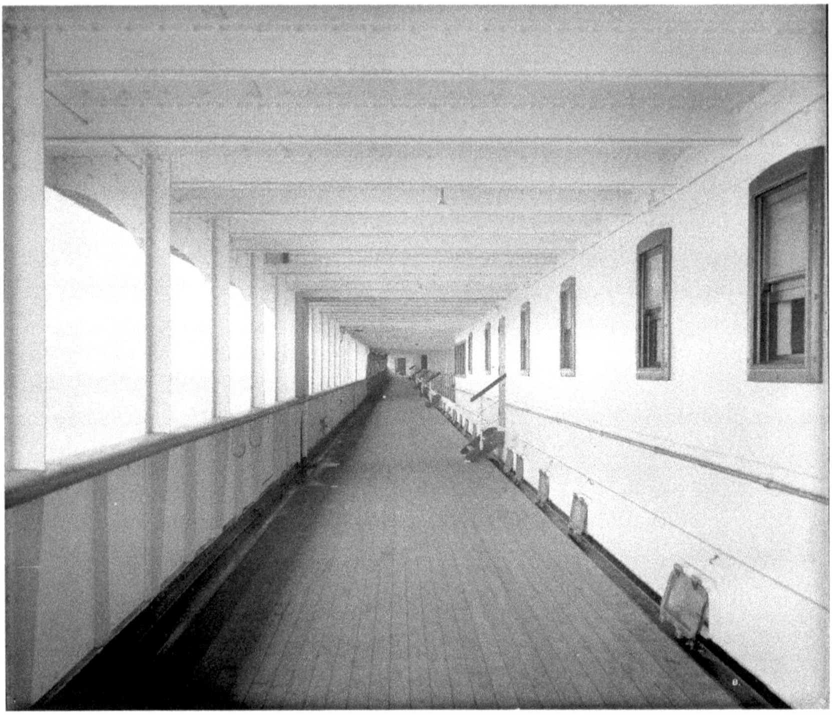

Figure 4.1 First Class Promenade on the *Aquitania* (1914). Photograph by Bedford Lemere & Co. Deck view on the passenger liner *Aquitania* (1914) showing the First Class Promenade, on the port side of the Bridge Deck (B Deck). A view looking forward towards the sheltered part of the deck. © National Maritime Museum, Greenwich, London (G10793).

Historically, conquering the seas, aided by evolving technology (i.e. reliable navigation systems) and an ever-growing confident and innovative art of shipbuilding, has been singled out as a telling index of the progress of civilisation in Smith's seminal text *The Wealth of Nations* (Smith 1981: 34). Following from this, as nations grew more dependent on ships for their defence and domestic and foreign commerce (i.e. water-carriage), attention to shipbuilding productivity and efficiency gained ground, with the development of more sophisticated design methodologies and materials.

Smith's *Wealth of Nations* played an instrumental role in the systematisation of the subject of economics, whose earlier exposition can be traced back to the work of English political economist Sir William Petty (1623–1687). In *Political Arithmetic* (1690), Petty discusses the favourable effects of the 'technical division of labour' on labour productivity and unit costs, by examining the case of Dutch shipping and the specialisation applied by the Dutch to ship production and outfitting processes (Aspromourgos 1996: 37, 39).

Petty's interest in shipbuilding went beyond his theoretical investigations of labour specialisation in *Political Arithmetic* and his deliberations on 'naval matters of all sorts' in his so-called *Treatise of Naval Philosophy* (McCormick 2009: 268). In 1660, the newly established Royal Society (1660–1663) under king Charles II (1630–1685) invited Petty and architect and polymath Sir Christopher Wren (1632–1723) to contemplate the subject of the 'philosophy of shipping.' Petty, once an apprentice on board a merchant ship, produced detailed designs for a 'double-bottom' (double-hulled) ship that aimed at outsailing its competition 'while requiring a smaller crew' and swiftly moved on to the construction of three prototypes between 1662 and 1664, *Invention, Invention II* and *Experiment*, with considerable scientific merit but little political success. Despite its eventual abandonment, Petty's scheme was successful in interlinking functional design with efficiency, optimisation and the rigorous pursuit of an economy of means and materials.[7]

During the 18th century, as a result of the increasing specialisation and natural division of labour that began to pervade the relevant literature on shipbuilding (Guy 2012: 11–12), architecture and naval architecture began to move towards different directions, after centuries of following intertwining trajectories, where shipbuilding came within the purview of the educated architect.[8] Early 20th century structural rationalism, championed by Le Corbusier and others, re-established the parallel between the arts of building and shipbuilding, with architects now looking at naval architecture for inspiration, as will become clearer in the following section.

The law of economy[9]

Presumably, what Le Corbusier saw in the poetry of linearity and horizontality epitomised in the image of the deck, besides the formal merits embedded in the rhythmical repetition of the ship's visible structural components, is a celebration of design/performance optimisation and efficiency that permeated the work of engineers at the time (1958: xxiii & 3)[10] and are deeply rooted in economic thought as economic efficiency or efficiency of industrial labour. Early on in *Vers une Architecture*, Le Corbusier commends his fellow 'industrialists, bankers and merchants' for:

> forging the tools of an era and creating throughout the world that host of very beautiful things wherein reigns the law of Economy, mathematical calculation combined with boldness and imagination.
>
> (2007: 97; 1958: 9)

Modern aesthetics – beauty, unity, harmony, minimum comfort, grandeur and also dignity – are governed by the laws of economy and nature that are epitomised in the design of the liner (2007: 158; 1958: 80),[11] mass-production housing (2007: 254; 1958: 187 & 192)[12] and standardisation (1958: 115), machinery (1958: 100)[13] or on-campus student accommodation, where the outdated and expensive poetry of an Oxonian College and its patron-led architectural tradition are replaced by the monastic 'cell' (2007: 286; 1958: 220).[14] Furthermore, the culturally-laden, elusive and subjective notion of beauty is linked to such mensurable and rational terms as utility and economy (1958: 113). Le Corbusier is not being specific about which 'laws of economy' apply to modern architectural design, but in *Vers une Architecture*, he hints repeatedly at neighbouring concepts, with efficiency standing out for being alluded to more frequently and openly at various places in the text. Indicatively, the American skyscraper for the working class is praised for attaining remarkable economies of scale, similar to those achieved by ocean liners,[15] by means of efficiency [efficacité] and economy of time and effort (1958: 43). Elsewhere, Le Corbusier provides the following description of what can be construed as a working definition of efficiency:

> The establishment of a standard involves exhausting every practical and reasonable possibility, and extracting from them a recognized type conformable to its functions, with a maximum output and a minimum use of means, workmanship and material, words, forms, colours, sounds.[16]
> (1986: 137)

Minimising means, workmanship and material without compromising the quality or the output of the end product alludes to improvements in the production process already introduced to certain aspects of human enterprise by the end of the 18th century. These entailed, among other measures, such as technological and infrastructure improvements, free trade and exploitation of economies of scale and scope (Wright 2002: 43, 212), the introduction of degrees of labour specialisation that characterised the evolving division of labour. Smith's well-known 'pin factory' example, expounded in the starting pages of the *Wealth of Nations*, functions as a lucid and indisputable illustration of how dividing a given manufacturing process into simpler, less time-consuming and more manageable tasks that require a narrower skillset – while triggering the production of specialised machinery – improves production in terms both of quality (increase in skill, dexterity and judgment of the labourer) and of quantity (productivity of labour). Smith's example of the pin factory is not merely as elaborate as the ensuing example of the woollen coat, where a more intricate network of interwoven tasks is outlined. However, Smith utilises the case of a 'very trifling manufacture' because housing all the different tasks in the same space provides for a strong visual argument (Smith 1981: 13–24).[17]

For Le Corbusier, an established standard develops gradually, first by eloquently stating the problem at hand and subsequently pursuing an optimum solution by means of a close reading and rigorous analytical reasoning, i.e. practical, rational, intentional, logical thinking and bold experimentation. Rival analyses establish a culture of commendable competition that mobilises human ingenuity and creativity and leads to an unceasing urge for upgrade and optimisation, towards achieving perfection, harmony and beauty beyond practicality. This is how progress had always been achieved. The ancient Greek temple and the motorcar present two disparate in time but comparable standards in human culture, with the Parthenon and the Delage Grand-Sport[18] being the refined end products of an evolutionary process 'of selection applied to a standard' (1958: 101–117; 1986: 129–148). Standardisation, as a social and economic imperative, regulates modern architectural design on different levels: in terms of units and measurements,[19] construction materials and building elements, such as windows. Le Corbusier's standardisation and Smith's specialisation are inextricably linked with processes that were already in place and aimed at increasing the productivity of labour. One might think that the space of the factory was the paradigmatic place of this increase. After all, Le Corbusier makes several references to modern factories in *Vers une Architecture*. In one of the lengthier mentions, he discusses the need for harmony that is the product of economy and physical necessity. This harmony can be observed in the transformative evolution of production processes and performances that 'come from the workshop or the factory [...] a whole world working with perception, intelligence and precision [...]' (Le Corbusier 1986: 102). Here as well, the strong visual stimulus of a carefully planned performance of mutually dependent tasks coming together under the same roof fuel the poetry of the division of labour. It could be argued, however, that the emphasis rests less with the space of the factory per se and more with a specialisation of labour that is marked, according to one understanding of Smith's work, 'by a plethora of small, independent trades that fit into one another without deliberate organization' (Fleischacker 2004: 11).

These irrefutable merits of the new epoch are not so readily apparent in the photographs of other public or private spaces from RMS *Aquitania*, namely the first class lounge (Figure 4.2), the drawing room, the smoking room, the dining saloon, the grill room, the long gallery, the 'swimming tank'[20] or the grand entrance, which were designed in different historical styles – Jacobean, Stuart, Queen Anne and Georgian (Wealleans 2006: 67; Kent Layton 2011) – that 'challenge[d] comparison with the best modern work in hotel or other buildings on land' (Davis 1914: 96). Supplementary artwork, such as a detailed reproduction of *The Colosseum and the Arch of Constantine* – an 18th century *veduta* by Italian painter and architect Giovanni Paolo Pannini (1691–1765) – that hang on the wall of the grand entrance staircase or the trompe-l'œil decorative paintings by P.H. Rémon & Sons – inspired by various architectural follies from the gardens of the Petit Trianon (1762–1768) at Versailles – that hid from the eyes the funnel casings at the 'Louis XVI Restaurant' (first class dinning saloon, Upper Deck/D Deck), added to a sense of scenographic euphoria that '[i]n 1914 a serious critic would have dismissed derisively [as] mock interiors' (Cantazuzino 1969: 397–398). It appears that RMS *Aquitania's* backward-looking, Beaux-Arts aesthetics (Hinchman and Yoneda 2016: 173)[21] attest to the 'increased awareness of visual national identity in [the] interior décor' of early 20th century design sensibilities[22] while reflecting the social stratification of Edwardian Britain (Wealleans 2006: 36). Nevertheless, this 901-feet long liner that accommodated 3,350 passengers and almost 1,000 crew was praised for her powerful engines, impressive manoeuvrability, fast docking, satisfactory average speed per crossing (23–24 knots), lack of vibration and economic consumption of coal (Kent Layton 2011). Furthermore, following the RMS *Titanic* disaster of 1912, she was fitted with such innovations as two radio-equipped motor lifeboats on top of her 80 regular lifeboats (Anonymous 1914a: 465).

In their twofold function, both as promoters of visual national identity and as brilliant feats of engineering, i.e. simultaneously looking towards the stylistic past[23] and the technological future, liners captured early 20th century imagination and became the sheer embodiment of their times (Cantazuzino 1969: 397–398) as well as experimental laboratories for contemporary design (Boucher 2017: 127–128). Indicative of their lasting effect is the special thematic issue [numéros spéciaux] on the evolution of transportation,

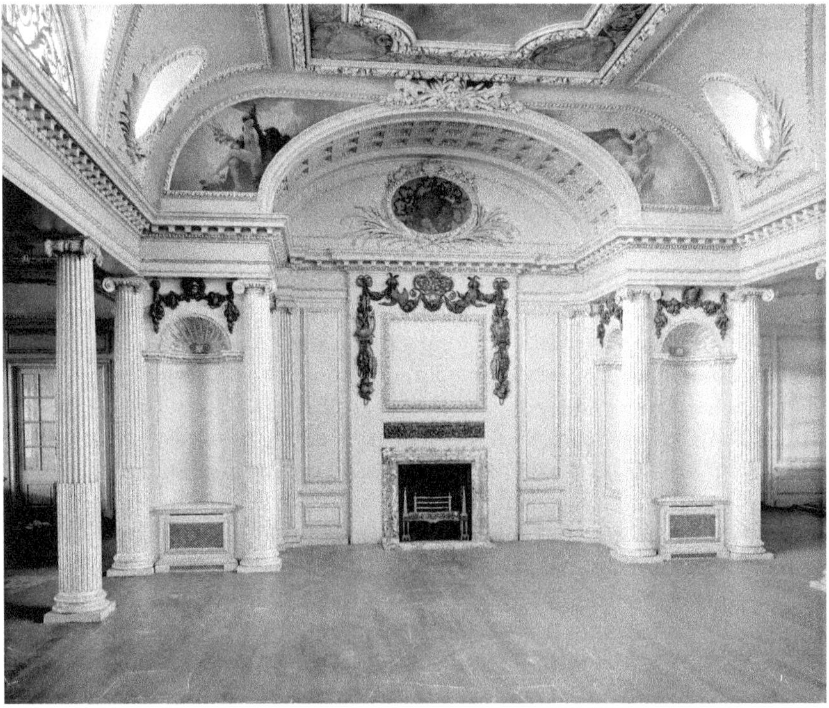

Figure 4.2 First Class Lounge on the *Aquitania* (1914). Photograph by Bedford Lemere & Co. Interior of the passenger liner *Aquitania* (1914) showing the forward end of the First Class Lounge, also called Palladian Lounge, on the Promenade Deck (A Deck), prior to completion of the fitting-out work. © National Maritime Museum, Greenwich, London (G10786).

hosted by the illustrious architectural journal *L'Architecture d'Aujourd'hui* (no.8, August 1935). There, alongside French architect and set designer Robert Mallet-Stevens' (1886–1945) critique of the SS *Normandie*[24] for its lack of stylistic innovation (1935: 27), French seascape painter and graphic designer Albert Sébille (1874–1953) discusses the aesthetic preconditions for contemporary liners accordingly: 'the element of "speed" implies above all submerged volumes of great finesse, and necessarily the completion of the hull, above the waterline, as an elegant whole.'[25] Thus, aesthetic concerns blend with practical considerations in order to lay the solid and rational foundations for a standard that serves, similarly to the motorcar, two different but complementary aims: speed and comfort (Le Corbusier 1956: 109).[26]

One of the most celebrated public spaces of RMS *Aquitania* was the first class, 150 feet long garden lounge on the port side of the Promenade Deck (A Deck) (Figure 4.3). Its decoration was carried out by the English furniture manufacturers Waring and Gillow in a manner that was 'suggestive of an old English garden, the walls of the deck house on one side of the lounge having been treated to represent stone covered with trellis in natural teak' (Anonymous 1914b: 462). However, Le Corbusier appears to be more interested in the 'ribbon window' (Eskilson 2018: 86), 'un mur tout en fenêtres' as he describes it (Le Corbusier 1958: 74), of the garden lounge, which featured sliding windows that could 'be slipped down out of sight as easily as the windows in your car,' thus transforming the lounge into a 'verandah of an ultra exclusive country club.'[27] This disappearing, linear window, and not the portholes or the rounded corners that were popularised by various instances of interwar modernism (e.g. Streamline Moderne), addresses both aesthetic and practical considerations in Le Corbusier's thinking. It could be argued that this garden lounge provided an early visual cue for the elongated window [fenêtre en longueur] that evolved into one of Le Corbusier's points of modern architecture, formulated in 1926 (Le Corbusier and Jeanneret 1967a: 128–129). Stephen Eskilson goes as far as to suggest that RMS *Aquitania*:

> provided a functioning example of another of Le Corbusier's core principles, in this case the "architectural promenade." The promenade acted for Le Corbusier as a type of implied itinerary in his buildings, a literal promenade whereby the viewer moved through a series of linked spaces and enjoyed the resulting perspectives.
>
> (2018: 86)

The idea of a carefully choreographed itinerary through varied embodied spatial experiences, shifting rhythmic transitions and a broad spectrum of framed vistas of both the interior and the surrounding landscape is intrinsically associated with Le Corbusier's *Villa Savoye* (1928) at Poissy and has formed a major component of his ensuing projects, as a form of initiation and a rhetorical mechanism for endowing architecture with

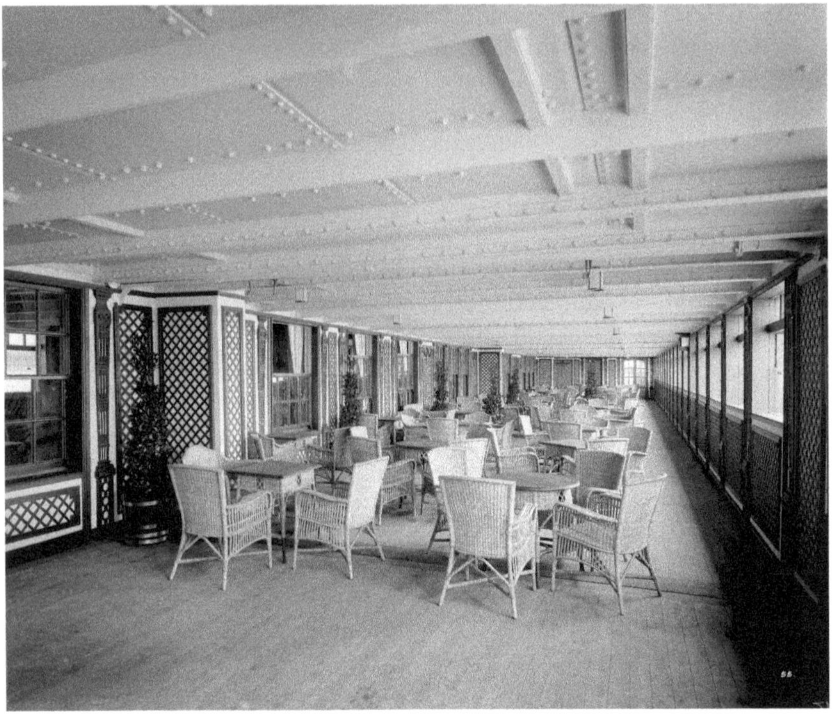

Figure 4.3 First class garden lounge on the RMS *Aquitania* (1914). Photograph by Bedford Lemere & Co. Interior of the passenger liner *Aquitania* (1914) showing the First Class Garden Lounge, on the port side of the Promenade Deck (A Deck). © National Maritime Museum, Greenwich, London (G10840).

meaning (Samuel 2010: 9–25). RMS *Aquitania's* promenade decks and garden lounge, despite their spacious layout and harmonic arrangement, are not semiologically rich enough to trigger such a complex notion. Instead, both the exterior promenades and the interior long gallery (A Deck), decorated in Adam style also by Waring and Gillow, appear to share a common archetypal reference to the 'long gallery' of the Elizabethan and Jacobean country house in England (Anonymous Undated). Long galleries, incorporated in the main structure of the manor, were particularly popular in the 16th and 17th centuries for combining effectively utilitarian and aesthetic functions (i.e. access, communication, recreation, exercise, reception of guests, appreciation of art).[28] These early multipurpose corridor/rooms present an interesting case of spatial configuration reborrowing from architecture to shipbuilding and back to architectural design that emphasises aspects of economy, such as layout efficiency and, indirectly, design optimisation.

Proto-modern efficiency

Early 20th century functionalism and the rhetoric of machine aesthetics sought eclectic relationships with naval architecture and shipbuilding. However, ships had been associated with optimal design and efficiency long before the advent of architectural modernity. Xenophon (430–354 BC), in his *Oeconomicus* from the 4th century BC, admires the organisational spirit and the effective management of space in a Phoenician merchant ship,[29] where:

> each kind of thing was so neatly stowed away that there was no confusion, no work for a searcher, nothing out of place, no troublesome untying to cause delay when anything was wanted for immediate use.
>
> (VIII, 11–14)

By contrast, houses that 'rest on solid ground' and are generously equipped with storage room 'fail to find a good and handy place for everything' (VIII, 17). The optimum solution to the stated problem is order that follows from the appropriate placement of the utensils of the household. Beauty proceeds from this order.[30] Furthermore, Xenophon's proto-functionalist discourse addressed aspects of design on top of questions on household and estate management, which also troubled Le Corbusier. The latter, in his 'Manual of the Dwelling' from *Vers une Architecture*, advises new tenants that economy alone should govern their actions and thoughts (1958: 96). Xenophon's ideal house featured simple rooms with few elaborate decorations, whose layouts are regulated by their intended functions.[31] Proper orientation and a bolted door to separate women's quarters from the men's conclude the list of traits that make for a practical and efficient house that has drawn valuable lessons from the Phoenician ship.

Early on in the 20th century, functionalism emerged as a potent vehicle for achieving efficient and economical results in architecture, with the founding fathers of modernism leading the crusade for a more practical approach to design. Le Corbusier, in particular, put into effective use and tested the validity of his theorisations in his many materialised projects, which included the 1929 design, with his cousin Pierre Jeanneret, of a cement barge,[32] an 80 meters long floating hospital/asylum [asile flottant] for The Salvation Army, that could accommodate up to 160 guests and boasted a hanging garden (Le Corbusier and Jeanneret 1967b). Despite Le Corbusier's fascination with liners, the design of the barge echoes his buildings on land, in the sense that it can be understood as a selective implementation of his five points of architecture, namely the roof garden, the horizontal window and the free façade, expounded a few years earlier.

The concept of function was neither unknown nor remained unchallenged in the history of architectural theory. From the early architectural treatises by Vitruvius[33] or Alberti[34] to the remarkable power of description demonstrated by Francis Bacon (1561–1626)[35] or the more rigorous and structured investigations by Carlo Lodoli (1690–1761),[36] it acquired various complementary meanings and served different purposes. On occasion, function outweighed such complex and historically contested notions as beauty[37] and even regulated aspects of ornamentation and decoration.[38] Hanno-Walter Kruft argues that it was not until late in the 18th century that function seized to be understood merely as usage and became the precursor of early 20th century functionalism.[39] At the very core of these investigations lie nature and the primal hut, whose conceptual explorations were furthered by 19th century American transcendentalism and instigated the forging of national architectural identities that steered away from the Greek and Gothic revivals. The work of American architect Asher Benjamin (1773–1845) provides an illuminating example of how aspects of efficiency are bound with national architectural autonomy. In *The Rudiments of Architecture* (1820), Benjamin, in discussing the proper application of the orders and their properties, is reluctant to assign specific proportions to the different types of columns, which up to the 18th century had been a major preoccupation of architectural theory.

> It would be absurd to make stone columns which support, besides their entablature, a whole story of a brick or stone building [...] as many diameters in height, as those which have only their entablature to support, and that, and the columns made of wood; which is the case with the greater part of columns in porticos and colonades, in this country.
>
> (1820: 58)[40]

This call for common sense and practical reasoning will formulate the basis for a more thorough, existential investigation of human habitation and meaningful dwelling. American sculptor and theorist Horatio Greenough, Ralph Waldo Emerson's fellow Harvard alumnus and intellectual interlocutor on aspects of nature, function and national identity, also places emphasis on materials and their efficient use, and advises against the ill-conceived appropriation of imported historical forms, namely the Classic or Greek Revival. In his writings on art,[41] Greenough expounds a 'modern' theory of functionalism based on an analogy between architecture and the organic form (DeZurko 1952: 98). He understood 'the promise of function' in 'the animal organisation' as the essential condition of beauty and sought inspiration from the wisdom displayed in nature. Inanimate objects also caught Greenough's attention. Anticipating in more than one way Le Corbusier, he expresses his admiration for bridges and ships;[42] structures that had replaced the subjective and arbitrary rules and laws of taste that guided decisions on form or proportion with the 'the great principles of construction' that are embedded in nature, 'not in the feather and in the flower, but in winds and waves' (1969: 61):

> Observe a ship at sea! Mark the majestic form of her hull as she rushes through the water, observe the graceful bend of her body, the gentle transition from round to flat, the grasp of her keel, the leap of her bows, the symmetry and rich tracery of her spars and rigging, and those grand wind muscles, her sails! [...] What Academy of Design, what research

of connoisseurship, what imitation of the Greeks produced this marvel of construction? [...] Could we carry into our civil architecture the responsibilities that weigh upon our shipbuilding, we should ere long have edifices as superior to the Parthenon [...] as the *Constitution* or the *Pennsylvania* is to the galley of the Argonauts.

(1855: 225)

Similar ideas are expressed by American art critic James Jackson Jarves (1818–1888) in *The Art-Idea* (1864), where, once more ocean-clippers and river-steamers become source of inspiration and set the framework of reference for architectural design, as the prized products of the owner, officer, sailor and manual labourer's love and pride, for their beauty, stylish appearance and performance. Jarves concludes that:

[a]s soon as an equal love is turned towards architecture, we may expect as rapid a development of beauty of material form on land as on the ocean.

(1865: 289)

However, Jarves romanticised outlook of the industry leaves little room for further technological advancement, which, according to Smith, is essential for the progress and prosperity of society. Indicatively, he expresses his reservations about the advent of the propeller, whose favour with the public is questionable and which 'art has yet to learn how to dignify and adorn' (1865: 289). This essentially technophobic take heightens Jarves' romanticism, instantiated in his admiration for an idealised past that is threatened by progress (i.e. machines that can replace manual labour), which, in turn, calls into question the overall pursuit of efficiency and design optimisation. Is there room for a rigorous investigation of the nature of efficiency and optimisation on the basis of concrete and tangible criteria, when so often subjective or even arbitrary aesthetic premises appear to shake the structural foundations of the proposed methodology?

Greenough is abundantly clear about his vision of an architecture that is tailored according to the particular needs and requirements of its occupants. He terms this architecture 'organic' and contrasts it against 'monumental architecture,' which appeals to different aesthetic and moral categories, namely sentiment and sympathy.[43] More importantly, he describes the product of organic architecture, each individual edifice, as a machine, for it has to 'obey a demonstrable rule' and 'must be formed with reference to the abstract type of its species' (1969: 65). This can be construed as a prefiguration of the emerging 'machine metaphor,' which, along with the puritan work ethic that has been thematised by Max Weber in his seminal study *The Protestant Ethic and the Spirit of Capitalism* (1904–1905), provided the general backdrop for the proliferation of early 20th century modernity.

For when asceticism was carried out of monastic cells into everyday life, and began to dominate worldly morality, it did its part in building the

> tremendous cosmos of the modern economic order. This order is now bound to the technical and economic conditions of machine production which to-day determine the lives of all the individuals who are born into this mechanism, [...].
>
> (Weber 1992: 123)

Weber's telling paradigm of the monastic cell functions here as a reminder of Le Corbusier's aesthetic and ethical worldview. His standards (types), standardised units, products and materials and design standardisation described in *Vers une Architecture* roughly outline the values and aspirations of a whole epoch. The way forward, the answer to the pressing call for progress is rigorous experimentation that maximises the results and minimises the effort. Greenough appears to be an inadvertent forerunner in this strive for optimisation:

> If we compare the form of a newly invented machine with the perfected type of the same instrument, we observe, as we trace it through the phases of improvement, how weight is shaken off where strength is less needed, how functions are made to approach without impeding each other, how the straight becomes curved, and the curve is straightened, till the straggling and cumbersome machine becomes the compact, effective and beautiful engine.
>
> (1855: 225)

Le Corbusier could have not put it more eloquently when discussing his established standards and their continuous refinement by means of selection as prerequisites for progress. Furthermore, Greenough's substitution of the engine, the device that converts energy into mechanical work (e.g. motion), for the machine, the apparatus that contains and is run by an engine, may signify yet another unintended allusion to the motorcar, the airplane and, more relevant to this chapter, the liner that has afforded so much room for speculation as to the origins and applications of efficiency in architecture.

Economic efficiency

Vitruvius's 'distributio,' which roughly translates to an efficient use of resources, an economy of means that, nevertheless, secures the anticipated results (book I, ch. II, 1997: 54–55), constitutes one of the earliest attempts to directly associate architecture with frugality, prudence and efficiency. Jean-Nicolas-Louis Durand (1760–1834) returned to the notion of economy [économie] from a radically different angle, in his *Précis des leçons d'architecture* (1802–1805). In his rendering of architectural functionalism, Durand understands economy, alongside convenience, as one of the two main principles of design, and ascribes to it a mixture of tangible and intangible qualities, such as symmetry [symmétrie], regularity [régularité] and simplicity [simplicité].[44] The latter suggests that any superfluous gestures are interpreted as useless and ought to be discarded in order to maintain simplicity (Kruft 1994: 274). This notion of economy in architecture echoes Smith's 'efficacy of human industry,' which often translates into the abandonment of time-consuming processes and the unceasing improvement of production by virtue of 'pretty machines' that facilitate this improvement (Smith 1981: 19–22).

The discussion on economy, albeit from a different scope, reignites across the Atlantic, a few decades later, with Henry D. Thoreau's philosophical investigations into the essence of a meaningful existence in *Walden; or, Life in the Woods* (1854) that also borders on household economy and estate management à la Xenophon's *Oeconomicus*.[45] Thoreau's explorations arise from the same natural, cultural and intellectual environment – Concord, Massachusetts and liberal New England – that gave birth to Emerson and Greenough's transcendental theorisations and Utilitarianism, a marked departure from orthodox Calvinism and Puritanism (Goodman 2019).

In what could be understood, in today's terms, as practice-based research,[46] Thoreau withdrew from society to Walden Pond, Massachusetts in 1845, where he sought solitude amidst nature for almost three years, on land owned by his friend Emerson. The first draft of *Walden*, an inquiry into what is essential and necessary for a life of simplicity and prudence, was completed there (Goodman 2019).[47] A considerable portion of *Walden*'s opening chapter, 'Economy,' draws on Thoreau's personal experience with building his ascetic cabin in the woods. Marc-Antoine Laugier's primitive hut as abstract conceptualisation of architecture's basic principles from his *Essai sur l'Architecture* (1756) reverberates in Thoreau's archaeology of the shelter (2004: 28–29). Land and house ownership are painted as sources of pain and tribulation, especially when they encourage a living beyond one's means. Meaningless and irresponsible consumption is also frowned upon, thus foreshadowing the postmodern critique of consumerism from a semi-theological standpoint. Luxury comes under heavy attack in any form and occasion, from the travelling habits of Thoreau's time to the furnishings of 'modern drawing rooms.' In this context, it is enticing to interpret the instance of the house with the frail structural frame as a metaphor for the potential destabilisation of society effected by a relentless pursuit of superfluous material possessions:

> When I consider how our houses are built and paid for, or not paid for, and their internal economy managed and sustained, I wonder that the floor does not give way under the visitor while he is admiring the gewgaws upon the mantel-piece, and let him through into the cellar, to some solid and honest though earthy foundation.
>
> (2004: 38)

Smith had also warned against the dangers of excessive luxury spending both for the imprudent individual, who foolishly mistakes 'present enjoyment' for the otherwise commendable 'desire of bettering [one's] condition,' and the nation (1981: 341). Even though governments rarely need to worry about the misconduct of few individuals, whose '"prodigality" takes away from the wealth of a nation,' frugality is strongly recommended as the way to go about conducting one's life (Fleischacker 2004: 87). According to an established tradition in economics, attributed, at least in part to Smiths' *Wealth of Nations*, self-interest, and not altruistic contribution to the community, provides the motivation for improving one's condition and optimum social progress at large (2004: 88). This, according to Smith, can happen in a 'vulgar' way that involves augmenting one's fortune by saving and accumulating (social betterment) (Smith 1981: 341–342) and a 'less vulgar' way that involves moral development (virtue, moderation, harmony).[48] Smith emphasises the fact that promoting moral development over social betterment will not reduce the real wealth of the society but would most likely promote frugality over prodigality and beneficent purposes over luxury (Fleischacker 2004: 88–89). In this sense, luxury that is manifest as superfluous or anachronistic decoration attests to society's poor moral judgment and could be construed as an obstacle to its moral development. Smith is abundantly clear about this distinction:

> The latter species of expense, therefore, especially when directed towards frivolous objects, the little ornaments of dress and furniture, jewels, trinkets, gewgaws, frequently indicated, not only a trifling, but a base and selfish disposition.
>
> (1981: 349).

This brings in mind Austrian-Czech architect Adolph Loos' (1870–1933) critique of Secessionist ornamentation in *Ornament and Crime* [Ornament et Crime] (1920),[49] where ethical and aesthetic judgments drive modern design towards a 'meta-language' of 'signs of complicity and adhesion with the common cultural bases of society' (Tournikiotis 2002: 24).

Thoreau's anatomy of the harsh reality many underprivileged Americans found themselves in and his acute diagnosis of their maladies prescribe an architecture that cuts down on ornamentation, satisfies the most pressing needs and capitalises on inexpensive, local materials (boards, shingles, lime and bricks) that can be found in abundance nearby and can be easily manipulated, without requiring skilled labour, to achieve the desirable result: a simple, modest, unassuming, yet safe and practical abode, fit to serve the individual requirements of the owner, who is also the architect and the builder (i.e. as far removed from the idea of labour division as possible). This asceticism is best pursued in close proximity to nature:

> The cart before the horse is neither beautiful nor useful. Before we can adorn our houses with beautiful objects the walls must be stripped, and our lives must be stripped, and beautiful housekeeping and beautiful living be laid for a foundation: now, a taste for the beautiful is most cultivated out of doors, where there is no house and no housekeeper.
>
> (Thoreau 2004: 38)

Thoreau's overall understanding of economy as a way of conducting one's life in harmony with nature, the precursor of American environmental philosophy (Goodman 2019), may have little relevance and limited applicability in today's world. However, his focused reworkings of such integral elements of architectural design as function and efficiency set the framework for a viable design economy and productivity that stands apart from the prevailing paradigm of early 20th century industrialisation, mechanisation and standardisation and is worth to be revisited from the viewpoint of current environmental concerns (i.e. sustainability and issues like carbon footprint).

In lieu of conclusion: Towards an 'augmented efficiency'

The 1960s and 1970s saw the rise of harsh criticism against the modern movement and its theoretical premises, on the grounds of its polemical stance towards variety or multiplicity, its canonical thinking and its crude reduction of the complexities of life and meaningful dwelling to questions of function. Unsurprisingly, Le Corbusier came under attack for his 'cold, standardizing logic and an uncompromising functionalism,' aspects for which his work was mostly known to the general public. However, the well-established by now criticism on modernism's underachievement – primarily with regard to city planning – fails to take into consideration other crucial parameters of Le Corbusier's work, namely its humanitarian and anthropocentric logic (Choay 1960: 14, 18–21). Thus, while economy and efficiency were understood mainly in terms of labour productivity and increase in volume, along the lines of Smith's theorisation of the division of labour in the *Wealth of Nations*, many of the visual cues utilised in *Vers une Architecture* reflect production processes that resist standardisation, specialisation and full mechanisation. Perfected standards, such as RMS *Aquitania* or the Delage Grand-Sport, linger somewhere between artisan and industrial manufacturing and cling to those facets of American transcendentalism that seek inspiration for design optimisation in nature.

Similarly, the theoretical and realised work of other exponents of interwar and post-WWII modernisms was critically reviewed and reappraised in the light of a newly introduced return to/of history, subjectivity, relativism, ideology and scepticism towards reason. One such attempt stands out for fighting, so to speak, against modernism from within, i.e. with the methodological toolset that was introduced and sharpened by interwar modernity. Lithuanian artist and founding member of Fluxus George Maciunas (1931–1978) published in 1964 his essay 'The Grand Fakers of Architecture: Mies van der Rohe, [Eero] Saarinen, [Gordon] Bunshaft, Frank Lloyd Wright,' which more or less accuses the protagonists of architectural modernity for faking rational reasoning and resorting to arbitrariness and preconceived conceptualisations about the end result of the design process. This brief essay presents in a schematic manner Maciunas's analysis of a single, telling example from the wide body of work of each architect,[50] logically arranged in a table that comprises three different columns: the 'pre-formed result' offered by the architect, the desired 'solution required by [the] client' and, finally, the 'resultant fraud and swindle.' The wording of the essay suggests that these examples are indicative of a wider and deeply rooted deficiency in modern architecture that borders on hypocrisy. Before embarking on his attack, in the introduction, Maciunas sets out to describe the theoretical framework that explains his criteria. There, one comes across three brief statements on 'value,' 'economy' and 'efficiency,'[51] which comprise the author's particular economic theory (Medina 2004: 274–276). Yet, in his relentless criticism, Maciunas appears to be neglectful of the valuable lesson from the ship's promenade deck, where the pursuit of efficiency, optimisation and economy of means and materials is based only in part on rational thinking. The other part rests with irrational thinking, instantiated in the example of SS *Normandie*, which could had been equally effective with just two funnels, but instead it was designed with three to satisfy the eye that *does* see (Sébille 1935: 32–33).[52] This explanation is not offered in justification of early modernist thinking, but rather as a belated acknowledgment of the mutual osmosis between rational and irrational thinking in early 20th century discourse on architectural rationalism.

Notes

1 *The Tempest*: 'O brave new world, That has such people in't!' (Shakespeare 1993: 21). Aldous Huxley was overtly critical of modern architecture. In his 1930 essay 'Puritanism in Art,' he comments with discontent that: 'Le Corbusier would compel us all to inhabit a mixture of green-house and hospital ward, furnished in the style of a dentist's operating chamber' (cited in Snyder 2005: 175).

2 First published: Le Corbusier-Saugnier. "Des Yeux qui ne Voient pas… Les Paquebots." *L'Esprit Nouveau*, no. 8, 1921, pp.846–855.

3 The Cunard Liner *Aquitania* was designed in 1913 by Cunard naval architect Leonard Peskett (1861–1924), author of the paper 'The design of steamships from the owner's point of view' that appeared in the *Transactions of the Institution of Naval Architects* in 1914. One of the pressing requirements of the times was, apparently, to design ships that could be made satisfactory by achieving economies of scale and cost-efficiency, hence their relevance to modern architecture. RMS *Aquitania's* generous and lushly decorated public spaces were designed by the Mewès and Davis firm of English architect Arthur Joseph Davis (1878–1951) and French architect Charles-Frédéric Mewès (1860–1914), mostly known for their hotel designs, such as the London Ritz Hotel (1901–1906) and the Hôtel Ritz Paris (1897–1898), respectively, who received their formal training at the École des Beaux-Arts in Paris. Several other firms were involved with the specialised interior decorations (Wealleans 2006: 67). RMS *Aquitania* set sail on her maiden voyage from Liverpool to New York in 1914. Having served and survived two World Wars, she was scrapped at Faslane, Scotland in 1950.

4 'La valeur d'un long promenoir, volume satisfaisant, intéressant; l'unité de matière, le bel agencement d'éléments constructifs, sainement, exposés et assemblés avec unité' (1958: 76).

5 The image now forms part of the collection of the National Maritime Museum, Greenwich, London. Source: https://collections.rmg.co.uk/collections/objects/20517.html (last accessed: 10/06/2020). Other images in *Vers une Architecture* from this collection include the flying bridge and the first-class garden lounge of RMS *Aquitania*.

6 Yet another alumnus of the prestigious École des Beaux-Arts in Paris.
7 As well as furthering Petty's investigations into Francis Bacon's (1561–1626) natural philosophy and the grounding of experimental science (McCormick 2009: 18, 150–156).
8 Vitruvius devotes the last chapter (XII) of book V to ports and shipyards (Vitruvii. 1997: 324–329), while Alberti discusses ships and shipping in chapter XII of book V (Alberti 1986: 96–98).
9 'The law of Economy necessarily governs our actions and our thoughts.' (Le Corbusier 2007: 88)
10 'L'ingénieur, inspiré par la roi d'Économie et conduit par le calcul, nous met en accord avec les lois de l'univers. Il atteint l'harmonie.' (Le Corbusier 1958: xxiii)
11 'Que les yeux voient: cette harmonie est là, fonction du labeur régi par l'*économie* et conditionné par la fatalité de la physique.' (Le Corbusier 2007: 158; 1958: 80)
12 'La loi d'Économie gère impérativement nos actes et nos conceptions ne sont viable que par elle.' and 'la loi d'Économie réclame ses droits.' In the outline of his argument, Le Corbusier introduces a slightly different but more potent wording: 'La loi d'Économie gère impérativement nos actes et nos pensées.' (Le Corbusier 1958: xxvi)
13 'La mécanique porte en soi le facteur d'économie qui sélectionne.'
14 'Classer, typifier, fixer la cellule et ses éléments. Économie. Efficacité.' Interestingly enough, Oxonian and Cantabrigian Colleges draw their origins and typologies (i.e. courtyard, dining hall, kitchen, church, library, college accommodation, etc.) from monastic life, while, in some instances, their foundations were laid over the grounds of former convents. Such is the case of Jesus College, Cambridge that was founded in 1499 on the site of a 12th c. Benedictine nunnery. John Alcock, Bishop of Ely and Founder of Jesus College, built the College

> from the foundation upwards on a ground-plan which even to this day recalls that of the nunnery; and in a position most agreeable to the Muses, who delight in quiet and seclusion; a position, namely, as far removed as possible from the noise and confusion of the Town.
>
> (Willis & Willis 1988, 115–119)

15 '[T]he larger the ship, the less the cost of carrying a ton of freight or a given number of passengers' (Anonymous 1914b: 461).
16 'Établir un standard, c'est épuiser toutes les possibilités pratiques et raisonnables, déduire un type reconnu conforme aux fonctions, à rendement maximum, à emploi minimum de moyens, main-d'œuvre et matière, mots, formes, couleurs, sons.' (Le Corbusier 1986: 137)
17 '[…] those employed in every different branch of the work can often be collected into the same workhouse, and placed at once under the view of the spectator.' (Smith 1981: 14)
18 Von Moos comments that the Delage Grand-Sport was not the best possible example of industrial standardisation, since it was not produced on the assembly line (2009, 63).
19 German architect Ernest Neufert (1900–1986) contributed greatly to this effort with his *Architects' Data* (Bauentwurfslehre), first published in 1936.
20 RMS *Aquitania* was the first to introduce a permanent swimming pool (Anderson 1998: 68).
21 RMS *Queen Mary* of the Cunard-White Star Line, which sailed on her maiden voyage in 1936, was the first British liner to adopt a 'restrained modern' design (Anderson 1998: 68). SS *Normandie*, which first set sail in 1935 for the French Compagnie Générale Transatlantique, must have paved the way for the stylistic

modernisation of the interior design of transatlantic liners with the inauguration of what came to be known as *Streamline Moderne*, an offshoot of the 1930s Art Déco style.

22 A reporter for *Scientific American* notes that the interior decoration of RMS *Aquitania* 'tells the traveler the history of the nation' (Anonymous 1914b: 462).

23 According to Anaïs Boucher, Georges Philippar (1883–1959), the President of the Compagnie des Messageries Maritimes, a French merchant shipping company established in 1871, campaigned for the formal emancipation of ship design from 'the great styles of the past,' such as Louis XIV or Empire, and the adoption of a 'truly modern' look, which, however, would not go out of fashion, as was the case with Art Nouveau interiors already by the mid-20s (2017: 126–127). Philippar's response to this dilemma was MS *Aramis*, launched in 1931 and torpedoed in 1942, whose public spaces were decorated in the presumably ageless style of Minoan Prehistoric (Bronze Age) Art, on designs by Georges Raymond. It appears that Philippar's modern vision involved the creative revocation of an even older past, one that inhabited the realm between reality and myth, distilled through Art Deco's formal (geometric) simplicity and stylisation (2017: 131–135). This was in tune with earlier developments in modern art, e.g. the attraction towards the prehistoric and the archaic, instead of the classical, that had fuelled many modernist vanguards early in the 20th century.

24 Many of her first class public spaces were designed by French architects Pierre Patout (1879–1965) and Henri Pacon (1882–1966), often associated with French Art Deco interiors, such as SS *Île-de-France* (1926) and SS *Normandie* (1932).

25 'Or l'élément "vitesse" implique avant tout une grande finesse des formes immergées; et obligatoirement par leur prolongemenut, au-dessus de la flottaison, une élégance de toute la coque' (Sébille 1935: 31).

26 Similar aspirations for modern architecture are also expressed elsewhere in Europe, namely Austria, Germany, and the Netherlands. The Deutscher Werkbund, later the Bauhaus and De Stijl represent, to a certain extent, complementary perspectives on architectural design and early 20th century trends of mechanisation, industrialisation and standardisation.

27 Cited in Kent Layton (2011) from a Cunard brochure.

28 For an in-depth study of the long gallery in England, see Coope (1986: 43–72 & 74–84).

29 Also admired by Smith, alongside the Carthaginians, for their skills in navigation and shipbuilding (1981: 34).

30 'There is nothing, in short, that does not gain in beauty when set out in order' (VIII, 20).

31 '[T]he rooms are designed simply with the object of providing as convenient receptacles as possible for the things that are to fill them, and thus each room invited just what was suited to it' (IX, 2).

32 Relevant technology was being developed during WWI and WWII, when shortages in steel led to the construction of concrete ships, such as those commissioned by the US Maritime Commission with McCloskey and Company (Philadelphia, Pennsylvania) in 1942. Interestingly, the second ship built by McCloskey in 1943 was named SS *Vitruvius*.

33 'Utilitas' is, according to Vitruvius, one of the three main principles of good architectural design, along with 'firmitas' and 'venustas,' roughly translated as strength and beauty correspondingly (1997: book I, ch. III, 2, 56–57).

34 Alberti devotes books IV and V of his *De re aedificatoria* (1452; 1485) to questions on function for different building types, i.e. those built for necessity, convenience or pleasure and some special purposes (1986: 65–110).

35 Francis Bacon, in his essay 'Of Building' (XLV, 1597–1625), makes the case for functional architecture, firstly by commenting on the building's location and

continuing with the arrangement its spaces, commenting on the Vatican and the Escorial as examples of flawed architectural design and describing his own standard (model) for a practical and functional palace (Bacon 2008: 179–183).

36 Venetian Franciscan friar Carlo Lodoli appears to be more systematic in his investigations of the notion of function. In his notes for a projected treatise on the art of building (c.1740s), Lodoli maintains that '[p]roper function and form are the only two final, scientific aims of civil architecture' (Mallgrave 2006: 130).

37 Indicative of this trend are the functionalist views of the first half of the 18th c., expressed in the work of Parisian treasury official Michel de Frémin *Mémoires critiques d'architecture contenans l'idée de la vraye & de la fausse Architecture* (1702) or abbé Jean-Louis De Cordemoy (1655–1714) *Nouveau traité de toute l'architecture* (1706) (Kruft 1994: 139–141). In addition, 19th c. revivalism revisited Gothic architecture 'as the product of function.' Eugène-Emmanuel Viollet-le-Duc's (1814–1879) *Entretiens sur l'architecture* (1863–1872) played an instrumental role in establishing this attitude towards the underrated European Middle Ages (Kruft 1994: 285). English architect Augustus Welby Pugin (1812–1852) and art critic John Ruskin (1819–1900) were equally involved in this effort.

38 Jacques-François Blondel (1705–1774), for example, in his *Cours d'architecture* (1771–1777) – not to be mistaken with *Cours d'architecture* (1675) by François Blondel (1618–1686) – clearly states that ornamentation should be dictated by 'expressive function,' i.e. the *caractère* of a building, drawing on Germain Boffrand's *Livre d'architecture* (1745). In an earlier work, from 1754, Blondel had championed for the allegorical, symbolic and arbitrary nature of ornament, but the consistency of his theorisations is a different matter (Kruft 1994: 149–150).

39 Kruft acknowledges the work of abbé Marc-Antoine Laugier *Essai sur l'architecture* (1756) as an important milestone in the transition towards a functionalist comprehension of architecture as structure, in correspondence to nature (1994: 153).

40 Such as the pillars that support the porches of Ralph Waldo Emerson's house in Concord, Massachusetts, purchased in 1835. Emerson describes to his brother William his experience with the house accordingly:

> I have dodged the doom of building & have bought the Coolidge house in Concord with the expectation of entering it next September. It is a mean place & cannot be fine until trees & flowers give it a character of its own. But we shall crowd so many books & papers & if possible, wise friends, into it that it shall have as much wit as it can carry. (1835)

41 Collected and published posthumously as *Form and Function, Remarks on Art by Horatio Greenough* (1947).

42 In his 'Letter to Washington Allston' (Oct. 1831), Greenough praises naval architecture for subjecting the 'abstract idea of form' to the 'wants and conveniences desired,' which is the most valuable lesson to learn from nature (quoted in Mallgrave 2006: 451).

43 On occasion, these two 'classes of buildings' coexist in the same edifice.

44 'Ainsi, la convenance et l'économie, voilà les moyens que doit naturellement employer l'architecture, et les sources où elle doit puiser ses principes, les seuls qui puissent nous guider dans l'étude et dans l'exercice de cet art' (Durand 1817, 6–8).

45 If only for his admiration for Phoenician navigators and merchants (2004, 20–21).

46 'I speak understandingly on this subject, for I have made myself acquainted with it both theoretically and practically' (2004, 40).

47 While in Waldon Pond, Thoreau also completed his first book *A Week on the Concord and the Merrimac Rivers* (1849).

48 This notion is expounded in Smith's earlier work *Theory of Moral Sentiments* (1976), first published in 1759.

49 The article was first published in French *at L'Esprit Nouveau* journal no.2 in November 15 1920 (159–168). For the history of this publication as well as an in-depth analysis of Loos's writings and projects, refer to Tournikiotis's *Adolf Loos* (2002: 23–27).
50 Ludwig Mies van der Rohe's Lake Shore Drive Apartments in Chicago (1949–1952), Eero Saarinen's MIT Auditorium in Cambridge Massachusetts (1952–1955), Gordon Bunshaft's Lever House in New York (1952) and, finally, Frank Lloyd Wright's celebrated Guggenheim Museum in New York (1956).
51 In architecture, 'efficiency of function and of being becomes a value: formed by reason, knowledge, inventiveness, ability' (Maciunas 1964).
52 '[A]insi, sur la plupart de ces navires, une des cheminées est postiche, dans le but, affirme-t-on, de satisfaire l'oeil.' (Sébille 1935: 32–33)

References

Alberti, Leon Battista. *The Ten Books of Architecture* [The 1755 Leoni Edition]. Dover Publications, 1986 [1485].

Anderson, Anne. "Fit for the Queens: Teawares for the Cunard Transatlantic Liners c1920–40." *The Journal of the Decorative Arts Society 1850–the Present*, no. 22, 1998, pp. 66–73.

Anonymous. "Long Gallery on the 'Aquitania' (1914)." Available online at: https://collections.rmg.co.uk/collections/objects/20592.html [last accessed: 10/06/2020].

Anonymous. "Motor Lifeboats of the 'Aquitania'." *Scientific American*, vol. 110, no. 23, 6 June 1914a, p. 465.

Anonymous. "The New Cunarder 'Aquitania'." *Scientific American*, vol. 110, no. 23, 6 June 1914b, pp. 461–462.Aspromourgos, Tony. *On the Origins of Classical Economics: Distribution and Value from William Petty to Adam Smith*. Routledge, 1996.

Bacon, Francis. *Complete Essays* [intr. O. Smeaton]. Dover Publications, 2008 [1597, 1612, 1625].

Bauman, Zygmunt. *Modernity and Ambivalence*. Polity Press, 1998 [1991].

Benjamin, Asher. *The Rudiments of Architecture*. R.P. & C. Williams, 1820 [1814].

Boucher, Anaïs. "The Ocean Liner *Aramis*: A Voyage to the Land of Minos and Art Deco." In *Cretomania: Modern Desires for the Minoan Past*. Edited by Nicoletta Momigliano and Alexander Farnoux. Routledge, 2017, pp. 124–156.

Cantacuzino, Sherban (ed.). "Queen Elizabeth II [special issue]." *Architectural Review*, vol. 145, no. 868, 1969, pp. 396–462.

Choay, Françoise. *Le Corbusier* [The Masters of World Architecture Series]. George Braziller, 1960.

Coope, Rosalys. "'Long Gallery:' Its Origins, Development, Use and Decoration." *Architectural History*, vol. 29, 1986, pp. 43–72 & 74–84.

Davis, Arthur. "The Architecture of the Liner: Planning, Decoration and Equipment." *Architectural Review*, vol. 35, April 1914, pp. 87–110.

DeZurko, Edward, Robert. "Greenough Theory of Beauty in Architecture." *The Rice Institute Pamphlet*, vol. 39, no. 3, 1952 [1951], pp. 96–121.

Durand, Jean-Nicolas-Louis. *Précis des Leçons d'Architecture* [vol. I]. École Polytechnique, 1817 [1802–1805]. Available online at: https://bibliotheque-numerique.inha.fr/viewer/7266/?offset=#page=12&viewer=picture&o=search&n=0&q=economie [last accessed: 10/06/2020].

Emerson, Ralph Waldo. *Letter to William Emerson*, 27 July 1835. Available online at: https://www.ralphwaldoemersonhouse.org/ [last accessed: 10/06/2020].

Eskilson, Stephen. *The Age of Glass: A Cultural History of Glass in Modern and Contemporary Architecture*. Bloomsbury, 2018.

Fleischacker, Samuel. *On Adam Smith's Wealth of Nations: A Philosophical Companion*. Princeton University Press, 2004.

Foucault, Michel. "Des Espaces Autres" [Of Other Spaces]. *Architecture, Mouvement, Continuité*, no. 5, 1984 [1967], pp. 46–49.

Goodman, Russell. "Transcendentalism." *Stanford Encyclopedia of Philosophy*, 2019 [2003]. Available online at: https://plato.stanford.edu/entries/transcendentalism/ [last accessed: 10/06/2020].

Greenough, Horatio. "American Architecture." *The Crayon*, vol. 2, no. 15, 1855 [1843], pp. 224–226.

Greenough, Horatio. *Form and Function: Remarks on Art* [intr. E. Loran]. Edited by H.A. Small, University of California Press, 1969 [1947].

Guy, Richard John. *First Spaces of Colonialism: The Architecture of Dutch East India Company Ships* [PhD dissertation]. Cornell University, 2012.

Hinchman, Mark and Yoneda, Elyssa. *Interior Design Masters*. Routledge, 2016.

Jarves, James Jackson. *The Art-Idea: Sculpture, Painting, and Architecture in America*. Hurd and Houghton, 1865 [1864].

Kent Layton, J. *The Edwardian Superliners: A Trio of Trios*. Amberley Publishing, 2011.

Kruft, Hanno-Walter. *A History of Architectural Theory from Vitruvius to the Present*. Zwemmer and Princeton Architectural Press, 1994.Le Corbusier. *Toward a New Architecture*. Translated by Fr. Etchells, Dover Publication, 1986 [1931].

Le Corbusier. *Toward an Architecture* [intr. J.-L. Cohen]. Translated by J. Goodman, The Getty Research Institute, 2007 [1928].

Le Corbusier. *Vers une Architecture*. Éditions Vincent, Fréal & Cie, 1958 [1928].

Le Corbusier and P. Jeanneret. *Œuvre Complete de 1910–1929*. Les Editions D'Architecture, 1967a.

Le Corbusier and P. Jeanneret. *Œuvre Complete de 1929–1934*. Les Editions D'Architecture, 1967b.

Le Corbusier-Saugnier. "Des Yeux qui ne Voient pass… Les Paquebots." *L'Esprit Nouveau*, no. 8, 1921, pp. 846–855.

Maciunas, George. "The Grand Frauds of Architecture: Mies van der Rohe, Saarinen, Bunshaft, Frank Lloyd Wright." *Fluxus 1*, no. 4, 1964.Mallet-Stevens, Robert. "Normandie 1935." *L'Architecture d'Aujourd'hui*, no. 8, August 1935, p. 27.

Mallgrave, Harry Francis (ed.). *Architectural Theory: vol. I: An Anthology from Vitruvius to 1870*. Blackwell Publishing, 2006.

McCormick, Ted. *William Petty and the Ambitions of Political Arithmetic*. Oxford University Press, 2009.

Medina, Cuauhtémoc. "Architecture and Efficiency: George Maciunas and the Economy of Art." *Anthropology and Aesthetics*, no. 45, Spring, 2004, pp. 273–284.

Peskett, Leonard. "On the Design of Steamships from the Owner's Point of View." *Transactions of the Royal Institution of Naval Architects*, vol. 56, 1914.

Petrovski, Henry. *The Pencil: A History of Design and Circumstance*. Alfred A. Knopf, 1990.

Samuel, Flora. *Le Corbusier and the Architectural Promenade*. Birkhäuser, 2010.

Sébille, Albert. "L'Esthétique du Paquebot d'Aujourd'hui." *L'Architecture d'Aujourd'hui*, no. 8, August 1935, pp. 31–33.

Shakespeare, William. "The Tempest." *The Complete Works*. Edited by W.J. Craig, Magpie Books, 1993, pp. 1–22.

Smith, Adam. *An Inquiry into the Nature and Causes of the Wealth of Nations* [vol. I]. Edited by R.H. Campbell & A.S. Skinner, Liberty Classics, 1981 [1776].

Smith, Adam. *Theory of Moral Sentiments.* Edited by D.D. Raphael & A.L. Macfie. Oxford University Press, 1976 [1759].

Snyder, Michael. "Premonitions of the Postmodern: Aldous Huxley's 'After Many a Summer Dies the Swan' and Los Angeles in the Thirties." *Aldous Huxley Annual: A Journal of Twentieth-Century Thought and Beyond*, no. 5, 2005, pp. 167–192.

Thoreau, Henry D. *Walden* [150th Anniversary Edition] [intr. J. Updike]. Edited by J.L. Shanley, Princeton University Press, 2004 [1971].

Tournikiotis, Panayotis. *Adolf Loos.* Princeton Architectural Press, 2002.

Vitruvii. *De Architectura* [books I-V]. Translated by P. Lefas, Plethron, 1997 [27–23 BC].

Von Moos, Stanislaus. *Le Corbusier: Elements of a Synthesis.* 010 Publishers, 2009.

Wealleans, Anne. *Designing Liners: A History of Interior Design Afloat.* Routledge, 2006.

Weber, Max. *The Protestant Ethic and the Spirit of Capitalism* [intr. A. Giddens]. Translated by T. Parsons, Routledge, 1992 [1930].

Willis, Robert & Willis, Clark. *The Architectural History of the University of Cambridge* [vol. 2]. Cambridge University Press, 1988 [1886].

Wright, Robert E. *The Wealth of Nations Rediscovered: Integration and Expansion in American Financial Markets, 1780–1850.* Cambridge University Press, 2002.

Τουρνικιώτης, Παναγιώτης. *Η Διαγώνιος του Le Corbusier.* Εκκρεμές, 2010.

Τουρνικιώτης, Παναγιώτης. «Σχόλια στην Ελληνική Μετάφραση του *Vers une Architecture*». *Για Μία Αρχιτεκτονική*. Μετάφραση Π. Τουρνικιώτης, Εκκρεμές, 2004, σσ. 247–257.

5 Resemblances and disjunctions

Art, mathematics and economic models[1]

Ragupathy Venkatachalam[2]

Introduction

The relationship between economic theory and the world of art is not immediately obvious. The former, often dubbed a dismal science, broadly deals with questions related to the creation and distribution of wealth through various modes of production, consumption and exchange. Art, on the other hand, is perceived to be the realm of the creative, expressing a wide range of ideas, skills, imagination and constantly challenging established boundaries. In the eyes of most people, the direct appeal of art to the senses, and matters of the heart and mind is perhaps far from the cold, unimaginative and calculating rationalism of economics.

One possible common ground between the two disciplines can be found in their engagement with representation. For instance, there is some level of art involved in creating a model of the economy. This sort of judiciousness involved, however, is not my direct focus here. Instead, the focus is on how works of art draw one's attention to selected aspects of what they represent or signify, which may not be obvious in the first place. Provocative artworks often shape perceptions to varying degrees by cleverly reorienting our attention, thereby stoking our imagination, creating a sense of wonder, appealing to our senses and even challenging our prevailing views of reality and the status quo.[3]

In the world of economic theory, the act of storytelling has, over the past century, increasingly moved towards employing mathematical models to represent relevant worlds or phenomena. Economic models range from those capturing aggregate macro-level phenomena such as growth, business cycles, inflation, unemployment and international trade to those dealing with micro-level issues such as consumption choices, labour supply, and situations of bargaining. Economic theories and the worlds they capture are often mathematically characterised. Once represented, a variety of features and associated consequences are closely examined. There is a lot of literature on modelling in economics that examines a range of questions, such as the ways in which idealisations and abstractions are employed (Morgan, 2008, 2012), the nature of the worlds that models create (Sugden, 2000), their ontological status, relationship with reality, ability to explain and limitations (Lawson, 2019).

DOI: 10.4324/9781003105435-8

Instead of attempting a detailed comparative exercise between art and economic theory as a whole, which is beyond my expertise, this chapter has a more modest goal: to find common ground between the methods and tactics employed by some artists and some mathematical economists and the way they use representation. More specifically, I focus on the theme of disjunction, manifested in the form of paradoxes, illusions, contradictions and impossibilities, both in economic theory and in art.

The reason to focus on such paradoxical results perhaps needs some justification. First, showing paradoxes and contradictions has played an important role in advancing our knowledge in virtually every field of academic inquiry. Their counter-intuitive character often draws the necessary attention of inquisitive minds and unleashes creative energies to further the investigation. They serve as effective instruments to highlight important disjunctions and issues within theories, thereby offering the necessary dose of scepticism. Paradoxes and illusions have a long history in art, and economics also has its fair share of counter-intuitive results and paradoxes (for example, Diamond-water paradox, Allais paradox, Ellsberg paradox, Edgeworth paradox).[4] Although the terms paradox, contradiction and impossibility are often used interchangeably, there is a need to distinguish between these different forms of disjunctions. A paradox or a contradiction draw attention to some aspects of inquiry. They may or may not always be of interest for the larger study or theory and not all of them have important consequences. However, some of them do and these are of interest for this chapter. Impossibility claims, on the other hand, are much stronger than claims of contradictions and paradoxes. As opposed to contradictions and paradoxes, they present universal (logical) assertions about certain properties of a theoretical system under consideration. In this chapter, I do not attempt to make an exhaustive typology of different cases and instead use the term disjunction in a more general sense to refer to the notions mentioned earlier. However, the usage of the term is distinct in character, where it specifically points to epistemological limits.

Starting from the realm of art, this chapter attempts to synthesise some common insights across selected works of René Magritte and M.C. Escher, both of whom employed disjunctions, paradoxes and illusions in their art. Building on them, it explores their relevance to understanding certain aspects of mathematical modelling in social sciences, especially in economics. It argues for a more prominent recognition and even a celebration of the relatively unsung virtue of modelling: to highlight paradoxes and impossibilities that lie beneath various representations. Despite their subversive character, creative disjunctions can play an important epistemological role by advancing our understanding of the nature and limitations of models while opening up the space for new concepts and conjectures. A case for the fruitfulness of such an approach in economics is illustrated by drawing examples from the works of Kenneth Arrow, Piero Sraffa and Vela Velupillai. Each of them, in their own way, used formal frameworks to show impossibilities, indeterminacies and undecidabilities, thereby forging new ways to think about economic problems (Figure 5.1).

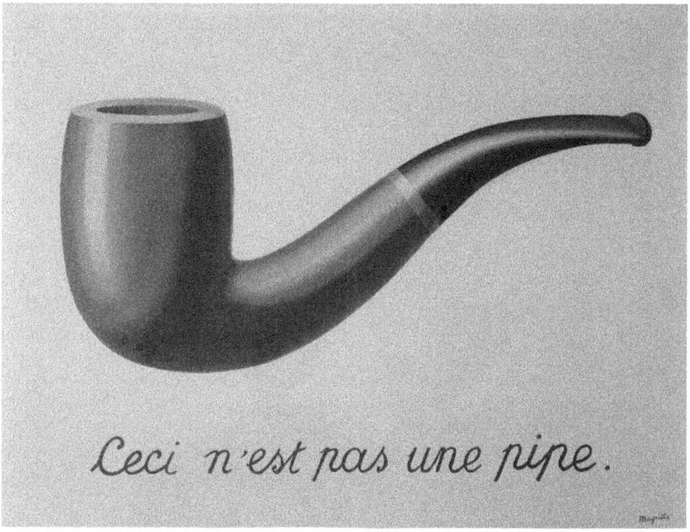

Figure 5.1 René Magritte's The Betrayal of Images: 'Ceci n'est pas une pipe', 1928–1929 (oil on canvas)

Magritte, Escher: Celebrating paradoxes

René Magritte, a celebrated Belgian surrealist artist, through his playful style raised many important questions concerning representations and the tensions that are born in transferring an idea across different mediums. Although he was a painter, his interest was in using artwork and paintings as a medium to meditate and communicate complex philosophical ideas.[5] Like many surrealists, Magritte did not like being referred to as an artist, preferring instead to be 'considered a thinker who communicated by means of paint' (Foucault, 1983: 2). Many of his paintings illustrate his keen interest in the tenuous, complex relationship between a representation and the object being represented.

More broadly, Magritte was deeply attracted to issues concerning resemblance, similitude, realism, sign and meaning; and explored these themes using disjunctions and disruptions. His famous painting, *The Treachery of Images* (1928–1929, also referred to as *The Betrayal of Images* or *Ceci n'est pas une pipe)*, can be seen as a classic example of this method. Like many others in the surrealist movement, he deftly utilised the method of juxtaposing objects and concepts in a way that resulted in a paradoxical image or a situation. For instance, in the case of *The Treachery of Images*, Magritte combines a readily recognisable image of a pipe together with a legend in text that declares *Ceci n'est pas une pipe* (this is not a pipe). This seeming contradiction between the verbal and the visual is utilised as a device to highlight the distinction between the *signifier* (i.e., the sign – the image or the word) and that which is *signified* (Figure 5.2).

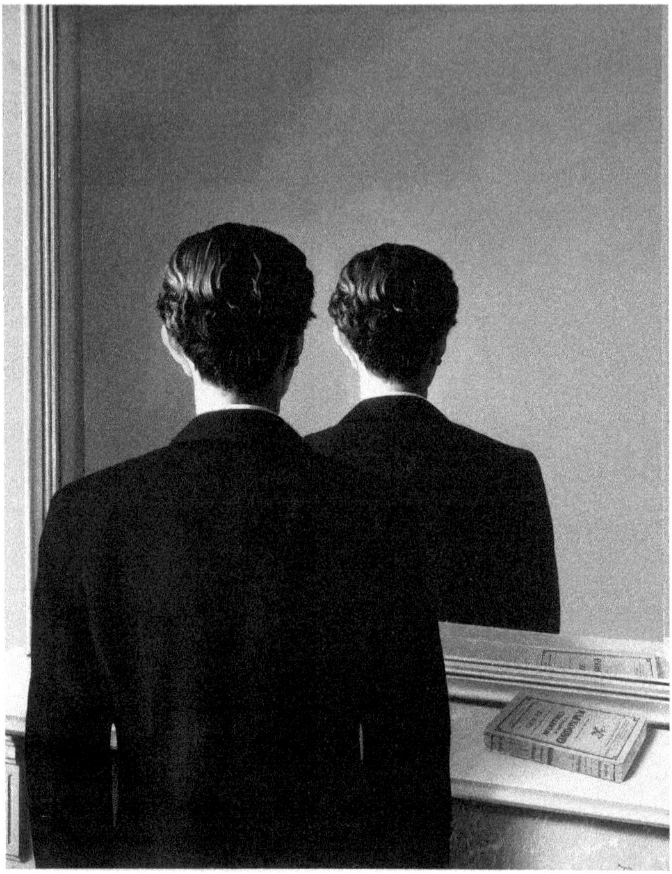

Figure 5.2 Recursion in Magritte and Escher. Left panel: Rene Magritte's Not to be Reproduced, 1937 © ADAGP, Paris and DACS, 2021. Right panel: M.C. Escher's "Hand with Reflecting Sphere" © 2021 The M.C. Escher Company-The Netherlands. All rights reserved. www.mcescher.com © ADAGP, Paris and DACS, 2021

Magritte seems to attack the uncritical equation of the essence of things with their representation, otherwise known as the object-representation divide. For Foucault, this also questions the implicit hierarchy presumed between the object and the representation, by focusing on the idea of similitude rather than that of resemblance. Similar paradoxical juxtapositions can be found in many of Magritte's paintings (*The Palace of Curtains III (1928–1929), The Use of Speech (1928), The Call of the Peaks (1943), The Human Condition (1933, 1935)*). The use of seemingly inconsistent juxtapositions or disjunctions is also seen elsewhere in logic and mathematics; these carefully exploit the reference relations and the ambiguity of language, thereby creating paradoxes that pave way for a deeper inquiry into the concepts under consideration (for example, Liar's paradox, Russell's paradox).[6]

Like Magritte, Dutch graphic artist Maurits Cornelis Escher too straddled the world of contradictions, disjunctions and paradoxes through his extremely original work. He had much in common with abstract Expressionism and Surrealism, even if he never acknowledged it, actively participated or thought of himself as a member of any particular group. Escher's works, often rendered in the form of lithographs, engravings, woodcuts and sketches, exemplify the possibilities of a romantic union between art and mathematics, in particular, geometry. He never had formal training in any advanced mathematics. Yet, his artworks were pregnant with mathematical ideas and interesting intuitions (Figure 5.3).

Escher constructed impossible worlds and interesting geometries and experimented with tessellations. However, of particular interest to him were depictions of infinity and reconciling the nature of the infinite with that of the finite (Schattschneider, 2010: 706). Hofstadter's famous book *Gödel, Escher, Bach: an Eternal Golden Braid* uses Escher's work to develop the idea of recursion and self-reference.[7] Escher meditated a lot on the myriad of 'paradoxes of perception in representation, playing with the ambiguity of the projective systems' (Ferrero et al., 2009: 307). Several examples of these impossibilities, inconsistencies and contradictions in his work invite one to think about perception and illusion. The appealing contradictions that emanate from the representation of higher dimensional objects in two-dimensional space are noteworthy (*Drawing Hands (1948), Möbius Strip II (1963)*, for instance). Similarly, he creates seemingly plausible representations of buildings and spaces, which cleverly embed impossibilities and contradict our perceptions (e.g., *Belvedere (1958), Convex and Concave (1955), Ascending and Descending (1960)*). They become instruments or telescopes to think about and grapple with profound intuitions concerning geometry and space. Consider his work Waterfall (1961), which captures a perpetual motion that blatantly contradicts the physical laws with which we are familiar. In this piece, created with inputs from Roger and Lionel Penrose (Schattschneider, 2010: 711–712), Escher presents an object that on the face of it looks physically plausible, only to reveal the impossibilities that emerge under careful scrutiny. The use of impossible objects in art and painting has had a long history prior to Escher, dating back at least four centuries in the Netherlands. For instance, *The Magpie on the Gallows* (1568) by the Dutch painter Pieter Bruegel, features a gallow that is very much in the same class as the Penrose triangle or the impossible construction in Escher's *Waterfall*.[8]

What underlies works like *Drawing Hands* (1948) is more than the mere visual ambiguity that one finds in Wittgenstein's famous 'rabbit-duck' diagram for instance. Rather, it is a kind of narrative ambiguity, whereby Escher 'ingeniously subverts of hierarchy, rendering level and meta-level perpetually reversible' (Rimmon-Kenan, 1982: 22). However, for both Magritte and Escher, creating these contradictions and impossibilities is not an attempt to

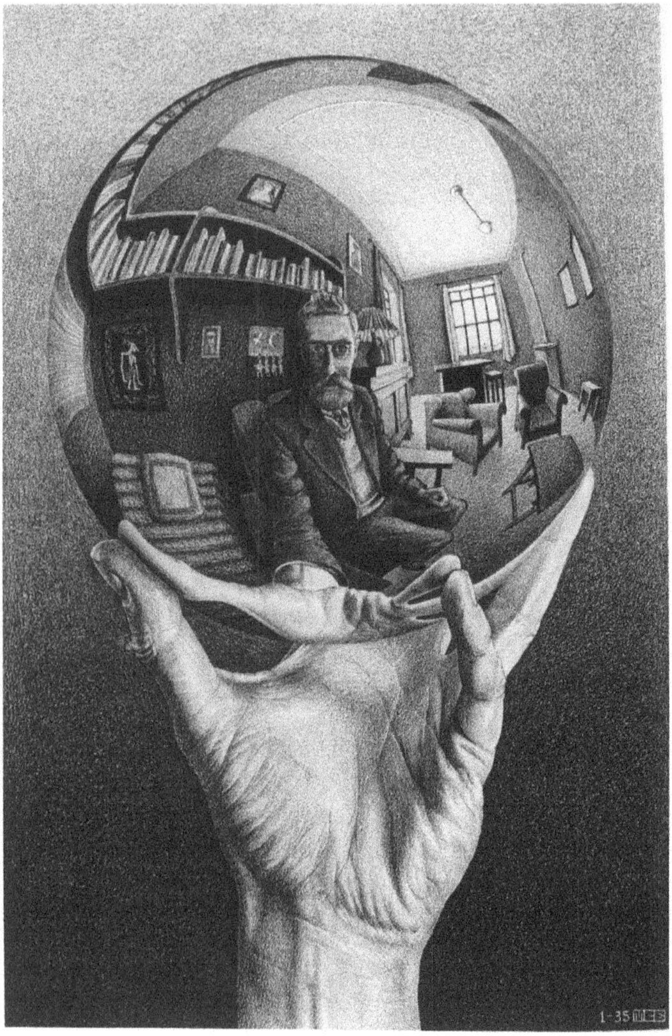

Figure 5.3 M.C. Escher's "Hand with Reflecting Sphere" © 2021 The M.C. Escher Company-The Netherlands. All rights reserved. www.mcescher.com

delve into alternative, imaginary worlds that are completely detached from ordinary experience. On the contrary, as the philosopher Alquié points out:

> Derealization of the everyday world was always, for the surrealists, in the positive hope of possession and discovery. Surrealism is not a flight into the unreal or into dream, but an attempt to penetrate into what has more reality than the logical and objective universe.
>
> (Alquié, 1965: 65)

What can these impossible worlds of Escher, and the carefully constructed disjunctions of Magritte, tell us about the study of economics? Their relevance concerns the methodology of economic analysis and specifically to the part of economic theorising that is concerned with the use of models.

Economic models: Mere resemblances?

The employment of models has been quite an important aspect of the methodology of economic analysis (both theoretical and empirical) for long, and they have acquired increasing prominence in the 20th century. Metaphors and analogical reasoning have been routinely employed in theorising about the economic world, and models, in their role as metaphorical and analogical devices aid the stories told by economists. In turn, empirical models have been seen as playing the role of fitting different theories to the world (more precisely to the data). Economists have tried to develop techniques that will aid them to identify the correct or true model among the many that are possible. Such models are supposed to help simplify the intricate, complex world of economic phenomena. A possible classification of economic models would be to see their roles as objects that (i) help facilitate fitting theories to the world, (ii) aid in theorising and (iii) serve as investigative instruments (Morgan, 2008). However, the distinctions between their roles as representations, metaphor or investigative instruments may not always be distinct, and this typology does not clearly define what constitutes a model and the features it embodies. In this chapter, I will focus on the use of mathematical models (not statistical or empirical models) in economic analysis, which may be seen as constituting a unique category.

Like many branches of science, economic models are closely allied to and benefit from metaphorical and analogical thinking. These metaphors range from mechanical, biological to fictional. For instance, economists speak of the: invisible hand (general equilibrium theory), rocking horses, pendulums, sunspots (business-cycle theory), predator and prey (class struggle), prisoner's dilemma, trembling hands (game theory), Robinson Crusoe, utility computers (microeconomics), turnpikes (growth theory), cob-webs, billiards players, random walks – just to name a few. Given that there is an inevitable loss of something that plagues every attempt at representation through a model, economic models are no exception. It is important to recognise and investigate the degree of sacrifice that may be involved in using them as analogue or heuristic devices. This, in turn, has important consequences for the correspondence or validity of the inferences drawn from the model to the original domain, which in this case is society.

Perhaps it is useful to briefly discuss the question of what one might mean by a model (as distinct from their use and role). Even if a precise definition may be elusive, Black (1962) provides a lucid characterisation: models are icons, analogues or abstract (symbolic) formulations that share similitude with the (real or imaginary) objects they embody. They strive to represent by preserving some properties of the original. Such invariant properties can range from relative proportions (as in scale models, e.g., miniature ships), structural properties (as in analogue models) or patterns of structural or functional relationships (as in mathematical models). François Quesnay's *Tableau économique* can be thought of as an early example of the latter class.

Theoretical models in economics predominantly belong to the class of *analogue models* more than to scale models. Therefore, desiring an exact resemblance or striving for a reproduction of all features in an economy is both impossible and unprofitable. Analogue models in economics are often mathematical, which attempt to map some selective properties of the economic system on to a mathematical or symbolic system. However, these analogue models need not exclusively be mathematical: The Phillips-Newlyn electro-mechanical hydraulic machine is a pertinent example of an analogue model that serves to capture the workings of the macroeconomic system.[9]

The choice of features to represent in a model may be guided by the structure or a part of the structure that is intended to be isomorphic with the model. Note that the notion of structure in practice can often be imaginary or a mere plausibility and not necessarily real. In a mathematical model, a social phenomenon or the structure of relationships is translated into a different medium (picture) or (symbolic) language. These models, by construction, are both simpler and more abstract than the economy.[10] One can argue that it is only by simplifying certain features, or by being unfaithful to the original in some aspects, will the model be able to serve its intended function. Thus, when looking at the Marshallian supply-demand diagram, the criticism that it does not capture *all* that is there in a market would perhaps be misplaced. It is true that the scissor-like figure does not accurately reflect or shine a light on the myriad of complex social relationships, context and institutional arrangements that underpin the process of exchange in an actual market. However, by virtue of being a 'model' of a market and as a heuristic fiction, it abstracts, simplifies and yet strives to map certain 'tendencies' concerning price movements. The ingenuity of the modeller then lies in the degree to which the inferences drawn from the representation can carry over to the original object of study and the level of universality that we can grant them. In this regard, it is worth noting that the kind of interpretations – whether fictitious or existential – that we employ concerning models are not trivial.

> The difference is between thinking of the electrical field *as if* it were filled with a material medium, and thinking of it *as being* such a medium. One approach uses a detached comparison reminiscent of simile and argument from analogy; the other requires an identification typical of metaphor.
>
> In *as if* thinking, there is a willing suspension of ontological unbelief, and the price paid, as Maxwell insists, is absence of explanatory power. Here, we might speak of the use of models as *heuristic fictions*. In risking existential statements, however, we reap the advantages of an explanation but are exposed to the dangers of self-deception by myths... (Black, 1962: 228, italics in the original).

Although these remarks were mentioned in the context of physics, they may be equally relevant for economic models, especially given the influence of physics in their development. With that brief discussion on the landscape of models in economics, we move to examine the productive role that disjunctions can play in models, methodology of economic analysis and in answering or posing ontological paradoxes.

Resemblances and disjunctions: In praise of subversion

The idea that models often entail simplifications, abstractions and projections on to a different medium is fairly easy to agree upon. Consequently, the possible loss of complexity and nuance involved in the original object inevitably opens up space for scepticism concerning the veracity of such representations. Based on such scepticism, one may conclude that economic models in the form of graphs, mathematical models, etc. are necessarily inadequate as authentic representations. A pertinent objection at this point would be that the veracity considerations should not require that all models should serve a photograph-like function. Instead, the verisimilitude (or the lack of it) cannot be judged independent of the purpose or the intended function of the model. Such a claim would be valid, of course, only as long as the omission in representation does not deprive us of useful insights into the phenomena it intends to explain.

Another relevant point here is the intended interpretation of the model that we discussed earlier. If economic models are taken to be existential representations (*as is*), this poses a more intricate issue when these models are used for policy decisions. The possibility of feedback loops, whereby the decisions based on the model end up affecting or influencing real-world outcomes, is of real concern. Similarly, some scholars point out the possibility of economic models playing a performative role in which models go beyond merely describing an economy. Instead, these models shape the social world they are meant to be describing. This critique is well articulated in MacKenzie, Muniesa and Siu (2007) and the vast subsequent literature it engendered.

The under-appreciated aspect of economic modelling that I wish to draw attention to is, at least in the face of it, subversive in nature. This concerns a model's ability to consciously generate *disjunctions* (i.e., showing inconsistency within the theoretical set up by highlighting paradoxes, contradictions, unsolvabilities and impossibilities) while serving as an exploratory or an investigative instrument.[11] A perception of disjunction – an apparent disconnect or contradiction between the entities involved – has often led people to declare such instances as paradoxes, impossibilities or inconsistencies. The surrealists have fruitfully employed this disjunctive device in their paintings, music, literature and theatre with admirable success. They used, *inter alia*, disjunctions to present interesting ideas in the realm of pure thought, challenge conventional perceptions and received wisdom, highlight neglected associations and advance philosophical discussions. Even though they were not economists, Magritte and Escher, regardless of their surrealist credentials, used disjunctions in *creative* ways to present contradictions.[12] They both opened up ways to challenge tacitly accepted concepts, especially those concerning the relationships between representations, perception, space, language and reality. It is this capacity of advancing new insights, concepts, hypotheses by unshackling existing perceptions and accepted conclusions that is powerful and needs to be celebrated. A modelling philosophy that focuses on identifying, constructing or deriving disjunctions in a framework or theory serves two functions: (i) to highlight aspects that are often hidden in a formal framework that sheds light on the limits of a chosen theoretical framework and (ii) contradictions and attempts at explaining, in turn, set the stage for *generation* of novel hypothesis and theories, which is the main business of any scientific enterprise.

Disjunctions perceived by the reader of the model can take many forms. A non-exhaustive list could cover the following: perception of a dissonance between the features of reality and its representation in the form of a model; a disjunction between the economic intuition and the implications of the model; disjunctions that present themselves as potential surprises in the form of impossibilities, inconsistencies between aspects or notions within a model. While all of these disjunctions are legitimate, the first two are perhaps the most recognised and characterise much of the critical engagement with economic theories and models. The latter category is relatively less emphasised. In these, the disjunction often concerns the internal consistency, ambiguity, indeterminacy and even the limits of the formal language (or the kind of mathematics) in which a model is clothed.[13] For the purposes of this chapter, only the last category of disjunctions that deal with formal aspects are considered. There are several instances where this approach has been employed and has yielded interesting results. Among these, three examples in the domain of mathematical economics are worth mentioning for our present purposes.

Arrow's impossibility theorem

Arrow's impossibility theorem (Arrow, 1950, 1951) is a landmark result that concerns welfare economics, social choice theory and political science, put forward by Kenneth Arrow, the cowinner of the Sveriges Riksbank Prize in Economic Sciences in Memory of Alfred Nobel in 1972.[14] Arrow investigated the idea of social choice (e.g. electing a prime minister, and voting for a specific policy or law as a society), ways to conceptualise it, principles to adhere to, and the possible rules or processes ('Social Welfare Function' in Arrow's terminology) by which such choices can be arrived at on the basis of preferences held by individuals in a society. Arrow's theorem showed that it was impossible to construct a mechanism or a social welfare function that was based solely on individual preference functions and at the same time satisfied a set of principles that were held as reasonable. In doing so, the impossibility theorem opened up the whole field of social choice theory and had a profound influence on the way welfare economics developed. According to Kelly (1978: 1), this 'deeply influenced theoretical welfare economics, moral and political philosophy, and mathematical approaches to microeconomic theory led to a whole new branch of welfare economics called social choice theory'. The history of this development can be found in Lützen (2019).

Arrow's impossibility theorem was one of the first impossibility results outside of mathematics and has been regarded among the more important results in the social sciences. Arrow's result also challenged the cardinal approach to welfare economics. Even though the axiomatic approach to ordered sets came into economics slightly before Arrow's work, through the work of von Neumann and Morgenstern (1947), Arrow's results drew the attention of economists to new mathematical and logical tools, which were hitherto uncommon to them. In particular, his reliance on order relations and a shift away from the use of the tools of calculus and analysis, at least in the context of welfare economics, was notable. Arrow seems to have learned about order relations and the relevant aspects of mathematical logic from the eminent mathematical logician Alfred Tarksi.[15]

To understand the context and the importance of the impossibility theorem, it is worth recalling some of the key questions in welfare economics before and around the time when Arrow was about to revolutionise the subject. Collective welfare and its maximum achievable level have traditionally been of interest to welfare economists. Cardinal approaches to welfare economics emanating from the Utilitarian tradition were dominant at the time and focused largely on collective welfare maximisation. The social state that achieved this highest level was thought to be an ethically appropriate benchmark. There were, however, several conceptual difficulties in measuring and aggregating individual utilities to arrive at a collective measure of social welfare. A competing approach – the ordinal approach – rejected the idea of having numerical values of individual utilities and aggregating them. Instead, it focused on how different possible scenarios are ordered (e.g., scenario A is preferred to B and so on, though it remained silent about answering 'by how much') and hence bypassing the issues of measurement and interpersonal comparison of utilities. Notions of the optimum in this tradition were defined without reference to cardinal values, such as the criterion by Pareto, as a potential solution. However, multiple such optimal positions were possible in principle, and some of these were ethically indefensible. The Bergson-Samuelson approach, often dubbed as the *new welfare economics*, was developed around the notion of a social welfare function (SWF). It tried to avoid cardinal measurements and tried to bridge the ordinal-cardinal divide.[16] SWF was a real-valued function, which was composed of many variables in principle; the idea was to rely on orderings as far as possible and to maximise this SWF with respect to a cardinal indicator.

Arrow completely rejected any reliance on a cardinalist approach and avoided the use of calculus and analysis, instead resorting to the machinery of order theory and logic. Instead of conceiving the social welfare function as a real-valued function that needs to be maximised using the tools of calculus, Arrow characterised preferences among different social states as weak orderings. In terms of mathematics, this indicated a shift from a continuous to a discrete analysis.

Given this background, we are now better placed to appreciate the counter-intuitive nature of the theorem. This theorem is more than just another paradoxical result concerning the theory of voting. In fact, paradoxes associated with choice and voting have a long history. For instance, the famous Condorcet paradox showed that collective preferences can be cyclical or intransitive, even if the individual preferences are transitive. Different voting methods have been proposed and examined in the past by many scholars, like Nicolas de Condorcet, Jean Charles de Borda, Duncan Black and others.[17] Arrow's unique contribution was in going deeper and beyond the paradoxes concerning aggregation issues and deriving a much stronger impossibility result.

Let us now move to the content of the theorem.[18] Consider x_1, x_2,..., which is taken to denote different possible social states, policies, projects or candidates among which a society has to choose from. Each individual i, who is a member of the society composed of N individuals, chooses an ordering relation R_i. This relation indicates their preference ranking over alternatives (say social states). Arrow departed from earlier cardinal approaches and reformulated the idea of a social welfare function as a *functional* relationship that determines an *aggregate* social ranking R on the basis of the collection of individual rankings $\{R_i\}$. The idea of rule or a process that maps individual preferences to the collective ordering of the social states is akin to a voting procedure that determines a winner from a collection of individual preferences over different candidates. The connection between voting theory and welfare economics can hence be clearly seen. The following principles or axioms can be seen as being an acceptable and reasonable requirement for a system of social choice based on democratic principles.

1 **Unrestricted domain:** for any logically possible set of individual preferences, there is a corresponding social ordering.
2 **Pareto principle:** If every individual prefers any x_1 to any x_2, then the society as a whole should prefer x_1 to x_2.
3 **Independence of irrelevant alternatives:** individual rankings of x_1 and x_2 alone determine the social rankings of x_1 and x_2.
4 **Nondictatorship:** There is no one distinguished voter whose preferences uniquely determine the outcome at the social level, regardless of the preferences of others.

A slightly simplified version of Arrow's impossibility theorem can be stated as follows (Maskin and Sen, 2014: 34):[19]

Theorem 1

(Impossibility theorem) *If there are at least three distinct social states and a finite number of individuals, there exists no social welfare function that can simultaneously satisfy all the axioms [1]–[4] above.*

One of the implications of this elegant and powerful theorem is that these seemingly reasonable axioms are not adequate to guarantee that an aggregation procedure to determine social ordering through democratic means exists. This also alerts us to the difficulties of evaluating axioms and their plausibility in isolation, without paying due attention to other axioms with which they are being combined. Overall, Arrow's impossibility theorem highlights a crucial disjunction between individual choices and social choices under reasonable conditions, by marrying voting theory and welfare economics. This can be seen and appreciated readily through a surrealist lens as well. Despite the theorem being a negative result, it ushered impressive amounts of research in the area of social choice theory, leading to many new insights (such as the Gibbard-Satterthwaite theorem), extensions, further relaxation of Arrow's conditions and an altogether deeper understanding of inherent tensions concerning aggregations and collective choice. As Lützen (2019: 85) observes:

> As a last driving force one can mention the creative force of impossibility or paradox. Indeed, despite their negative nature, impossibility theorems rarely bar progress. On the contrary, they often result in vigorous activity. For example, the discovery of incommensurability (the first rigorous impossibility proof) led the ancient Greeks to a great number of important theories. Similarly, the discovery of the unsolvability of the quintic led to the development of Galois theory and much of modern algebra. In the same vein, much of the activity in voting theory was a reaction to Condorcet's paradox, and the development of social choice theory can be (and has been) considered a response to Arrow's impossibility theorem. To circumvent the impossible has always been a strong driving force in many areas of life.

Piero Sraffa and indeterminacy

A second example that demonstrates the inherent limitations in some economic theories is the critique developed by Piero Sraffa in his magnum opus, *Production of Commodities by Means of Commodities* (Sraffa, 1960).[20] The subtitle of the book indicates that it was a *Prelude to a Critique of Economic Theory.* Sraffa represents the economy as a production system. His choice of representation was very much in the classical and physiocratic tradition, wherein production is viewed as a circular process. Given the *methods of production* and by taking one of the distributive variables – i.e., wage or profit rate – as being exogenously given, Sraffa resolves some important issues concerning value and distribution.

Sraffa's critique is based on the idea of a self-replacing system and self-replacing prices, wages and profit rates. Self-replacing is the condition in which production can continue to take place as it did during the previous production cycle. This condition enables an exclusive focus on prices and distribution of the surplus, where produced physical quantities remain unchanged. Within this framework, Sraffa searches for those exchange-values (relative prices) between different commodities that would allow the prevailing production structure to repeat itself in the future.

Sraffa's system: A brief sketch

A very brief sketch of Sraffa's system is presented below for expository purpose.[21] Sraffa assumes an annual cycle of production and at the end of the production cycle there are n produced commodities:

$$b = [b_1, b_2, \dots b_i, \dots b_n]^T \quad i = 1, 2, \dots, n. \tag{5.1}$$

The method of production producing the commodity b_i is a linear combination of means of production and labour:

$$a_i^1, a_i^2, \dots a_i^j, \dots a_i^n, l_i \rightarrow b_i \tag{5.2}$$

where a^j_i denotes the means of production produced by industry j used in the production of commodity i and l_i the labour used in the production of b_i.

In the case where the system produces more than the minimum amount which is necessary for replacement, one ends up with a surplus that needs to be distributed. Let s_i be the surplus of commodity i available for distribution after the quantities $\{a_i^j\}$ have been put aside for the next year's production. In compact matrix notation, we have

$$\mathbf{S} = (\mathbf{B} - \mathbf{A})^{\mathbf{T}}\mathbf{e} \tag{5.3}$$

where e is the $n{\times}1$ unit or summation vector (each element is 1); T is the transpose operator; S is the $n \times 1$ Physical Surplus vector or Physical *Net National Product*; B is the diagonal matrix composed of gross production b as its diagonal elements. Given the knowledge of the methods of production used during the previous annual production cycle (and assuming that the same methods will be used), Sraffa solves for uniform prices that would allow the system to replicate these commodities during the next production cycles. If this is our problem setup, the accounting balance would require that:

$$(\mathbf{I} + \boldsymbol{R})\, \boldsymbol{Ap} + \boldsymbol{Lw} = \boldsymbol{Bp} \tag{5.4}$$

where **I** is the identity $n \times n$ matrix; $\boldsymbol{p} = [p_1, p_2, \ldots, p_n]^T$ is the price vector, $\boldsymbol{R} = \text{diag}(r)$ is the diagonal matrix, whose diagonal elements are the rate of profits in each single industry, $r_1, r_2, \ldots, r_i, \ldots r_n$; A is the $n \times n$ matrix denotes the means of production $\{a_i^j\}$; L is the $n \times 1$ vector whose elements $\{l_i\}$ are the labour used in production.

The system of equations in (5.4) is indeterminate. Sraffa simplifies the problem by assuming that the rates of profits are uniform. In that case, the n rates of profits are assumed to be equal to a single rate of profits: $r = r_1 = r_2 = \ldots = r_n$.[22] Here, there are n equations and the number of variables is reduced to $n + 2$ (i.e., n prices, a wage rate w and a uniform rate of profits r). The system is still indeterminate and it can be closed only by adding some additional exogenous elements. We can chose the physical surplus S as the *numéraire* (as Sraffa does). The economic system is described in terms of $n + 1$ equations (i.e., n equations in (5.4) and the *numéraire* equation). With the uniform rate of profits assumption, we have $n + 2$ variables $\{p_1, p_2, \ldots, p_n, r, w\}$. In this case, there is only one degree of freedom and one of the $n + 2$ variables has to be exogenously given.

Indeterminacy and the critique

Using this representation of the economy, Sraffa has shown using constructive methods that the natural prices of the commodities, in this case, are not unique and they simultaneously determine the distribution of the physical surplus.[23] Moreover, the values of gross or net output and the value of capital are themselves a function of prices and hence of distribution.

Sraffa chose a system in which the analysis relied only on quantities of goods that are used, produced and exchanged, all of which are observable in principle. He first shows that the system represented in such a manner is not determinate. There is a unique association between prices and the distribution of the physical surplus in his system. In particular, he has shown that values (i.e., self-replacing prices) and distribution cannot be computed independently of each other. Venkatachalam and Zambelli (2021) argue that this indeterminacy is at the very core of Sraffa's message. He deftly uses the classical framework to show there is a deeper indeterminacy that persists, which in turn raises uncomfortable questions for the neoclassical theory of distribution. His work constituted an important part in the famous *Cambridge Capital Controversy*, which has been regarded as one of the important debates within economic theory in the last century. This is an example of how representations cleverly geared to show indeterminacies and impossibilities – in Sraffa's case, the impossibility of determining prices and distribution, independent of each other – can pose credible challenges for conventional wisdom and foster new avenues of thinking.

It is necessary to acknowledge the pervasive temptation that exists to get rid of such indeterminacy by 'closing' the system through additional assumptions. However, such attempts miss the point and the virtue that lies beneath the choice of representations to highlight these important features. The representation provided by Sraffa is not to be mistaken for yet another system, like that of general equilibrium models that provide a mechanical description of how the world works. That would be a mistaken view in my opinion. The same holds for uncritically adopting Sraffa's choice of simplifying assumptions, such as the uniform rate of profits, the absence of money and so on, as defensible positions and to treat his representation as the final word. That these elements were not strictly necessary for the critique that he was developing does not automatically imply that the framework he presented has no place for these elements.[24] An awareness of the modelling philosophy advocated in this chapter, and one that Sraffa employed fruitfully, could possibly diffuse some of the fierce, but ultimately misguided, battles.

Some justification may be warranted for what has been claimed to be Sraffa's ultimate aim in his choice of representation. To this end, let us briefly consider the discussion in the correspondence between him and Pierangelo Garegnani. In 1962, the latter was preparing a review of PCMC and discussed the relation between the profit rate and the money rates of interest in his letter to Sraffa. Garegnani wonders whether the issue of the profit rate as determined by the money rates of interest is valid and provides a plausible argument. However, Sraffa was clearly wary any such mechanical ways of determining distribution within the system and states categorically that it is not the intention in his book.[25]

It is quite evident that the negation that Sraffa emphasises is the indeterminacy issue and that he is not interested in having this as a positive, mechanical model that also renders everything determinate.

> [...] in general I only wanted to send out some signals to **avoid anyone to think** that the system [of PCMC] is presented [by me] as a "foundation" for a theory of relative supplies of capital and labour! It is the *negation* that seems important to me: as to the *affirmative* I have no intention of putting forward yet **another mechanical theory** which, in one form or another, reinforces the idea that distribution is determined by natural, or technical, or perhaps even accidental circumstances, but such as to render **futile** whatever **action**, from one side or the other, aimed to **modify the distribution**.
>
> (Sraffa Papers, D3/12/111/149, translation by Stefano Zambelli, in bold emphasis added).[26]

Undecidability and uncomputability in economic theory

The third example, one that has been close to my own research interests, concerns the distinction (and a dissonance) between the proof of existence of an entity (concerning economic models) and the ability to compute or construct these. This is relevant since not everything that has been proved to exist can be computed, sometimes even in principle, unless the choice of formalism admits only those proofs that establish existence through explicit constructions. In general, proving existence in classical mathematics does not guarantee that the mathematical object in question can be computed. This has important epistemological consequences and highlights the gulf between what we can 'prove' to exist and the possibility of computing them effectively (or decide membership). This alerts us to the importance of representations and associated possibilities and limitations. The set of assertions that can be established as being true can depend on whether a model is expressed within a specific mathematical framework (e.g., classical mathematics or constructive mathematics), the kind of logic that underpins them, and the modes of reasoning they admit. What may be valid, admissible or true for a model in one kind of mathematics may fail to hold in another.

To understand the relevance and importance of this, it may be useful to take a brief detour into the nature of mathematics used in economic theory. To date, classical mathematics – by which I refer to set theory (Zermelo-Fraenkel variety, with the axiom of choice), real analysis and classical logic – remains the predominant kind of mathematics employed in major areas and even in the frontiers of mathematical economics. There has also been a strong reliance on the use of the axiomatic method in post-war era developments in mathematical economics. Many scholars identify these developments as having been heavily influenced by the Formalist school and the Bourbakian school of mathematics.[27] The dominant mode of theorising in this tradition has been to axiomatise an economic theory (in classical mathematics) and pose questions concerning the existence, uniqueness and stability of various forms of static or dynamic equilibria. Within this enterprise, the methods of proof and persuasion are often devoid of numerical content. Once these mathematical objects are proved to exist, these results are then utilised for applied and policy purposes by devising algorithms to compute them using digital computers.

The idea of computing is intimately connected to the notion of algorithms and it may not be possible to devise algorithms to compute all objects that are proved to exist. Computability theory or recursion theory is a branch of mathematical logic that, among other things, delineates what can and cannot be computed through a mechanical or effective procedure. Similarly, there are varieties of mathematics that may fit the bill even when we are interested in the algorithmic aspects (Martin-Löf, 1982). For instance, the mathematics of the computation is often also seen through different forms of *constructive mathematics*, which stand in contrast to classical mathematics by allowing only *constructive* proofs to establish existence.

There are important differences between these formalisms and consequently the results that we can obtain within these. For instance, the nature of the domain of numbers typically utilised in classical mathematics and analysis (real numbers) is different compared to recursion theory (*rational* numbers).[28]

Note that even though almost all economic quantities that we encounter are at best *rational* numbers, they are uncritically and routinely characterised as real numbers. Similarly, the notion of an algorithm or constructive procedure is central to computability theory and constructive mathematics, but they aren't central to the formalist approach to mathematics, which in turn pays very little regard to the notion of computation and numerical implementation.[29] Even such simple differences can have important consequences concerning whether the results of a model carry over across different frameworks.[30]

All of these highlight the dependencies on the choice of representation and the importance of investigating the universality (or the lack thereof) of the results obtained in mathematical economics. In other words, how immutable are the truths and insights of mathematical economic models once we change the *kind* of mathematics that is used to represent economic problems? Similarly, questions concerning the appropriateness of certain type of mathematics in relation to the economic problem at hand and the limits of purely mathematical approaches become relevant as well.

For the last four decades, Vela Velupillai has examined these important issues systematically through his research program on computable and constructive economics. Velupillai recasts many traditional economic theories, concepts and models using alternative mathematical and logical formalisms – mainly computable and constructive – and investigates the implications. Many cornerstone results that are taken for granted in mathematical economics turn out to be invalid in alternative mathematical formalisms, or that they easily cannot be translated or meaningfully computed. Velupillai (2009) presents several undecidability and uncomputability results concerning a variety of topics in mathematical economics ranging from the rational choice, general equilibrium to Nash equilibria of finite games. These results highlight the limits of specific mathematical formalisms and distinguish the different kinds of mathematical foundations and their implications. A selection of these results (many by Velupillai, but also other scholars) is presented below (see Velupillai, 2009; Velupillai, 2010: 470–471):

- Nash equilibria of finite games are *constructively indeterminate.*
- Computable General Equilibria are *neither computable nor constructive.*
- The Two Fundamental Theorems of Welfare Economics are *Uncomputable and Nonconstructive*, respectively.
- There is *no effective procedure* to generate preference orderings.
- Recursive Competitive Equilibria (RCE), underpinning the Real Business Cycle (RBC) model and, hence, the Dynamic Stochastic General Equilibrium (DSGE) benchmark model of Macroeconomics, are *uncomputable.*
- There are games in which the player who in theory can always win cannot do so in practice because it is impossible to supply him with effective instructions regarding how he/she should play in order to win.[31]
- Inductively *effective* policy formalisations are impossible for complex economies.

It is evident that these results concern some of the foundational aspects of modern economic theory. Some of these results specifically highlight the presence of *undecidable disjunctions* (in the logical sense) in economic models, which cannot be made constructive. Let us briefly consider one of the results from the above list, which can help highlight the essential aspects of the narrative developed in this chapter.

Undecidability in the rational choice model

The result concerns the standard rational choice model employed in neoclassical economics. In the preference-based approach to choice, a (binary) preference relation R defined over a set of alternatives X is said to be *rational*, if it is complete and transitive.[32] The notion of *rational choice* is often understood to be synonymous with the idea of choosing the best preferred or maximal alternatives from a set of alternatives, on which preference orderings are generated through pairwise comparison. This model remains a cornerstone of neoclassical microeconomics and decision theory. In this framework, consistency of chosen outcomes matter more than all else and it is famously silent on the procedural aspects of decision making. Velupillai starts with standard axioms and definitions concerning choice, with an aim to unearthing the procedural aspects and make them explicit. The concept of a process is formalised in terms of an *effective procedure* or *mechanical procedure* (assuming the validity of the Church-Turing thesis) as understood in recursion theory. In doing so, he shows a formal equivalence between the rational choice behaviour of economic agents and the computational activity of a suitably programmed Turing machine.

Having established this equivalence, he further demonstrates that there is no effective procedure to generate preference ordering (i.e., there is no algorithm to systematically evaluate alternatives) by showing the choice function in question is uncomputable in general. Even if we are given a class of choice functions to generate preference orderings associated with picking maximal choices, he shows that there is no algorithm to decide whether or not an arbitrary choice function belongs to this class. In other words, the demands placed on the rational choice by human beings in the neoclassical model of choice surpasses the power of even the ideal computing machines. This immediately begs the question of its relevance in understanding actual human behaviour and forces one to think about relaxing the requirements we place on rational behaviour. Note that a demonstration of non-effectivity of generation of preference orderings does not imply that agents do not have or use preferences. On the contrary, it highlights the limitations of the representation in question.[33]

But our interest is in the methodological aspects of showing uncomputability and undecidability. By recasting the same questions using a different kind of mathematical framework (in his case, recursion theory) and thus bringing together two different worlds, Velupillai points us to the limitations of a specific formalisation and prompts us to think in new ways.

Velupillai's results, like those of Arrow's, may seem subversive or negative but only at the outset. A careful examination of these opens up new vistas of thinking about economic theorising and it has given rise to a research program on computable and constructive approaches to economic theorising. More interestingly, it points us to the dissonance between the pseudoprecisions of the mathematical models on the one hand and the 'conceptual fragility of the economic underpinnings' (Velupillai, 2015) on the other. Similar tussles are based on disjunctions in mathematical philosophy, where attempts to reconcile formal mathematics and intuitive notions have resulted in deep debates that have clarified the scope and limit of mathematical knowledge (Horsten and Welch, 2016).

Conclusion

Magritte often indulged in a deliberate method to obscure things from the observer, 'forcing us to question and think for ourselves about the world' (Day, 2018). Escher experimented with infinities, recursions and employed carefully constructed deceptions in his geometric objects that make us question about the nature of space and reality. The examples discussed in the domain of economics in this chapter point to remarkable similarities in terms of the meta *methods* employed by these artists and the economists.

Velupillai's style of demonstrating tensions that arise between different choice of underlying mathematics – i.e., medium of representation – bears a lot of similarity to the way in which Magritte demonstrates the tension between the visual and verbal mediums in *The Treachery of Images*. Sraffa's attempts to showcase indeterminacies and the inescapable simultaneity (of prices and distribution) inherent in some theoretical models of the economy can be fruitfully interpreted through the techniques employed by Escher in his *Hand with a reflecting sphere*. Likewise, the device employed by Arrow to highlight the emergence of impossibilities from seemingly plausible or standard premises are similar to the way Escher demonstrates (architectural) impossibilities in an otherwise normal or innocuous setting in the *Waterfall*.

That said, there sure are important differences between them and that these similarities cannot be stretched too far beyond reason. Nor do these individuals seem to have had any explicit influence on each other concerning the method discussed here. However, they all share a common ground in questioning representations, employing disjunctions creatively to show certain limitations. Through these examples discussed above, I hope to have persuaded the reader that there is at least a case to see these attempts in economic modelling as sharing similarities in character between themselves and with these artists. In my opinion, they all echo the spirit in which Magritte claimed that de Chirico's painting *Le chant d'amour* (1914) showcased the 'ascendance of poetry over painting'. There is much that economists can learn from various forms of art, and I believe that it can help them understand their own quests and methods better.

I conclude with a succinct reflection by Velupillai on the approach fostered by his mentor, the economist Richard Goodwin, who was also an artist:

> To be skeptical is an art – but it can be fostered, paradoxically, by the formalism of a mathematics of ambiguity, entirely based on the Erlanger Program. It was, in art, fostered by Escher, trained in geometry by Coxeter.
>
> …*I believe geometry can be harnessed to teach and represent economic indeterminacy and ambiguity in fruitful ways.* This was why Goodwin was aware of the need for rigorous approximations of the conceptual bases of economic theory. He recognized that **our concepts are always an approximation to a reality, the appearance of which was always deceptive, never completely encapsulable in any formalism** – that was something he had to grapple with as a painter, every time he put canvas on easel, and, then, brush to canvas.
>
> (Velupillai, 2015: 1494, emphasis added)

Notes

1 This paper is meant to be a tribute to Prof. Vela Velupillai. He always infused copious art, poetry and music in all his lectures, especially on the most technical subjects, which made them highly enjoyable for me. The panache and elegance with which he did so will forever be an elusive standard for most. A preliminary version of this paper was presented at the workshop on 'Economics & The Plastic Arts', held at Goldsmiths, University of London, during 4–5 July 2019. I thank Constantinos Repapis, Ivano Cardinale, Sarath Jakka, Divya Pant, Astrid Van den Bossche and Yohan John for helpful discussions on related topics, even if they may not agree with the views expressed here. I also thank participants from the above workshop for useful comments and clarifications. They are not responsible for any errors, which remain my own.

2 Institute of Management Studies, Goldsmiths, University of London, London, UK. Email: r.venkatachalam@gold.ac.uk

3 Equally, knowledge of various traditions of perception that exist across different societies can influence by reorienting and redefining one's prevailing view of art. I thank Velupillai for pointing this out.

4 I use the terms paradox, contradiction and impossibility interchangeably and there is a need to distinguish between them. A paradox or a contradiction may or may not always be of interest and not all of them have important consequences. However, some of them do and these are of interest for this chapter. Impossibility claims are much stronger than claims of contradictions and paradoxes. I use the term *disjunction* in a more general sense to refer to these different notions; however, it is distinct in character by pointing specifically to the associated epistemological limits.

5 This outlook, which signifies 'ascendence of poetry over painting', seems to have been inspired by Giorgio de Chirico. In particular, the painting *Le chant d'amour* (1914) seems to have influenced Magritte decisively (Gablik, 1970: 25).

6 A simple way to illustrate the Liar's paradox is as follows:

> The following sentence is true.
> The previous sentence is false.

The above example is purely in the verbal realm, exploiting disjunctive device to highlight the treacherous role played by self-reference.

7 Magritte too can be seen playing with the idea of recursion in his painting *Not to be reproduced* (1937), which fits naturally alongside Escher's *Hand with Reflecting Sphere* (1935).

8 I am unsure whether Escher was directly influenced by the work of Pieter Bruegel.

9 This is also referred to as the Monetary National Income Analogue Computer (MONIAC). For a collection of articles that cover various aspects of MONIAC, see the special issue of the journal *Economia Politica* (Vol. XXVIII, no. 1, 2011) that commemorates the 60th Anniversary of the Phillips machine.

10 An accessible outline of the procedures concerning the use of mathematical and theoretical models can be found in Black (1962: 224–225, 230–231).

11 For instance, see Kao et al. (2012).

12 Magritte, however, was not completely detached from the economic issues, at least from a specific political viewpoint:

> The only way that poets and painters can fight against the bourgeois economy is to give their works precisely that content which challenges the bourgeois ideological values propping up the bourgeois economy.
>
> (Magritte, 2016: xiv)

13 Although it is worth noting that strict adherents of intuitionistic-constructive mathematics broached by L.E.J. Brouwer would demur that mathematics itself is a languageless activity and that language can only provide a description of that activity.

14 For a biographical article on Kenneth Arrow, see Velupillai (2019).

15 Arrow is acknowledged in the preface of Tarski's 1941 book, *Introduction to Logic and to the Methodology of Deductive Sciences*, for his help with proofreading the English translation.

16 Note that the social welfare function, in this case, refers to something different from the sense in which Arrow conceives it. For an accessible history of this approach, see Lützen (2019: §3).

17 Charles Dodgson, popularly known as Lewis Carroll, was an important contributor to this area and his work on the theory of voting was rediscovered by Duncan Black.

18 This is a simplified exposition of the theorem to focus on the main ideas and it departs from Arrow's original version in some aspects. It closely follows Maskin and Sen (2014: 33–35).

19 Arrow originally referred to this in his book as the *General Possibility Theorem*, apparently on the advice of Tjalling Koopmans (Maskin and Sen, 2014: 58).

20 The ideas and exposition in this section draw from Zambelli (2018); Venkatachalam and Zambelli (2021a).

21 For a detailed version, see Zambelli (2018).

22 Zambelli (2018) discusses this assumption. The uniform rate of profits is obviously a special case. This assumption is justified in PCMC, which is meant as a *Prelude to a Critique of Economic Theory*. See Velupillai (2008) for a discussion on the constructive nature of Sraffa's arguments.

23 See Velupillai (2008) for a discussion on the constructive nature of Sraffa's arguments.

24 See Zambelli (2018) and Venkatachalam and Zambelli (2021a) on extensions of Sraffa's framework to include non-uniform rate of profits and credit and debt, respectively.

25 For a detailed argument, see Venkatachalam and Zambelli (2021a: §3).

26 The text in Italian:

> [...] io non ho inteso dir niente di molto impegnativo, e in generale ho solo voluto metter fuori qualche segnale **per evitare che si creda** che il sistema viene presentato come "fondamenta" per una teoria delle offerte relative di capitale e lavoro! E' la negazione che mi sembra importante: quanto
> alla affermativa non ho nessuna intenzione di mettere avanti **un'altra teoria meccanica** che, in una forma o nell'altra, ribadisca l'idea che la distribuzione sia determinata da circostanze naturali, o tecniche, o magari accidentali ma comunque tali da rendere **futile** qualsiasi **azione**, da una parte o dall'altra, per modificarla.
>
> (Sraffa Papers, D3/12/111/149, in bold emphasis added)

27 For instance, Gerard Debreu, one of the important mathematical economists who made fundamental contributions to mathematical general equilibrium theory, explicitly states (Debreu, 1984: 395):

> After having been influenced at the Ecole Normale Superieure in the early forties by the axiomatic approach of N. Bourbaki to mathematics, I became interested in economics toward the end of World War II. ...To somebody trained in the uncompromising rigor of Bourbaki, counting equations and unknowns in the Walrasian system could not be satisfactory, and the nagging question of existence was posed. But in the late forties several essential elements of the answer were still not readily available.

Also see Velupillai (2012) on the influence of Bourbaki on mathematical economics.

28 Computable analysis is a branch of mathematics that examines analysis from the viewpoint of computability and extends the Turing machine model to real numbers.

29 See Mathais (1992).

30 For instance, Bolzano-Weierstrass theorem, which is valid in real analysis and one that is often invoked either explicitly or implicitly in many mathematical economics models, is not valid in constructive analysis.

31 This is due to Michael Rabin (see, Rabin, 1957).

32 See Mas-Colell, Whinston and Green (1995: 6).

33 Velupillai (2000: 40–41) addresses this:

> It is quite possible that economic agents are able to rationalize their preferences using nonrecursive functions. Computable economics is, at least in part, about delineating the boundaries between the effective and noneffective process.

To what extent, then, can we firmly theorise about decision making if its procedural aspects are not accessible even to idealised forms of intuitive calculability (as captured by Church-Turing thesis)? Wittgenstein's closing remarks in the *Tractatus* may offer one answer: '*Whereof one cannot speak, thereof one must remain silent*'.

References

Alquié, F., *The Philosophy of Surrealism*, Ann Arbor: University of Michigan, 1965.

Arrow, K. J., A Difficulty in the Concept of Social Welfare. *Journal of Political Economy*, vol. 58, no.4, 1950, pp. 328–346.

Arrow, K. J., *Social Choice and Individual Values*, 1st edition, New York: Wiley, 1951

Black, M., *Models and Metaphors: Studies in Language and Philosophy*, Ithaca, NY: Cornell University Press, 1962.

Day, S., The Contradictory World of René Magritte. *Medium*, 2018. https://medium.com/@susanday_25940/the-contradictory-world-of-ren%C3%A9-magritte-49d542eefeb2

Debreu, G., Economic Theory in the Mathematical Mode. *The Scandinavian Journal of Economics*, vol. 86, no. 4, 1984, pp. 393–410.

Ferrero, G., Cotti, C., Rossi, M. and Tedeschi, C., Geometries of Imaginary Space: Architectural Developments of the Ideas of MC Escher and Buckminster Fuller. *Nexus Network Journal*, vol. 11, no. 2, 2009, pp. 305–316.

Foucault, M., *This Is Not a Pipe*, Los Angeles: University of California Press, 1983.

Gablik, S., *Magritte*, London: Thames and Hudson, 1970.

Horsten, L. and Welch, P., *Gödel's Disjunction: The Scope and Limits of Mathematical Knowledge*, Oxford: Oxford University Press, 2016.

Kao, Y. F., Ragupathy, V., Velupillai, K. V., and Zambelli, S., Noncomputability, Unpredictability, Undecidability, and Unsolvability in Economic and Finance Theories. *Complexity*, vol. 18, no. 1, 2012, pp. 51–55.

Kelly, J. S., *Arrow Impossibility Theorems*, New York: Academic Press, 1978.

Lawson, T., Mathematical Modelling in Economics: Seeking a Rationale. In Francesca Gagliardi and David Gindis, eds., *Institutions and Evolution of Capitalism – Essays in Honour of Geoffrey M. Hodgson*, Cheltenham: Edward Elgar Publishing, 2019.

Lützen, J., How Mathematical Impossibility Changed Welfare Economics: A History of Arrow's Impossibility Theorem. *Historia Mathematica*, vol. 46, 2019, pp. 56–87.

MacKenzie, D. A., Muniesa, F., and Siu, L., eds., *Do Economists Make Markets?: On the Performativity of Economics*, Princeton, NJ: Princeton University Press, 2007.

Magritte, R., *René Magritte: Selected Writings*. Minneapolis: University of Minnesota Press, 2016.

Martin-Löf, P., Constructive Mathematics and Computer Programming. In: L. Jonathan Cohen, Jerzy Łoś, Helmut Pfeiffer, and Klaus-Peter Podewski, eds., *Studies in Logic and the Foundations of Mathematics*, vol. 104, pp. 153–175, Amsterdam: Elsevier, 1982.

Mas-Colell, A., Whinston, M. D. and Green, J. R., *Microeconomic Theory*, Oxford: Oxford University Press, 1995.

Maskin, E., and Sen, A. *The Arrow Impossibility Theorem*, New York: Columbia University Press, 2014.

Mathias, A. R. D., The Ignorance of Bourbaki. *The Mathematical Intelligencer*, vol. 14, 1992, pp. 4–13.

Morgan, M. S., Models. In: Steven N. Durlauf and Lawrence E. Blume, eds., *The New Palgrave Dictionary of Economics*, 2nd edition, 2008 (online version).

Morgan, M. S., *The World in the Model,* Cambridge: Cambridge University Press, 2012.

Rabin, M. O., Effective Computability of Winning Strategies. In: *Contributions to the Theory of Games III (Annals of Mathematics Studies, No. 39),* pp. 147–157, Princeton, NJ: Princeton University Press, 1957.

Rimmon-Kenan, S., Ambiguity and Narrative Levels: Christine Brooke-Rose's Thru. *Poetics Today*, vol. 3, no. 1, 1982, pp. 21–32.

Schattschneider, D., The Mathematical Side of MC Escher. *Notices of the AMS*, vol. 57, no. 6, 2010, pp. 706–718.

Sraffa, P., *Production of Commodities by Means of Commodities*, Cambridge: Cambridge University Press, 1960.

Sugden, R., Credible Worlds: The Status of Theoretical Models in Economics. *Journal of Economic Methodology*, vol. 7, no. 1, 2000, pp. 1–31.

Velupillai, K., *Computable Economics – The Arne Ryde Memorial Lectures*, Oxford: Oxford University Press, 2000.

Velupillai, K. V., Sraffa's Mathematical Economics: A Constructive Interpretation. *Journal of Economic Methodology*, vol. 15, no. 4, 2008, pp. 325–342

Velupillai, K. V., Uncomputability and Undecidability in Economic Theory. *Applied Mathematics and Computation,* vol. 215, no. 4, 2009, pp. 1404–1416.

Velupillai, K. V., *Computable Foundations for Economics*, Abingdon: Routledge, 2010.

Velupillai, K. V., Bourbaki's Destructive Influence on the Mathematisation of Economics. *Economic and Political Weekly*, vol. 47, no. 3, 2012, pp. 63–68.

Velupillai, K. V., Perspectives on the Contributions of Richard Goodwin. *Cambridge Journal of Economics*, vol. 39, no. 6, 2015, pp. 1485–1496.

Velupillai, K. V., Kenneth Joseph Arrow. 23 August 1921–21 February 2017. *Biographical Memoirs of the Fellows of the Royal Society*, vol. 67, 2019, pp. 9–28.

Venkatachalam, R. and Zambelli, S., Money and Distribution, Ch. 15. In: Ajit Sinha, ed. *A Reflection on Sraffa's Revolution in Economic Theory*. London: Palgrave Macmillan, 2021. ISBN 9783030472054.

Venkatachalam, R. and Zambelli, S., Self-Replacing Prices with Credit And Debt. *ASSRU Discussion Papers*, No. 2021–3, 2021.

von Neumann, J. and Morgenstern, O., *The Theory of Games and Economic Behavior*, Princeton: Princeton University Press, 1947[1944].

Zambelli, S., Production of Commodities by Means of Commodities and Non-Uniform Rates of Profits. *Metroeconomica*, vol. 69, no. 4, 2018, pp. 791–818.

6 Fragments, *spolia* and economic texts

Constantinos Repapis

Introduction[1]

One of the important questions that has been at the centre of economic thinking at least since the work of Adam Smith is the development of systems of analysis that are able to give a rational, coherent and definitive picture of the social and economic world. The importance of this enlightenment programmatic vision in the development of the discipline of economics cannot be understated – it is behind the formation of the classical, neoclassical and Marxist conceptions of the economy that are the basis of most of the theoretical output in economics that spans the last 200 years. In these traditions, the link between economic theorists and idealist philosophers has been explored extensively in the literature. There is a substantial corpus of work that shows the influence of enlightenment philosophers on the physiocrats, or Hegel's influence and importance on Marx's thought to name two obvious examples.

Nevertheless, this broad philosophical tradition of system builders who organise and make explicit the links that hold together the fabric of reality in a structurally coherent and defined, in its totality, system of analysis is one way to theorise and attempt to come up with a refined understanding of social reality. In contradistinction to this approach, the romantic writers and theorists point to another way – a way that focuses on capturing the complexity of society through the impression of its different facets by using tools that are more open ended in their approach and suggestive rather than definitive in their findings. As Elizabeth Millan-Zaibert notes, this should not be seen as a primitive and unsuccessful effort to build a system, but as a radically different way to do analysis and provide insight. She writes:

> One important reason why the early German Romantics have gone unnoticed by most philosophers is that their work is read as part of the tradition of classical German Idealism, and in the company of grand system builders such as Fichte, Schelling and Hegel, their work which was not designed to result in grand theories at all, is often dismissed as incomplete and unimportant, as nothing more than a collection of

DOI: 10.4324/9781003105435-9

> dilettantish efforts … to deal with philosophical problems that were much more 'professionally' addressed by their contemporaries, Fichte, Schelling and Hegel.
>
> (Millan-Zaibert 2007: 44).

Instead, however, of trying to assign to the Romantics practices, modes of expression and ends that are not their own, it is important to attempt to explore their own programmatic vision and armoury of tools. They focus on a complex layering of meaning that allows many interpretations of a literary passage, without settling necessarily on only one, through mediums of expression that include the use of irony and even incompleteness in the form of the fragment. In this sense, we can argue that:

> The themes of incompleteness and incomprehension we find in their work are reflected in the literary forms they used to present it; the use of the fragment, for example, was not a result of a lack of resolution, a blameworthy incompleteness, in the sense of something that was meant to be finished and never was. Early German Romantic philosophy is incomplete not because the Romantics failed to finish their work but rather because they were convinced that a complete system could not be built.
>
> (Millan-Zaibert 2007: 46).

This lack of commitment to a system view should not be seen as an inability to theorise, but rather as an effort to not be tied to one way of seeing things. Schlegel admits "It is equally fatal for the spirit to have a system and to have none. It will simply have to decide to combine the two" (Millan-Ziabert 2007: 47). The fragment allows at one end an openness that could lead to new understandings, and at the other touches the negation of all knowledge, a nihilism that nothing can be truly known. But against this nihilism what we have is the plurality of possible understandings. The abandonment of a monolithic view of the nature of human society is not equivalent to the abandonment of all knowledge. In fact, properly operationalised, it allows the development of a plurality of perspectives that would address different aspects of social reality and offer innovative solutions to problems old and new.

Therefore, what this chapter will explore is how we can bring together these different visions in a new and coherent space and at the same time explore the poetics of this new kind of theorising and also the new kind of "organised thinking" this open-ended approach can give rise to. For this end, I will attempt to make a connection across three disparate literatures, which are literary and architectural theory and economic texts. The chapter has the following structure: The next section argues that Schlegel had a consistent and modern view on the importance of the fragment in understanding contemporary reality. This view of the fragment as a stand-alone element of reality defines the romantic perspective and imbues the objects or text it glorifies with a meaning that is suggestive rather than definite. The section *from fragments to spolia* will link the concept of the romantic fragment to that of the *spolium*, as used in architectural theory and practice, and see how physical objects such as buildings can come together by an assemblage of pre-existing fragments. The next section will present a tangible form of this concept of *spolium*-assemblage, the Arch of Constantine, built during (or before?) the 4th century AD, and will discuss both the use of *spolia* as fragments that display their association with their past, and as promises that these will become a basis for some new symbolism pregnant with an imagined future. We then consider how the example of the arch and its use of *spolia* to convey a complex and layered message to a disparate audience can be used as a way to approach theoretical texts in economics and especially Keynes' *General Theory (GT)*. The argument is that a text, like an architectural object, rests on *spolia* of meaning that connects it with its intended audience. By not hiding the nature of its message and its disjoined or open-ended threads of argument and reflection, the GT steeps the reader in the context that they bring with them, and they take as given, in order to construct an understanding of the text which is both deeply personal and through shared context, universal as each reader discovers their own meanings and associations. This process refocuses the attention from the fragmentary text and its incomplete message back to the reader and the interpretive tools they bring with them and develop in order to decode the text. It allows the reader to imagine new spaces of meaning and build radically new future understandings.

Schlegel on fragments: Completeness was a mirage of the past

The idea that the fragment is not an object that needs to be completed in a particular way to take a tangible and definite (and therefore understandable) form is historically linked with the Romantic Movement.[2] In a way, the romantic reconceptualisation of the fragment moves us beyond the dichotomy of either something being complete, understandable and rational, and as such within the realm of comprehension and knowledge, or being incomplete, disjoined and irrational, holding little meaning other than a glimpse of loss, chaos and incomprehension. This dichotomy implicit in the enlightenment viewpoint with its pursuit of certain truths, is either abolished or reinterpreted in new ways. It reorients our pursuit of knowledge from that of an objective and complete picture to the possible different expressions that a fragment can take and the further ideas, concepts or understandings it can give rise to.

In this transformation, Schlegel's work adds an interesting perspective. Schlegel theorised that modernity is defined of fragments. The ancient past left behind only its fragments – and therefore we look at the past only though the fragments that have survived, and we need to imagine what the whole was like. A whole that is constantly reshaped as our imagination forms new understandings and takes in new perspectives. If we admit this central aspect of the past, as a world lost, at the beginning of a linear conception of time that moves forward (rather than seeing reality in cyclical time, when history, human society, even artistic effort repeats itself, much as the seasons do), then we can adapt the definition of fragments in the following interesting way. If we start building something today, it is only a fragment of a future yet to be realised, and a future that is to some degree unknown. This is true not only when we are constructing a tangible object (e.g., a building) but also when we are developing a theoretical corpus, whose complete argument and the ramifications of the argument and the ideas it will give rise to are yet to be determined.

Therefore, fragments as an approach to reality become the basic hermeneutic tool of our epoch – they define our viewpoint of the past and of the future. The present is seen both through the traces the past has left behind, and as the start of new beginnings, whose shape is yet to be determined. As Schlegel writes "Many of the works of the ancients have become fragments. Many modern works are fragments as soon as they are written" (*Athenaeum* Fragment n. 24 in Schlegel 2002b: 246).[3]

The importance of this realisation is that the attempt to have a complete objective meaning of an artefact or a text (a poem, a piece of literature – even a theoretical work) remains outside the realm of the possible and, at its core, is not a valid pursuit. Even when we think that this has been achieved, it is clearly the outcome of defining the scope of our viewpoint upon reality narrowly enough to see a fragment as a complete understanding. As Tanehisa notes "Schlegel posits, works that appear to possess unity at a glance in fact do so only superficially and, in the negative sense, fail to be more than a mere fragment" (Tanehisa 2009: 60). Interestingly, in 1797, Schlegel writes his essay *On Lessing,* the following

> The most interesting and the most penetrating in Lessing's works is intimation and suggestion [Winke und Andeutungen]; that which is the ripest and the most complete in his works are fragments of fragments… His accurate reasoning is generally little more than a string of witty ideas.
>
> (Tanehisa 2009: 61).[4]

Thus, the fragment is complete simply because it functions as a vehicle for new ideas, for the space it gives to the reader/viewer/interpreter to imbue it with meaning and develop new avenues of thought. In short, it captures the dynamism of our epoch, its march towards a future whose contours are constantly re-drawn and re-imagined, at every point in time. This brings forth a new type of object or text, one that does not purport to be complete or unidimensional in what it attempts to convey but acts more as a support in the journey an individual takes as they construct meaning of the natural and social world around them.

From fragments to *Spolia*: Re-possession as a way to shock and involve the reader/viewer in narrative creation

The romantic fragment, as conceived, is a concept that tries to allow the opening up of space through its dissociation from its surrounding text and its attached context.[5] Schlegel writes "A fragment, like a miniature work of art, has to be entirely isolated from the surrounding world and be complete in itself like a porcupine" (*Athenaeum* Fragments, no. 206 in Schlegel 2002b: 251). And yet, while, in theory, this allows the maximum freedom for the reader to build their own understanding and unleash their imagination, this is exactly what a fragment can never do. By broadcasting its incompleteness, the knowledge that it is a broken part of a whole which we do not know the full contours of, it invites the reader/viewer to add from what they know and lean on associations they have from other texts or readings to complete its message. In an odd twist, the suspended empty space that Schlegel exults as enveloping a fragment is no-where to be found. Even though the fragment appears liberated on the page from elucidations that an author would feel obliged to do, it becomes embroidered in context the moment it meets the eye of the reader.

At a more basic level, every fragment is either by construction or through the act of interpretation by the reader a *spolium* – an attempt of appropriation and internalisation of the phrases of someone else, who either left it by intention incomplete (as the Romantic authors did) or became incomplete and reinterpreted in the act of reading.[6] Thus, the Romantic poet imbues the fragment with many and at times contradictory meanings which come from external associations, from the surrounding world that they have torn it away from, but of which the fragment remains a vessel and a memory. These associations may be constructions of the individual reader, and yet, the power of the fragment to hold some distinctive element, and therefore a memory of a broader – rather than entirely personal – meaning, cannot be denied.

Here, architectural theory can give us not only a new viewpoint on exploring this aspect of a fragment's message but also an armoury of definitions and concepts to deal with its many facets. Architectural historians and archaeologists have extensively worked on the concept of *spolia*.[7] *Spolia* comes from the Latin "spoils of war",[8] and is an architectural term used for stones repossessed from one building or ruin and embedded into another. In its use in architectural theory, the focus is not on the non-descript repossessed stone but on the stone that displays the fact that it comes from another building or structure.[9] In short, it displays, or does not hide, that it is a fragment of another whole, violently removed.[10] That whole may have become a ruin, or was a building that was taken down and dismembered with its material becoming structural and ornamental blocks for other projects.

The story of *spolia* is as long and varied as human history itself. It stretches to the very beginning of human building work. In times that pre-date the industrial revolution the repossession and re-use of blocks performed not only an aesthetic but fundamentally a practical function as disused or dilapidated buildings were used as quarries for new ones. The consistency of building techniques and material used across time made this exercise an obvious labour-saving activity when building something new, instead of quarrying for new stone or creating new building material, both of which usually entailed substantially more labour cost.[11]

That this activity of re-purpose and re-use would be more prevalent in time of economic hardship or in periods of depopulation and decline when the cost of entirely new material to build or repair something would be seen as prohibitive is obvious but should not simply be assumed. It would tend to separate economic realities from other social processes happening at the time. In fact, in most cases, this re-use and re-possession appears not only to be fulfilling immediate practical needs, nor should it be interpreted as simply an indication of economic decline. *Spolia* carry with them part of their past, their own aesthetic and other signifiers and point into meaning and association that these repositions do not obliterate, and at times are meant to celebrate or use for new purposes. *Spolia* become part of the language of the new object by extending it, and an element of its identity and meaning. This meaning does not admit a single interpretation exactly because it is composed of allusions to many different buildings, ages, people and aesthetic and other languages. However, exactly because *spolia* could be used for many reasons and purposes, the concept can be used to denote very different activities and, has been used in this way among architectural historians working in this field. For the purposes of this chapter, we will concentrate on one specific and celebrated example, the *locus classicus* of *spolia* literature, the Arch of Constantine in Rome.[12] The point is to see how a celebrated building and one of the best-preserved ancient buildings in Rome stood the test of time, being itself a *spolium*, a great survivor whose message changed over time to fit the times. More generally, however, we will attempt through it to gain a broad understanding of the complex layering of meaning that *spolia* can imbue a building or architectural object with.

The Arch of Constantine: *Spolia* and the veil of seeing a complex object

There is arguably no other architectural object that has occupied the field of *spolia* studies more than the Arch of Constantine in Rome. The Arch of Constantine is a (probably) 4th century AD building dedicated during the early years of Constantine the Great's reign, on the ancient *Via triumphalis* of Rome very close to the Colosseum. It was part of the programme by the new emperor to beautify the city and establish his new authority over Maxentius, the discredited predecessor, and the tetrarchy system that Constantine inherited and effectively abolished.

Temporally, the arch stands at the end of the ancient world and its transition to the medieval period. Constantine was the first emperor to convert to Christianity and the emperor who moved the capital from Rome to

Constantinople. The arch is one of the last triumphal arches build in Rome (and in this case, contrary to custom, build for a triumph over a Roman rival Maxentius, instead of an external enemy which was the ancient norm for building arches) and, also the first that uses so extensively parts of existing buildings both for its construction and its decoration. This extensive use of *spolia* is an emblematic feature of the arch which has attracted attention since its creation. Archaeological analysis has shown that Constantine's arch has repossessed *spolia* and other decorative elements from a number of monuments of previous eras, and especially from the building projects of the "good emperors" of the past, particularly, Hadrian, Trajan and Marcus Aurelius.[13] This creates a complex visual language that according to some modern scholars associates Constantine with the exploits and successes of these emperors, and the stability and wealth that the Roman Empire had then. In this visual language, Constantine adds his own stamp both by re-curving his face on the decorative *spolia* of the previous eras (defacing the "good emperors" by altering their image to his own)[14] and by inserting a frieze composed after 303 CE and using the artistic style of the period, instead of the classical style of the age of the "good emperors".[15]

All this high relief creates a complex and varied visual language that the viewer is confronted with. This has presented new challenges in the understanding of the arch and its multi-faceted message. Archaeologists as well as art historians have debated two interlinked questions: (1) What did the contemporary viewer make of the arch and its complex visual language and symbolism? (2) How have viewers since then viewed the arch, and decoded its meaning?

There is no agreed answer to either of these questions, but an indication of the answers could move us some way towards understanding the type of interpretative lines that this object has given rise to. On the first question, i.e. the message received by contemporary viewers, archaeologists and historians have argued different lines. La Rocca and Zanker (2007) seem to suggest that the arch's message was aimed at an "uncultured" audience and its mismatch of styles and whatever subtle message that implied, was secondary to the overall overbearing impression of wealth and power all these sculptural elements created. They further note that contemporary viewers would be unaware of the complex allusions the arch implicitly builds. In this line of argument, Liverani notes that the monument was directed towards "*un pubblico assai più vasto e popolare*" (Liverani 2004: 401) and Curran writes that "it is even more difficult to believe that the two most important viewers of the monument, Constantine and the Roman populace, would have understood the significance of such a subtle composition" (Curran 2000: 87).

This line negates the complex language that *spolia* built as assemblage art. That is the visual outcome of the contrasting styles of the decorative elements drawn from different eras and using a mismatch of symbolic languages. The argument effectively sees even the decorative elements as building material in the crudest form – they add ornamental detail that lacks any deep association or meaning, other than "looking imposing" in the most obvious sense. The interpretative line that sees this composition of *spolia* as an assemblage of imposing carvings only is equivalent to saying that there was a complete break with the past (e.g., Rome lost a war, its citizens all killed and a foreign power taking over the city and its monuments) and a new ruler took what they liked and built a new arch for themselves – completely oblivious of any meaning other than its striking beauty.

The alternative line has been argued by Sande (2012) who notes that "The Arch of Constantine must have given different messages to different spectators according to their status and education" (Sande 2012: 287). Sande notes that the dismissal of the education of the viewer of this era is linked with the overall belief in "late antique art being somewhat inferior" (Sande 2012: 287). Thus, this interpretative line indicates that the multi-faceted arts of Constantine's era, which had moved away from the realistic representations of the classical period and into a new symbolic language in the representation of the body, the composition of the crowd and its appearance, are indications of decline, not only of art but also of artistic understanding.

In a way, this negates what we think Constantine and the senate tried to achieve with this arch – i.e., instead of seeing it as a symbol of the return to the "good times" of the reigns of the emperors whose *spolia* Constantine appropriates, *spolia* become the symbol of how far the Roman empire had declined. The decline is so serious that the only worthy art is *spolia* from the past, which share space with inferior contemporary art of late Diocletian's and Constantine's period. This way of seeing the Arch forms an important and even constitutive narrative of how we think of the history of western art since the Renaissance.

It is not coincidental that one of the first recorded viewers of the arch after the Middle Ages is the painter, Raphael. Raphael writes a famous report for Pope Leo X in about 1519, where he notes the following:

> Although literature, sculpture, painting, and almost all the other arts had long been declining and had grown worse and worse until the time of the last emperors, yet architecture was still studied and practiced according to the good rules and buildings were erected in the same style as before .... Of this there are many evidences: among others, the Arch of Constantine, which is well designed and well-built as far as architecture is concerned. But the sculptures of the same arch are very feeble and destitute of all art and good design. Those, however, that come from the spoils of Trajan and Antoninus Pius are extremely fine and done in perfect style.
>
> (Translated in Elsner 2000: 149)

This interpretative line of seeing the arch remains a powerful one. A modern re-statement by Berenson (1954) is somewhat more refined in that it explicitly claims that his interest on the arch is to examine the decorative elements "and while doing so, we shall ignore history, whether spiritual or material, social or political" (Berenson 1954: 2). He builds a framework of interpreting art on how realistic representations are and argues that "they must allow me, however, to insist that in my point of view decline is decline and not simplification, symbolization, sublimation or any other –ation…" (Berenson 1954: 3). From this perspective, the use of *spolia* may be due to a "hurry to get things ready in time" but he adds there is

> a feeling that nothing could be done then and there as worthy of the occasion. Explain it as you will, it was a confession of inferiority to the past, whether economic or artistic, as happened long before when Ramses II had statues of earlier Pharaohs rededicated to himself.
>
> (Berenson 1954: 14).

It is easy to trivialise such assessments from a modern theory of art perspective. However, this viewpoint has some currency across lay viewers throughout history and until today, because of the transformation of western art that has been the bedrock of our visual language since the Renaissance. Significantly, one real problem of this perspective is that it imposes a particular conformist line of viewing the object, suppressing what could be seen as its complex and multi-level message that could open a new understanding both of the times the object was created in and, by reflection, of our own.

Another way to interpret the object's complex visual symbolism is to wonder why it was built in this way. Our interest lies in the opposite direction to Berenson's, its artistic message is of importance to us exactly because it is situated in a particular historical and social context and not as an exercise to describe artistic forms from today's vantage point. From there, we can deduce not only that the arch appealed to different viewers who had necessarily a different level of education as Sande (2012) argues, but that at a more fundamental level, we see a fragmentation of the very artistic language that had defined the ancient Roman world since its early antiquity and association with classical Greece. The beginning of Christianity as a more established religion brought with it (and/or coincided with) deep changes in art, this kind of (what was in more ways than one) underground art brought with it a language that cannot be seen as a simplification of classical art in cheaper mantle, lacking details and refinement, but essentially part of the same visual universe. It is distinct enough to be viewed as new and here to cater to other needs and impulses.[16] Thus, you have, for example, the highly dynamic and animated scene of the *spolia* in the central passage of the Arch, which depict Trajan's battle with the Dacians, in contrast with the stocky, static and substantially less subtle and more class conscious in a forward-looking medieval sense, soldiers of the later frieze.[17] Constantine himself is depicted in different ways, as if he himself occupies different spheres of existence, power and even social and spiritual positions. For example, his head was recurved on the *spolia* of the good emperors in the antique manner – dispossessing them of their bodies and also of the visual language of the tableau and the classical grandeur that surrounds a Roman Emperor, the first citizen and soldier of the state. In contrast, on the later frieze, he hands alms (or gifts) to his people seated on a throne that resembles medieval kings without any of the subtle signals of the emperor being "the first of Roman citizens".[18] Even in military depictions, we can see significant differences between the compositions. For example, compare the highly animated battle scene of Trajan's tableau, where the emperor is in the thick of the battle, triumphant over the enemy combatants, heroically depicted but still as another combatant, with the new frieze with him seated on a chariot in procession at the back of the army entering Rome, with ranks mirroring the social strata of society.

All these mixed messages are there because this subtle composition may serve a complex purpose. This is alluding to the past and drawing from it authority, power and reassurance that the period of internal strife is over, and at the same time hinting that things have changed. One possible interpretation is that the arch does not hide that it is heralding a new order, and this new order is here to stay and will bring with it stability and prosperity that can match the past. This complex message cannot easily be communicated through one visual language and one set of symbols. It needs the parallel languages that are part of the very fragmentation of the ancient world in this period in time to deliver its message. Its intention is also to appeal to different parts of the population through its complex symbolism. To the new Christian underclass, possibly the lower strata of population, the new emperor may, through the frieze, speak in a language they would be familiar with and recognise.[19] The alms are to the many, the many can look to the one for their protection and guidance. The parallel to the Christian symbolism of one saviour/one king is an iconography that will define much of the Middle Ages and may be in its first steps here. The "new" symbolic art that adorns the catacombs, modest altars and funerary monuments of the first Christians has now a place in the most formal of buildings, the triumphal arch of the emperor.[20] And to the Roman educated elite, the monument speaks a different message – a message of a Roman Emperor who respects tradition, assimilates it, is a noble and will treat nobles by their rights. He is here to unite under him the people, plebeian and patrician against a common enemy, foreign invaders and their internal supporters. This reading of the monument means that the emperor and the senate knew very well what they were trying to do, heal the divide that was rupturing the ancient world and try to give different messages to different parts of society, all through one medium, the arch. The assemblage of *spolia* and new sculpture was not haphazard, it was the only way at that point in time and in that society to display this complex multi-layered message. In this way, we can also understand the arch's somewhat peculiar inscription which reads:

> To the emperor Flavius Constantine, the Great, pious and fortunate, the Senate and People of Rome, because by divine inspiration and his own

> great spirit with his army on both the tyrant and all his faction at once in rightful battle he avenged the State, dedicated this arch as a mark of triumph.
>
> (Translated by Claridge 1998: 272)

The much-analysed phrase "by divine inspiration" (*INSTINCTV DIVINITATIS*) is nebulous enough to please all viewers – both pagan and Christian who would be looking for some clear allusion to the new faith, without offending either or explicitly taking sides.[21] This text displays the very same characteristics that are observed in the pictorial composition of the arch- tradition and innovation, stock phrases and expressions[22] with new, open-ended meanings and messages. Maybe by managing to have different viewers see the message they were looking for and by making the arch speak to them, Constantine achieved his purpose of uniting a fragmented people. The inscription, like the whole arch itself and its complex pictural imagery, "reveals a deliberate ambiguity designed to achieve reconciliation and tolerance" (Pierce 1989: 407).

From this standpoint, a re-appreciation of the arch can convey to the modern viewer similar messages of permanence and transience, multiple meanings without necessarily security in finding a final key that will unlock all questions relating to the monument. The interplay of different visual impulses is the challenge we face to understand them, theorise and see their association. Its message, made of fragments, *spolia* that archaeology and other interpretative fields (art history, etc.) uncover, is constantly changing, reflecting sensibilities of the present. The fact that the monument has managed to survive since antiquity and has captured the interest of the successive generations of art lovers, even when the appreciation of the monument itself, its sculptural universe and its meaning remain contested and constantly changing, speaks to the success of this composition. The debates on some of the key questions about this monument: What was the intended message? What did viewers see? What does it tell us about the society of the 4th century AD? may never be conclusively resolved, but they are not debates looking for such resolution and definitive answers. Through the questions this object poses, new spaces of meaning and understanding emerge, and this is part of the legacy and enduring message of the arch of Constantine.

The General Theory: Reading a text that displays its "spolia" and argues with its readers

Spolia, in the direct way discussed above, can be defined as *spolia in se*, i.e., the real thing, pieces removed and placed in a different building than the one they were originally a part of. Brilliant (1982) used this term to distinguish this kind of *spolia* from *spolia in re*, which are "monuments or works of art purporting to belong to an earlier period by using typology, proportions or styles of the past" (Sande 2012: 287). It is interesting that Constantine's arch displays both types of *spolia*. As we saw in the quote by Raphael, he praises the proportions of the arch and its overall construction, as it clearly follows the architectural example of the previous eras, and is thus an example of *spolia in re*,[23] while at the same time, some of its ornaments are *spolia in se*. This creates a complex set of allusions that blurs the lines of what is new and what is old, what is true and what is make believe.

Furthermore, this distinction is very useful if we move the object of enquiry from the question of buildings to that of texts and use the terminology of *spolia* there. Liverani (2011) attempts such transference by keeping *spolia in se* in its traditional definition by Brilliant but stretches the application of *spolia in re* to "the domain of metaphor" and iconic operation (Liverani 2011: 47). With this, Liverani places direct citations, allusion, copying of sentences, etc. in the domain of *spolia in re* – arguing that all this activity of textual reproduction and allusion is distinct to the original concept of appropriation by destruction of the previous edifice or object.

However, this taxonomy by Liverani is not granular enough to allow us to operationalise the *spolia* concept in interesting ways when doing literary analysis. As Liverani argues, simply saying that quotations in a text are *spolia*, and by extension that a text with quotations is an act of assemblage, does not take us very far. But if we attempt to refine our vocabulary, this perspective can help us arrive at more interesting insights. Another way to look at it is to build on this distinction between *spolia in re* and *spolia in se* as different types of *spolia* in a written text. We can therefore separate between a direct quotation or reference, the insertion of another text into the host text or an explicit appeal to some external text or author by mimicking the other text's characteristics. This could mean mimic the language, structure, type of argument, that makes the text strongly allude to a specific literature or other text and almost, even, trying to pass as a piece of it. This can be even more pronounced if the allusion is to texts of a previous era or of a particular community, and the host text tries to borrow from those texts not only their style and overall structure of argument but also "social" elements (the culture, internal relations and modes of thought and articulation, etc.), which it uses for its own purpose. In this case, *spolia in se* are the quotes and direct references, with the usual explicit paraphernalia of attribution being precise in convention and clear and fairly unambiguous notes to readers, and *spolia in re* become more elusive parts of the written text that allude to specific literature but are linked with it through intimation and suggestion, to use the terms of the Romantics. These two elements together, the explicit and the suggestive, constitute the rich textual bedrock on which readers build associations of the meaning of texts.

How can this analysis help us get an entry point into a text on economic theory? This is a difficult question that relates to the use of hermeneutics in understanding a text and decoding its meanings. The purpose of this section is to see if the insights of the concepts of fragments and *spolia* developed in the previous sections can shed new light on our understanding of a particular text in economic theory, Keynes' *General Theory*.

I have argued elsewhere (Repapis 2020) that Keynes' *General Theory* is more an exploration of the methodology an economist uses to solve or tackle problems in the real world than an attempt to create a set system of analysis, a treatise that completely defines and builds an exhaustive scheme at the level of theory which intends to be definitive. It is not devoid of theory, in fact, the book has little else; but what has puzzled readers since its publication in 1936 is how the different theory sections fit together and what is the overall structure of the argument.

Much work has gone into ascertaining how the relevant chapters fit together into one coherent whole and whether each chapter or some parts should be seen separately.[24] This has made the book not only difficult to comprehend for readers who are looking for a treatise in the tradition of classical and neoclassical economics but has also been the charge against it as an incomplete or contradictory, even ill-developed, piece of theoretical work, and therefore inferior to the classical treatises in economics by Adam Smith and David Ricardo, that it attempts, purportedly, to emulate. The holy grail of reading it in this way is to find the one key that would make all sections fall into place and give the work the singular unity on the plane of theory a classic treatise in economics and political economy is expected to display.

However, if we attempt to see this kind of reading that well-intending readers have attempted since the *GT's* publication in relation to the arch of Constantine, we can see that it may be a futile project. In both cases, the attempt to find a single key that encapsulates the complete and final message of both text and object runs quickly aground as all unidimensional narratives fail to account for some element of the composition. As noted in the previous section, there is reason to believe that the arch of Constantine is nebulous in its message exactly because its pictorial and other elements were intended to be read in different ways by different viewers and not appeal to the same sensibilities in all viewers.

In the case of the *General Theory*, this characteristic comes through by a variety of means. It comes through by the use of different modes of expression, where the language shifts from axiomatic assertions and analytical prose, occasionally fused by mathematical argument, to broad discussions in a conversational manner, historical examples and generalisations, and even the use of asides, vignettes, irony and self-negation.[25] Thus, one finds the following passage:

> VI. With the aid of the notation introduced in chapter 20, we can, if we wish, express the substance of the above in symbolic form.
>
> Let us write MV=D where M is the quantity of money, V is its income-velocity (this definition differing in the minor respects indicated above from the usual definition) and D the effective demand…
>
> (Keynes 1936: 304)

And a few pages before, the book directly refers to this passage with the following words:

> The object of our analysis is, not to provide a machine, or method of blind manipulation, which will furnish an infallible answer, but to provide ourselves with an organised and orderly method of thinking of particular problems; and, after we have reached a provisional conclusion by isolating the complicating factors one by one, we then have to go back to ourselves and allow, as well as we can, for the probable interactions of the factors amongst themselves. This is the nature of economic thinking. Any other way of applying our formal principles of thought (without which, however, we shall be lost in the wood) will lead us into error. It is a great fault of symbolic pseudo-mathematical methods of formalising a system of economic analysis, such as we shall set down in section VI of this chapter, that they expressly assume strict independence between the factors involved and lose all their cogency and authority if this hypothesis is disallowed; whereas, in ordinary discourse, where we are not blindly manipulating but know all the time what we are doing and what the words mean, we can keep 'at the back of our heads' the necessary reserves and qualifications....
>
> (Keynes 1936: 297)

Thus, the book has both formal mathematical language, which is a needed vestment for transmitting its ideas to a professional class of economists but at the same time cautions the reader, in the strongest possible terms, about accepting these very constructs, and asks them to think outside these terms, which are not really vital to the argument. Keynes does not only play between verbal narrative and mathematical symbolic formal language but also discusses what kind of narrative would suit different types of questions. For example, he writes:

> So far we have been primarily concerned with the way in which changes in the quantity of money affect prices in the short period. But in the long run is there not some simpler relationship?
>
> This is a question for historical generalisation rather than for pure theory.
>
> (Keynes 1936: 306)

The text shifts between different types of narrative that it appropriates for its different and sometimes conflicting insights. These can be seen as attempts of *spolia in re*. The form of expression is used so that the reader, by association, admits this text within the company of texts that it emulates and indirectly borrows legitimacy from. For example, the reader is expected to understand the rules of mathematical modelling, verbal theorising and historical digression and admit these as accepted forms of argument and information transmission. Each has its remit and specific purpose, both as an act of rhetoric, to convince the reader, and as a vessel of information that carries a message. The final text is an act of assemblage of these different narratives exactly because it does not try to paper over the differences when presenting them to the reader, or even to hide that its use of these alternative forms of expression is partly a rhetorical device, and the reader may not have to take part of the text too seriously. The text warns and even argues with the reader on the very theory the text is trying to transmit. Therefore, the final work is by construction formed by parts, whose fit is far from perfect, and that, itself, is part of the message.

The effort of the text to display scepticism about the very forms through which it tries to relay its message is part of a deeper agenda on how Keynes sets and orients his book. The very first chapter of the GT starts with a broad claim on the nature of this theoretical exercise:

> I shall argue that the postulates of the classical theory are applicable to a special case only and not to the general case, the situation which it assumes being a limiting point of the possible positions of equilibrium. Moreover, the characteristics of the special case assumed by the classical theory happen not to be those of the economic society in which we actually live, with the result that its teaching is misleading and disastrous if we attempt to apply it to the facts of experience.
>
> (Keynes 1936: 3)

From its title and first pages, the book makes the claim that it intends to provide a more general theory of the economy to what existed before, which it intends to assimilate as a special case. In the first footnote, it mentions by name the theorists that form this classical corpus of economic theory, and Keynes writes the following:

> The classical economists was a name invented by Marx to cover Ricardo and James Mill and their *predecessors*, that is to say for the founders of the theory which culminated in the Ricardian economics. I have become accustomed, perhaps perpetrating a solecism, to include in the classical school the *followers* of Ricardo, those, that is to say, who adopted and perfected the theory of Ricardian economics, including (for example) J.S. Mill, Marshall, Edgeworth and Prof. Pigou.
>
> (Keynes 1936: 3)

Keynes in this footnote achieves a double purpose. First, he puts himself on par with Marx, saying outright that he can recompose past economics and their theoretical output into a new grouping that does not respect existing lines of demarcation. The act of delineating schools of economic thought is not any more an objective exercise but one of personal choice. An act of solecism that a writer can enforce, and Keynes, without apology does, to reveal new insights. Second, by this re-ordering, Classical and Neoclassical theory become fused in one canon, with writers that stretch from Ricardo to Pigou. This act has shocked and bewildered even some prominent Keynesians since publication, who have returned to the usual demarcations of Classical and Neoclassical schools trying to fit Keynes' theory sometimes in the first and sometimes in the second grouping, politely ignoring the parts of the text that do not go with the specific reading they are imposing on the book.

It is useful here to think again of the *spolia in se* category, which has the closest association with the violence of the act of despoiling an old building to beautify a new one. In its essence, the shock tactic employed by Keynes is not very different. He dissociates these prominent writers from their customary groupings and the normal way their theoretical output is viewed and forces them together to form this new theoretical pillar that his book stands in opposition to. He uses them in the same way that Constantine's Arch despoils Trajan's Arch, chisels his face on Trajan's body and puts the re-worked *spolium* in his arch to celebrate both him and Trajan. It is both an act of sacrilege and an act of homage.

However, it should be noted that Keynes does not do this re-ordering in order to impose a new dogmatic reading of all these writers and weave a definitive theoretical scheme of the economic system. Instead, he advocates an open-ended approach to the economy that asks the reader to train in several modes of thought and expression and use their judgement for the questions they need to tackle. This gives the book the particular position within the canon of classic texts in economics it inhabits today. At one end, it is obviously a treatise of economic theory that proposes a new catholic view of the social and economic order of society. At the other end, it is a very different book to the treatises of Adam Smith, or John Stuart Mill or David Ricardo, or Alfred Marshal. Here again, the parallel with Constantine's arch may be useful as an exploration on the peculiarity of Keynes' text. The arch is without question an ancient Roman triumphal arch, and yet there is a world of difference between that arch and those of the "good emperors" it tries to associate with and even in parts emulate. Equally, the *General Theory* is a grand work in economics, the same way the arch of Constantine is a Roman imperial arch. But its message is more layered, complex and demanding for the viewer than other works, and its form, although sharing many similarities of language, style and purpose with the classical treatises of economics, is, at the same time, a very different construction. The difficulty is not that it asks readers to get accustomed to a new symbolic language which they have not encountered before, as perhaps other theoretical works in mathematics or economics require. Its difficulty is that it references a whole ecosystem of literature which the reader must have encountered and assimilated prior to attempting the *General Theory*. It requires good knowledge of Classical and Neoclassical theory for the reader to be able to penetrate somewhat this book – in the same way that the viewer of the arch would understand more about it if they knew where the *spolia* that are so visible, came from.

The *General Theory* asks the reader not to a nuovo learn a new language, but the more difficult task of reflecting on the language the reader already speaks, see it anew, and question its limits. More importantly, because of this game of intimation and suggestion, rather than straightforward instruction and indoctrination to a new mode of thought and expression, both the arch and the *General Theory* appear inexhaustible and, although so context bound and therefore fragile because of their demand of knowledge of outside sources, great survivors. They are survivors exactly because each period and each reader/viewer is inspired to form their own readings and message of the text, with the objects offering their spoils to frame the spectator's imagination in a dynamic way with no expiry date. Constantine's arch has been discussed since the Renaissance both as an indication of the falling standards of the classical era and recently in more complex ways. But it has always been discussed without intermission. *The General Theory* has also had a varied reception since publication, and for reasons that mirror the discussion of Constantine's arch, it has divided its readership, but it has never ceased to excite interest and offer readers new insights.

Conclusion: Classical texts and modernity

This chapter tried to forge links between three different literatures, the literature on the romantic fragment, architectural investigations on *spolia* and economic theory. The broader unifying thread that connects these disparate literatures is, to some degree, the fact that they may be part of a different canon of philosophical thinking to the one that focuses on completeness, objectivity, systemic thinking and knowledge acquisition in a direct and unproblematised way. As Schlegel argues, "A classical text must never be entirely comprehensible. But those who are cultivated and who cultivate themselves must always want to learn more from it" (Critical Fragments no. 20 in Schlegel 2002a: 239). It is interesting to observe that both Schlegel and Keynes spoke of the importance of principles of thought, or formal theorising, and yet both found this to be not the end but the beginning of an exploration into the nature of reality. Formal systems are treated by these authors in the same way that the architectural principles of building a triumphal arch is a necessary prerequisite in order to understand Constantine's arch. But it is only a first step in a very long process of trying to decode the object.

The intellectual and aesthetic tradition of the romantics, and their method of thought and investigation, added new tools and perspectives on the canon of western thought. The singularity of modernity does away with the principle that general rules can be used to mimic and thus represent reality. Unidimensional representations do not seem to suffice anymore, because reality has become complex in ways that has no counterpoint in previous eras. This realisation both celebrates the artistic and literary heritage of the past and brakes resolutely with it in mode of thought and expression.

The importance of fragments at this juncture should not be understated. As articulations, they become an elemental building block of understanding.

In this way, we return to Schlegel's message that even complete systems of analysis are fragments of a greater whole, never realised, and whose shape constantly changes as the future unfolds. Keynes' book exemplifies this reasoning. By moving the message of *the General Theory* from the realm of theory to more explicitly that of methodology and ontology, Keynes is able to appropriate whole systems of theoretical analysis and their armoury as *spolia* that signify fragments of a complex social reality that can never settle into one definitive narrative. The book admits that it cannot provide us with a compact theoretical system that can act as the definitive theoretical apparatus in the field of economics but intends to make the reader start a personal journey of exploration and reflection that excites and develops the reader's imagination.[26] In this, it constantly argues with its readers and their preconceptions, undermining every effort to take a single message as the one key to the text. It acts as a reflective piece that intends to make the reader aware of the various languages that can be developed in economics and the limits these languages have. The nature of this approach allows the opening of new spaces of theory and theoretical experimentation that can be added to the *General Theory* as blank pages yet to be written, as *spolia* from the future the book enabled to come into existence and thus retrospectively appropriates as the text and its communicated message unfold through time.

Notes

1 I would like to thank Foteini Lika, Sheila Dow, Victoria Chick, Geoff Harcourt, Stratos Myrogiannis, Ragupathy Venkatachalam, Ivano Cardinale and especially Dale Kinney and the participants of the economics and plastic arts workshop for valuable feedback and suggestions. This work has improved substantially due to their kind remarks and thoughtful comments.

2 As D. Rauber notes in his seminal contribution "the fragment can be viewed as that form which more completely than any other embodies romantic ideals and aims" (Rauber 1969: 212).

3 Another translation by Otabe Tanehisa of the same fragment is "many works of the ancients have become fragments. Many works of the moderns are fragments at the time of their origin" (Tanehisa 2009: 59).

4 This re-asserts the key role that fragments play in creating an alternative interpretative tradition and also a counterpoint to the Enlightenment viewpoint. Janovich notes

> amongst the German writers associated with the Jena School and the journal *The Atheneum* (1798–1800), the fragment structure was held up by literary theorists as the model for a new kind of poetic originality freed from the constraints and forms of the classical genres.
>
> (Janowitz 2001: 479)

5 The Athenaeum Fragments, which first appeared in June 1798, where written as stand-alone aphorisms by different authors. This is one visual textual representation of the autonomy of each fragment as a separate self-supporting entity.

6 This is exactly what Schlegel does when he says that a text is effectively an agglomeration of fragments. He writes "A dialogue is a chain or garland of fragments. An exchange of letters is a dialogue on a large scale, and memoirs

constitute a system of fragments...." Atheneum fragments no. 77 (Schlegel 2002b: 248). Therefore, Schlegel interprets what he reads in a fragmentary way as a reading strategy. Fragment becomes the tool through which he approaches works of literature of any tradition that would be conceived, through conventional means, as complete- or at least as non-fragmentary.

7 See (Brilliant and Kinney 2011, Kinney 2019) as possible entry points to a huge literature.

8 Greenhalgh writes *spolia*

> in the strict classical sense refers to armour and weapons ..., which were taken from the defeated then preserved and displayed. The most prominent were the *spolia opima*, spoils taken by a Roman commander-in-chief from a defeated monarch and displayed in a triumph.
>
> (Greenhalgh 2011: 78)

As Greenhalgh notes that the term is emotionally charged, it does not only mean disposition and appropriation but it also signals victory and defeat. And yet these complex layers are not so easy to disentangle – in a building a stone that displays its association and makes clear reference to the previous owner isn't itself a story of victorious survival? What *spolia* at the very least do is bring any past association into the present. This association becomes a living dialogue and part of present reality.

9 It would be impossible here to offer a succinct definition of the term that captures almost all its use and avoid controversies. I have tried to despoil a reference for a good enough definition but to no avail. The field has become so broad that the term is both quite specific and at the same time so multi-faceted that it must remain somewhat undefined. Kinney aptly writes "this returns us to the categorical definition of *spolia*, a definition that grows even more elusive as the field continues to expand" (Kinney 2019: 349). Kinney (2019) is probably the best starting point to give a broad survey of the current state and use of the term *spolia*.

10 Violence is part of the definition and it's one of the ongoing discussions in the literature, if *spolia* as a term should be replaced by the less emotive term of "re-use". There is disagreement if these terms should be used interchangeably, and most theorists do not use them in such a way. For the purposes of this chapter, the term *spolia* is more apt – it speaks more of the layers of intention when there is this reuse alluding also to the complex nexus of meanings intentional reuse of older material entails – destruction, symbolism, functionality, power, association, historical memory, etc.

11 This general condition does not mean that all buildings of the past used *spolia*, as other cultural, material and aesthetic realities played a role. But the general argument is that it made more sense when there was some repetition in building materials and techniques across time and epochs, and that changed to a large extent by the industrial revolution and the way primarily materials are used from then on. The creation of industrial standardization makes reuse and spoliation, in most cases, a more expensive process, than simply using new material that reproduces a prefabricated result. For modern buildings to assimilate part of pre-existing ones either *in situ* or by quarrying older buildings in the vicinity for anything other than ornamental purposes entails a substantial cost. This leads me to the generalisation that modern *spolia*, when present, are not of necessity but of intent, whereas previous eras used *spolia* for a variety of purposes, that merged functional and ornamental use.

12 This claim is made by (Kinney 2012: 5).

13 See Elsner (2000) and Feris (2013) for a detailed description.

14 A practice which makes the whole symbolism of what he is trying to do more difficult to comprehend, i.e., defacing those emperors of the past you try to associate yourself with. If Constantine ordered this naively to use the spoils hoping viewers will not know of his act of *damnatio memoriae*, this would be odd since if viewers did not know where he took these *spolia* from this action alone negates his fairly obvious effort of association with the past. If they do, and he hoped they would not notice, it excites ridicule from the viewers he tries to impress. If he does this to show how he can surpass and deface even the good emperors in glory, then it is an act of delusion that would again, possibly, alienate his viewers and make the message complex if somewhat original. This reading of this act makes the jarring symbolism of a triumphal arch against another Roman (already ethically difficult waters) a triumphal arch against all roman history, and the city of Rome itself. Perhaps, it intended to intimidate anyone who questions his authority, in covert ways that we miss today. Maybe, it was an underhand effort by the senate, who was overseeing the construction of the arch, to pass a message of discontent and disobedience or irony, negating in subtle ways the purported message of a thankful and servile senate on the arch. Who can tell? It would be interesting to contemplate another possibility. That this emblematic building which does not intend to simply reproduce the artistic forms of the past, also intends to signal a break with the mores of the past. It intends to tell the viewer that the previous era of classical Rome has morphed into something new in political, moral, religious and aesthetic terms and this necessitates the pillaging and repossession of the past in ways that would have been impossible before. In the same way that this arch and its sculptural universe could not be erected in the times of Marcus Aurelius, so we can say that the morals of what you can and cannot do symbolically in the times of Marcus Aurelius shifts by the times of Constantine. Too much had happened, and this is a new era. The intention is exactly to display this message, as clearly as possible, even if this is done with some violence.

15 In a very recent contribution Rose (2021) argues that the frieze itself that has until now been attributed to Constantine by almost all scholars as a new sculpture of this period probably made directly for the arch is, in fact, (mostly) from a slightly earlier decade, most probably commissioned by Diocletian for his Vicennalia in AD 303, for a triumphal arch for him that was not completed. This would make almost all the art on Constantine's arch repossessed from other buildings, which itself would be a very interesting result. The argument that the arch itself as a building is older than Constantine's reign has been noted before – see endnote 23 below for the relevant literature.

16 Elsner rightly notes that the interpretative line that speaks of decline in form did in fact make an important point – that of fundamental change in Roman art. As he writes

> the Arch did precipitate a fundamental and radical set of changes in Roman visual practice which the style merchants may have identified in ways that now seem outmoded and inappropriate, but which none the less did happen.
> (Elsner 2000: 152)

17 As Ernst Kitzinger perceptively notes "[In the frieze] differences in the physical size of figures drastically underline differences of rank and importance which the second-century artist had indicated by subtle compositional means within a seemingly casual grouping. Gone, finally are elaboration of detail and differentiation of surface texture. Faces are cut rather than modelled, hair takes the form of a cap with some superficial stippling, drapery folds are summarily indicated by deeply drilled lines" (Kitzinger 1977: 8).

18 *Liberalitas* was a well-established custom by this time, practiced by Emperors throughout the centuries, so the act itself would not be a novelty. However, it is interesting to consider how this custom was depicted in different ages and the changes in iconography. On the frieze, the depiction is both realistic, actual distributing of coin, and symbolic, in that the bodies, composition of scene, etc. do not have the realism of the older fragments but are in the new style.

19 It would again be interesting to consider the problem of the frieze's provenance. If it is from an unfinished arch devoted to Diocletian as Rose (2021) argues, that the Roman population would know about, then the frieze would be coming directly from the time of the Diocletian edicts against the Christians. If this is true, then the intended message through this spolium could have the opposite outcome than approaching the Christian population, but instead implicitly alienating it, and signal something very different. Then, again, if it is a spolium from Diocletian that Constantine appropriates and adds his head where Diocletian's was, this could be seen as an act or undoing a wrong. It can even be read as the triumph of Christianity over the persecutions. The vail of history is too thick to pierce. We will never know what exact interpretation this spolium took in the minds of contemporary viewers if indeed all viewers decoded it in one way, which seems unlikely.

20 It is worth noting here Deichmann's observation that there was a new aesthetic preference for diversity and pattern in the developing Christian architecture. In the new basilicas, *spolia* columns constituted a new "order" that replaced the visual universe of the old Roman and Greek orders (see Diechmann 1940).

21 Pierce notes that the monument has no clear explicit Christian symbols (Pierce 1989: 406). What we are left with is suggestion and interpretation of "odd" novelties. This itself points to the kind of romantic notion of never being entirely sure – one can develop an argument and yet the opposite argument is equally plausible. Constantine did not really make any allusions to Christianity but was simply using what material he had available to build an arch in the traditional manner. Neither narrative can be completely proved, and the power of the monument is exactly that – that it allows new interpretative lines without putting to rest the old ones.

22 As Pierce perceptively writes "by the time of Marcus Aurelius the virtues of the emperor had become something of a cliché" (Pierce 1989: 410) and therefore reaffirming them in pictorial compositions on the arch showed the continuation of ancient traditions – a reassuring note to the upper classes who were looking for stability and respect of customs in the new order.

23 Assuming, of course, that the arch was not created before Constantine's time. This is disputed by some archaeologists, see Frothingham (1912, 1913, 1915a, 1915b), although the current consensus is that it was made during Constantine's time (see Kleiner 2001). But this adds to the interesting discussion on *spolia in re*, if they could make a building at the time of Constantine that could mimic so perfectly an arch of previous eras, we cannot claim that the age had been so unable to continue the artistic tradition of the past – therefore the use of the past, as well as the use of *spolia* signifies something else. More importantly, *spolia in re* create a category that adds to the ability of the object to relate to previous eras in new ways by playing on the very nature of time and authenticity. It instigates a complex dialogue with the viewer, not through decontextualisation of its message and appeal to a universal artistic language but by creating complex allusions to other periods and styles and involving the viewer on the question of what is original, what is new and what is the difference.

24 I will not review this voluminous literature here, but perhaps the best entry point is Harcourt and Riach (1997) which has extensive discussions connected with specific chapters of the book.

25 Irony plays an important part in the romantic literature. The whole concept of fragment and the inability to reach a completeness that is always elusive brings forth irony. Schlegel writes that "[irony] contains and arouses a feeling of indissoluble antagonism between the absolute and the relative, between the impossibility and the necessity of complete communication", Critical Fragments no. 108 (Wheeler 1984: 43). Thus, irony is embedded in the process of understanding – the reader understands part of the message the text attempts to convey, but at the same time they become aware that they do not have a complete understanding, a full picture and are constantly betrayed by the text as soon as they try to move closer to this end.

26 Imagination is a key concept both for Keynes and for the Romantics. As Rauber notes,

> we have already touched indirectly upon the supreme importance placed by the romantic mind on the creative imagination, as it applies to reader as well as to poet. But the fragment is a peculiarly potent means of eliciting an active imaginative response.
>
> (Rauber 1969: 221)

Therefore, both the Romantics and Keynes looks to the reader as an equal to the writer, asking the reader to complete the intellectual journey with the text acting only as the starting point.

References

Berenson, B. (1954) *The Arch of Constantine, or the Decline of Form*, London: Chapman and Hall.

Brilliant, R. (1982) "I piedestalli del Giardino di Boboli", *Spolia in se, sporia in re, Prospettiva*, 31, pp. 2–17.

Brilliant, R. and D. Kinney (2011) *Reuse Value*, London and New York: Routledge.

Claridge, A. (1998) *Rome: An Oxford Archaeological Guide*, Oxford: Oxford University Press.

Curran, J. (2000) *Pagan City and Christian Capital*, Oxford: Oxford University Press.

Diechmann, F. W. (1940) "Säule und Ordnung in der frühchristlichen Architektur", *Roemische Mitteilungen*, 55, pp. 114–130.

Elsner, J. (2000) "From the Culture of Spolia to the Cult of Relics: The Arch of Constantine and the Genesis of Late Antique Forms", *Papers of the British School of Rome*, 68, pp. 149–184.

Ferris, I. (2013) *The Arch of Constantine*, Stroud: Amberley Publishing.

Frothingham, A. L. (1912) "Who Built the Arch of Constantine? Its History from Domitian to Constantine", *American Journal of Archaeology*, 16 (3), pp. 368–386.

Frothingham, A. L. (1913) "Who Built the Arch of Constantine? II: The Frieze", *American Journal of Archaeology*, 17 (4), pp. 487–503.

Frothingham, A. L. (1915a) "Who Built the Arch of Constantine? III. The Attic", *American Journal of Archaeology*, 19 (1), pp. 1–12.

Frothingham, A. L. (1915b) "Who Built the Arch of Constantine? IV. The Eight Medallions of Domitian", *American Journal of Archaeology*, 19 (4), pp. 367–384.

Greenhalgh, M. (2011) "Spolia: A Definition in Ruins", in R. Brilliant and D. Kinney (eds.), *Reuse Value*, London and New York: Routledge, pp. 75–96.

Harcourt, G. C. and P. A. Riah (1997) *A Second Edition of the General Theory*, 2 volumes, Routledge: London and New York.

Janowitz, A. (2001) "The Romantic Fragment", in Wu Duncan (ed.), *A Companion to Romanticism*, Oxford: Blackwell, pp. 479–488.
Keynes, J. M. (1936) *The General Theory of Employment, Interest and Money*, London: Macmillan.
Kinney, D. (2012) "Instances of Appropriation in Late Roman and Early Christian Art", *Essays in Medieval Studies*, 28, pp. 1–22.
Kinney, D. (2019) "The Concept of Spolia", in Conrad Rudolph (ed.), *A Companion to Medieval Art*, Oxford: Wiley-Blackwell, pp. 331–356.
Kitzinger, Ernst (1977) *Byzantine Art in the Making: Main Lines of Stylistic Development in Mediterranean Art, 3rd–7th Century*. Cambridge, MA: Harvard University Press.
Kleiner, F. S. (2001) "Who Really Built the Arch of Constantine? - Patrizio Pensabene and Clementina Panella, Arco di Costantino Tra Archeologia e Archeometria (Studia Archaeologica 100; L'Erma di Bretschneider, Rome 1999). 228 pp., 139 figs., 8 black-and-white and 2 color foldout pls. ISBN 88-8265-036-7", *Journal of Roman Archaeology*, pp. 661–663.
La Rocca, E. and P. Zanker (2007) "Il ritratto colossale di Constantino del Foro di Triano", in P. Palombi and S. Walker (eds.), *Res bene gestae. Ricerche su storia urbana di Roma antica in onore di Eva Margareta Steinby*, LTUR Suppl. IV, Roma, pp. 145–159.
Liverani, P. (2004) "Reimpiego senza ideologia, La lettura antica delgi spolia dall'arco di Constantino all'eta carolinga", *RM*, 111, pp. 383–434.
Liverani, P. (2011) "Reading Spolia in Late Antiquity and Contemporary Perception", in R. Brilliant and D. Kinney (eds.), *Reuse Value*, London and New York: Routledge, pp. 33–52.
Millan-Zaibert, E. (2007) *Friedrich Schlegel and the Emergence of Romantic Philosophy*, State University of New York Press: New York.
Pierce, P. (1989) "The Arch of Constantine: Propaganda and Ideology in Later Roman Art", *Art History*, 12 (4), pp. 387–418.
Rauber, D. F. (1969) "The Fragment as Romantic Form", *Modern Language Quarterly*, 30 (2): 212–221.
Repapis, C. (2020) "The Place of The General Theory in the Economics Canon", *Iberian Journal of the History of Economic Thought*, 7 (1), pp. 79–92.
Rose, C. B. (2021) "Reconsidering the frieze on the Arch of Constantine", *Journal of Roman Archaeology*, 34 (1): 175–210
Sande, S. (2012) "The Arch of Constantine – Who Saw What?", in S. Birk and B. Poulsen (ed.), *Patrons and Viewers in Late Antiquity*, Aarchus: Archus University Press, pp. 277–290.
Schlegel, F. (2002a) "From 'Critical Fragments' (1797)", in J. Bernstein (ed.), *Classic and Romantic German Aesthetics (Cambridge Texts in the History of Philosophy)*, Cambridge: Cambridge University Press, pp. 239–245.
Schlegel, F. (2002b) "From 'Athenaeum Fragments' (1798)", in J. Bernstein (ed.), *Classic and Romantic German Aesthetics (Cambridge Texts in the History of Philosophy)*, Cambridge: Cambridge University Press, pp. 246–260.
Tanehisa, O. (2009) "Friedrich Schlegel and the Idea of Fragment: A Contribution to Romantic Aesthetics", *Aesthetics* (The Japanese Society of Aesthetics), 13, pp. 59–68.
Wheeler, Kathleen M. (1984) *German Aesthetic and Literary Criticism: The Romantic Ironists and Goethe*, Cambridge: Cambridge University Press.

Part III

Reflections on economics, society and art

7 Art as experience

The aesthetic dimensions of meta-economic concerns in E. F. Schumacher's work

Sarath Jakka

Introduction

In 1969, Erik Lundberg presented the first Sveriges Riksbank Prize in Economic Sciences (in Memory of Alfred Nobel) to Ragnar Frisch and Jan Tinbergen for their pioneering efforts "in the development of economics into a mathematically-specified and quantitatively-determined science" (Lindbeck 1992: 4). In his presentation speech, Lundberg sought to distinguish between a "vague, more 'literary' type of economics" with its "arbitrary 'naming' of causes of cyclical fluctuations" and its "concentration upon certain simple chains of causal connection" with an economics that was primarily the study of "mathematical systems that state the mutual relationships between economic variables" (Lindbeck 1992: 3). In effect, the Economics Nobel confirmed and conferred a ceremonial validity to a disciplinary turn towards what Lundberg approvingly called the "mathematical stringency", lent by Frisch and Tinbergen to economic theory (Lindbeck 1992: 3).

As Avner Offer and Gabriel Söderberg have elaborated in a study locating the prize in its political and economic context, the "Nobel Prize in economics came out of the strife between Social Democracy and business elites in Sweden, a local instance of class conflict in the West more broadly" (Offer and Söderberg 2016: 13). The prize thus also indicated another turn in "the historical chess-game between the two doctrines: On the one hand, Social Democracy, a political movement which set out to reduce insecurities and inequalities for most of the population (...) (o)n the other, a neoliberal economic doctrine (neoliberal in doctrine, market- liberal as a wider social movement), committed to undoing these reforms", with the Nobel decisively marking the victory of the latter over the former (Offer and Söderberg 2016: 10–11).

Of course, the 1969 prize did not herald "the quantitative age" in economics as such; for that, we would have to go back a few centuries. As William Deringer has shown in the case of England, "(T)he rise of calculation within British civic epistemology" (Deringer 2018: 29) was well underway around the turn of the 18th century, in the face of changing

DOI: 10.4324/9781003105435-11

political structures, practices and problems. During the late 17th and early 18th centuries, he argues,

> Britain's financial system became dramatically larger, more varied, and more technically complex. Politicians, corporate leaders, and projectors engineered an array of untested financial ventures. These included new market instruments (annuities, lotteries, tontines), public finance techniques ('equivalents,' 'engraftments,' 'sinking funds'), and regulatory schemes (international trade liberalization, interest rate reductions).
>
> (Deringer 2018: 30)

What is common to both the earlier quantitative age and the later mathematical turn was that the quantitative realm was privileged with claims to a numerical innocence, a "numbers don't lie" dogma. That this professed innocence, this strident concern and fear that economic concerns ought not to be contaminated with ideological doctrines and corruptible agendas was, ironically, a rhetorical move that was itself shaped by a specific set of ideological concerns and corruptible agendas, tacit and explicit. Accordingly, Deringer shifts the emphasis from previous histories of social and economic quantification that concentrate on debates over the kinds of numerical strategies that constituted the authentic and the impartial, to a historical treatment of the use – and usefulness – of calculations and quantities as an "instrument of dispute" (Deringer 2018: 9) in the political culture of its time. He argues that calculations were employed not just as a tool of rhetorical persuasion in 18th-century Britain, but also "proved useful for a whole range of other argumentative tasks: to interrogate, measure, judge, flatter, needle, undermine, and insult" (Deringer 2018: 10). Calculations, he writes,

> [B]ecame a medium not just for making arguments, but for *having* arguments, a way for political adversaries to fight out problems. As this happened, numerical calculations also gained new power as a way to make knowledge about the social world. They gained not only rhetorical authority, but epistemological authority.
>
> (Deringer 2018: 10–11)

The disposition of the earlier quantitative age as sketched by Deringer has an obvious resonance with the mathematical dominance heralded by the Economics Nobel of 1969. Lundberg's characterisation of economics as an attempt to map "relatively systematic interrelations, for which one can find a more or less regular repetitive pattern" among "historically unique events and disruptions" (Lindbeck 1992: 3), was marked by the conviction that the pursuit for economic objectivity was in line with developments in natural sciences like physics and chemistry, domains that already had annual Nobel prizes to celebrate their achievements. The project to cast as the subject of objective observation, the complex and ever evolving dynamics of global and national economies would inevitably be undercut by an irony, an irony not only difficult to ignore but also difficult to acknowledge. Offer and Söderberg delineate the presumption on which economists' arguments have tended to rest as follows:

> The arguments of economists are supposed to have a special authority, quite different from the pleadings of other parties: they are the counsel of reason, disinterested and objective. They stand apart from the claims of sectional and private self-interest; and also from those that emanate from metaphysical sources like religious sanction or the people's will. There is an irony here, which economists rarely acknowledge: they consider private self-interest to be the prime motivator, but not of their own advice.
> (Offer and Söderberg 2016: 2)

By drawing attention to the ironic yet unreflective disposition of its discipline, Offer and Söderberg neatly encapsulate the paradox that haunts the language game of neoliberal economics: that it is a neutral and expert view that dictates the economy centres around self-interest, so that those arguing for furthering their private interests do not have to invoke self-serving aims in order to do so. Rather, one is encouraged to pursue their own interests for the cumulative – and beneficial – effects they have on the collective, the larger economy as a whole. This irony allows for an ambiguous space to emerge, private desires and ambitions concealing themselves as neutral claims made on the public domain, of self-interest dressed up either as collective interest or as a mathematically informed disinterest. The obverse, and otherwise quite obvious, view that prioritising private interests may be antithetical and damaging to the well-being of the collective becomes a sideshow at best, a secondary concern whose legitimacy can only be forcefully invoked and mobilised during periods of deep crisis.

This irony, and its attendant consequences, was not lost on the British economic advisor, public intellectual and author Ernst Friedrich Schumacher (1911–1977). In 1973, a few years after the Economics Nobel was instituted, Schumacher published *Small Is Beautiful*, a guide to an ecologically attuned economic paradigm. This alternative-economics manual sought to address the problem of scale as the central problem of economics by presciently laying out the second and third order effects that the neoliberal paradigm's relentless emphasis on economic growth would have for the dignity of labour and the nature of work, the well-being of global and national communities and the environment at large. It also presented alternative economic schemes that were taken up by sustainability and de-growth advocates in various local initiatives and experiments across the globe. Satish Kumar, an activist and founder of the Schumacher Society (UK), characterises the Schumacherian view as one of a "reverential economy" (Schumacher 1999: 4), in which the primary approach is one of deep reverence towards the economy and the environment rather than analytical domination. For Schumacher, it was essential to place limits on individual and collective needs; to interrogate deeply the desire for economic growth, the employment of technologies for production and the extraction of natural resources. The limits were not to be driven solely by utilitarian concerns about the well-being of future generations; they had to be arrived at by a reconstruction of social values, in which the cultivation of awareness, contemplation and an aesthetic appreciation of the living framework that sustains us would allow individuals and communities to lead meaningful and fulfilling lives by embracing those very limits.

It is understandable, then, that Schumacher would decry the economics discipline's "addiction to purely quantitative analysis" that assumed (at least until the reality could no longer be completely ignored) "a virtually limitless variety of goods and services, produced and consumed by an equally limitless variety of people" (Schumacher 1999: 32). He recognised that the nature of problems that mathematical operations sought to resolve were of a fundamentally different character from, and incommensurable with, the more difficult, paradoxical and intractable problems of social life, problems that the ends of economics had to seriously consider before any mathematical methods might be applied in order to best execute a chosen social objective.

Blind spots and the limits of abstraction

Schumacher's distinction between economic and meta-economic concerns

In order to illustrate this incommensurability between the quantitative and qualitative aspects of economic and social reality, Schumacher makes two related sets of distinctions, that between convergent and divergent problems on the one hand, and those between economic and meta-economic considerations on the other. Convergent problems are those for which a solution can be arrived at by "a process of abstraction (…) can be written down and passed on to others, who can apply it without needing to reproduce the mental effort" that was initially involved in framing and solving the puzzle (Schumacher 1999: 75). Convergent problems, such as those encountered in mathematics and the physical and natural sciences progress cumulatively, each generation employing, nuancing or transforming an inherited collection of problems and solutions. Divergent problems, on the other hand, were often constituted by irreconcilable differences, tensions and dilemmas which could not be resolved in abstraction but had to be taken on as they arose in a living situation such as those encountered in the daily contexts of familial and cultural life, politics, education and so on. Schumacher gives as examples of divergent problems, the concerns faced by a teacher or a parent in modulating the tension between freedom and discipline in the context of raising a child, or the opposition between planning and freedom in economics (Schumacher 1999:

75–77). Such a problem could not have an unequivocal or clearly delineated solution that was provided beforehand, rather engaging with it involves attuning to, appreciating and handling the unique patterns, relationships and paradoxical oppositions that arise in a particular environment. Acting on such problems involves cultivating an awareness and a relation to social reality and the environment that takes one beyond present limits, beliefs, assumptions and power relations regarding the manner in which the world and its inhabitants behave, or ought to behave.

Similarly, in order to foreground the limits of abstraction in economics, Schumacher draws a distinction between economic and meta-economic concerns. He was concerned about the myriad qualitative relations economics sidelines or omits in its quest for quantitative proficiency over human behaviour and resource management. Meta-economics, for Schumacher, deals with the realm of mankind and nature that exists prior to and beyond their economic valuation, and from which economics derived its subject matter. Quantification was thus a derivative operation where every possible manner of already existent life processes and entities are reduced to the measure of price and seen as subject to the unitary set of market laws of supply, demand and bargain-hunting regardless of whether the resource in question might be renewable or non-renewable, manmade or natural, or whether the goods in question were a service or a manufacture. Schumacher pointed to the incommensurability between a renewable resource and a non-renewable one, and that between a manufactured good and a natural resource, and the dangers that arise from treating them as being equally subject to the same market laws of pricing. As he explains:

> The illusion of unlimited powers, nourished by astonishing scientific and technological achievements, has produced the concurrent illusion of having solved the problem of production. The latter illusion is based on the failure to distinguish between income and capital where this distinction matters most. Every economist and businessman is familiar with the distinction, and applies it conscientiously and with considerable subtlety to all economic affairs—except where it really matters: namely, the irreplaceable capital which man has not made, but simply found, and without which he can do nothing.
>
> (Schumacher 1999: 4)

The use of irreplaceable capital, resources that exist in nature prior to any human intervention and which cannot be replaced once they are extracted and consumed, required to be handled with special consideration given the serious consequences their overuse has on the ecosystem as a whole. If such a stark concern was ignored within economic theorisation, then Schumacher was right to suspect the epistemic imagination – and the incentive structure that sustained the dominance of such an imagination – that prioritised mathematical rigor as the mainstay of economics. A mathematical dominance belied an impatience to emphasise economic concerns and its ties to the matters of living – whether in its social and environmental dimensions – as a series of convergent problems. What seemed to matter was not so much the material ramifications of reducing a particular process, material, or activity, each with very specific roles or entanglements to the world in which they were situated, but the formulation and application of a reducing operation – of characterising an economic entity in terms of pricing – as if it were prior to any other considerations that might have to be taken into account. An important example which Schumacher returned to in the context of conflating income with irreplaceable capital was the case of fossil fuels. Regarding the economic categorisation of fossil fuels, Schumacher summarises:

> Let us take a closer look at this "natural capital." First of all, and most obviously, there are the fossil fuels. No one, I am sure, will deny that we are treating them as income items although they are undeniably capital items. If we treated them as capital items, we should be concerned with conservation; we should do everything in our power to try and minimise their current rate of use; we might be saying, for instance, that the money obtained from the realisation of these assets—these irreplaceable assets—must be placed into a special fund to be devoted exclusively to the evolution of production methods and patterns of living which do not depend on fossil fuels at all or depend on them only to a very slight extent.
>
> (Schumacher 1999: 5)

A pragmatic and careful consideration of the use of fossil fuels from a societal standpoint that accounted for the dangers of overuse and sought to develop renewable alternatives which would allow us to reduce our dependence on irreplaceable resources would involve not just mathematical calculations of the quantities involved in such an exercise but the more challenging and "divergent" task of building a political and social consensus, and institutional integrity that would allow for such a moderation and futurity to come to fruition. By prioritising convergent concerns, the more difficult divergent challenges become increasingly obscured until a crisis of unmanageable proportions forcefully makes visible what was *repressed*.

Fossil fuels are only one aspect of the earth that we depend on and not nearly as necessary as air or water without which it is impossible for life to sustain itself. "Even more important", Schumacher notes,

> is the recognition of the existence of 'goods' which never appear on the market, because they cannot be, or have not been, privately appropriated, but are nonetheless an essential precondition of all human activity, such as air, water, the soil, and in fact the whole framework of living nature.
>
> (Schumacher 1999: 35)

Such "goods", unlike say a manufactured product, have to be considered as being prior to but also above economic consideration, significant enough to be protected from the effects of economic activity. This would involve a radical prioritising of air, water and the living environment such that economic activities take place only to the extent that they don't have harmful effects for the former. This social vision of prioritising meta-economic considerations – the integrity and value of the living framework which allows economics to exist in the first place – over economic activity would involve overturning the assumptions and even the legitimacy of the dominant economic paradigm. As Schumacher laid out in his characteristically urgent tone:

> Until fairly recently the economists have felt entitled, with tolerably good reason, to treat the entire framework within which economic activity takes place as given, that is to say, as permanent and indestructible. It was no part of their job and, indeed, of their professional competence, to study the effects of economic activity upon the framework. Since there is now increasing evidence of environmental deterioration, particularly in living nature, the entire outlook and methodology of economics is being called into question.
>
> (Schumacher 1999: 35–36)

But Schumacher recognised that the marginalisation of meta-economic issues was neither an innocent act of ignorance nor a mistake of method that might be rectified when recognised because "the real strength of the theory of private enterprise lies in this ruthless simplification, which fits so admirably also into the mental patterns created by the phenomenal successes of science" (Schumacher 1999: 216). Schumacher links the reductionism prevalent in economics to the dominant epistemological values of our era in which "[t]he strength of science, too, derives from a "reduction" of reality to one or the other of its many aspects, primarily the reduction of quality to quantity" (Schumacher 1999: 216). Economics, in its aspirations to become a respected science, also borrowed the latter's horizon of a permanence that transcended human and geographical limits.

A group of physicists and philosophers seeking cross-disciplinary engagement, Adam Frank, Marcelo Gleiser and Evan Thompson note the blind spots of scientists with reference to the experience of time. "Scientists", they note,

> have taken physical time to be the only real time – whereas experiential time, the subjective sense of time's passing, is considered a cognitive fabrication of secondary importance. The young Albert Einstein made this position clear in his debate with philosopher Henri Bergson in the 1920s, when he claimed that the physicist's time is the only time
>
> (Frank, Gleiser and Thompson 2019)

The economic possibility or assumption of limitless growth can be seen as an analogue of the physicist's absolute conception of time. For Frank, Gleiser and Thompson, the "presumption that physical time, with an absolute starting point, is the only real kind of time", not only

> distorts the truth, but creates a false sense of distance between ourselves and the world. That divide arises from what we call the Blind Spot, which science itself cannot see. In the Blind Spot sits *experience*: the sheer presence and immediacy of lived perception.
>
> (Frank, Gleiser and Thompson 2019).

This recognition of the neglect of experience – "the sheer presence and immediacy of lived perception" – that is inevitable when certain scientific presumptions are the order of the day, will always gain a delayed acknowledgment from actors within science, given that the exploration of the intellectual questions they set themselves *depend* on being insulated from the "noise" of experience. What makes these problems urgent and political, however, is the dominance such presumptions exert over the entire cultural field and the world at large.

Hannah Arendt, Schumacher and the return to earth

Schumacher understood the cataclysmic implications that would follow when such blindspots were not only ignored but even taken to be intellectual virtues and actively encouraged. For Hannah Arendt, writing prior to Schumacher in the late 1950s, this technological and scientific dominance and its public inscrutability was the most pressing political concern for contemporary human societies. This question is one of the central engagements of her ambitious work *The Human Condition* where she starkly lays out the problem as follows:

> [T]he situation created by the sciences is of great political significance. Wherever the relevance of speech is at stake, matters become political by definition, for speech is what makes man a political being. If we would follow the advice, so frequently urged upon us, to adjust our cultural attitudes to the present status of scientific achievement, we would in all earnest adopt a way of life in which speech is no longer meaningful. For the sciences today have been forced to adopt a "language" of mathematical symbols which, though it was originally meant only as an abbreviation for spoken statements, now contains statements that in no way can be translated back into speech. The reason why it may be wise to distrust the political judgement of scientists *qua* scientists is not primarily their lack of "character" - that they did not refuse to develop atomic weapons - or their naïveté that they did not understand that once these weapons were developed they would be the last to be consulted about their use - but precisely the fact that they move in a world where speech has lost its power. And whatever men do or know or experience can make sense only to the extent that it can be spoken about.
>
> (Arendt 1998: 3–4)

If the reality – the sense of immediacy, perception, significance and value – of experience, action, intuition and even understanding as Arendt points out, cannot be meaningfully captured in the language of mathematical symbols – however much the latter might contribute to the shaping of our projects – then casting these very symbols as the most important criterion for validating theories and decisions on social reality practically render us mute, silencing, overriding or denying the richness of concerns and the merit of questions that arise in our immediate experience. In this sense, the dominance of mathematics over experience is not so much an exercise in accurately capturing our social habitations and our environments as much as an *escape* from the crucial difficulties and possibilities of our lived realities. This escape is often celebrated as a victory over natural limits but acquires tragic dimensions as it colonises our understanding of ourselves and supersedes any relations to the environment that we might have otherwise intended to cultivate. Arendt's reflections in the prologue begin with the strange reactions to an event that occurred a year prior to the publication of *The Human Condition* – the launch of Sputnik 1, the first artificial Earth satellite. She observes that

> this joy was not triumphal; it was not pride or awe at the tremendousness of human power and mastery which filled the hearts of men, who now, when they looked up from the earth towards the skies, could behold there a thing of their own making.
>
> (Arendt 1998: 1)

Rather, as she notes, "(t)he immediate reaction (...) was relief about the first 'step toward escape from men's imprisonment to the earth'", a sentiment that was resonant with "the extraordinary line (...) carved on the funeral obelisk for one of Russia's great scientists: 'Mankind will not remain bound to the earth forever'" (Arendt 1998: 1).

Science's escape – or rejection – of the earth is also a submission to powerful human interests that distance themselves from accountability by taking recourse to an anonymous, inaccessible horizon. As Margaret Canovan notes while introducing Arendt's work,

> [B]y escaping from the earth into the skies, and through enterprises such as nuclear technology, human beings are successfully challenging natural limits, posing political questions made vastly more difficult by the inaccessibility of modern science to public discussion.
>
> (Canovan 1998: x).

In line with Arendt's terrestrial sympathies, Schumacher's meta-economics involved a return to the earth – literally – for soil too like air, water and other meta-economic entities was a precious resource that has been exploited and abused as a result of being taken as a resource in the abstract. But the earth was a condition that the limitless horizons of economics sought to escape from, the soil bearing value mostly in terms of profit like any other commodity or factor of production rather than as an essential for nourishing life. Alienated from a relation with the soil, economic expertise, Schumacher asserts, necessitates a philosophy that can only indulge in a narrowly-defined prioritisation. He writes,

> Nothing could be clearer. If agriculture does not pay it is just a "declining enterprise." Why prop it up? There are no "necessary improvements" as regards the land, but only as regards farmers' incomes, and these can be made if there are fewer farmers. This is the philosophy of the townsman, alienated from living nature, who promotes his own scale of priorities by arguing in economic terms that we cannot "afford" any other.
>
> (Schumacher 1999: 92)

Having travelled across nation states emerging from colonisation such as India, and having witnessed a variety of indigenous cultivation practices, Schumacher was right to suspect arguments regarding the economic infeasibility of an agriculture that was not of an industrial scale or largely machine driven. As he made clear, not caring for the soil was not a matter of the unprofitability of such an enterprise, or of a lack of expertise; rather, it could be ascribed to a meta-economic sensibility, or the lack thereof:

> There are no technical difficulties and there is no lack of relevant knowledge. There is no need to consult economic experts when the question is one of priorities. We know too much about ecology today to have any excuse for the many abuses that are currently going on in the management of the land, in the management of animals, in food storage, food processing, and in heedless urbanisation. If we permit them, this is not due to poverty, as if we could not afford to stop them; it is due to the fact that, as a society, we have no firm basis of belief in any meta-economic values, and when there is no such belief the economic calculus takes over. This is quite inevitable. How could it be otherwise?
>
> (Schumacher 1999: 92–93)

The examples of fossil fuels and soil allow us to draw out a larger insight that Schumacher is pointing to. Because both fossil fuels and soil are mainly valued in their potential to deliver profit, social priorities are aligned in such a manner that any other attitude or relation to these entities lose their significance. Having served in the British National Coal Board for over two decades, his projections of the future consequences of the ravenously excessive use of fossil fuels demonstrate the extent of his foresight. With the benefit of hindsight, we can see that Schumacher's anticipation of future disaster and his advocacy for alternatives provide a far more sobering and accurate account of the present global situation compared to the clueless visions of his more reputable colleagues in the economics profession who were his contemporaries, many of whom believed increased efficiency and technological development will herald a future with greater leisure, health, equity and cooperation. But Schumacher's consequentialist accounts do not mark the end of his inquiry, rather it is an initial move in the imagining of a different kind of economic orientation.

If economics was preoccupied with the efficiency of outcomes, Schumacher was inviting us to consider a view of economics that started out at the opposite end, what might be seen by more conventional economists as an uneconomical economics. Such a "reverential" economics, one of practicing gratitude towards the "generous" earth is alien to the arithmetic of efficiency and increased scale where growth is seen as a non-negotiable prerequisite. While such arithmetic legitimises itself with an appeal to objectivity or neutrality, in effect, it behaves projectively in that it seeks to both reduce and exhaust its object. Meta-economic reality is first reduced into an economic calculus and its discursive authority is then projected to be an exhaustive view which has greater claims on the former than any other possible outlook. This double operation, of the projective that takes on the mantle of the objective, and the reductive that takes on the mantle of the comprehensive sets in motion a dynamic that occludes the possibility of what Schumacher refers to as a "firm basis of belief in any meta-economic values" (Schumacher 1999: 93). Therefore, Schumacher's analysis is to not be solely valued for his capacity to anticipate events, but for recognising the fundamental priority of having a *relational* attitude to our communities and our environment rather than starting out with what we can ironically term a neutral or objective bias.

Play and the relational making of reality: Donald Winnicott and Schumacher

Before turning to his suggestion of what meta-economic values might involve, let us dwell a little more on how relations *make* social reality, i.e., rather than attempting to predict social outcomes based on what *is* economic social reality, Schumacher understands that we *make* social reality based on how we relate to others and our environment. Through his wide-ranging ruminations on play as a schema of experience, the British psychoanalyst Donald Winnicott can provide us an illustration of how social reality is fundamentally a potential space that is made and remade through relations. For Winnicott, after the child's initial feeding phase where there is little or no sense of a distinction between internal and external worlds, they begin to recognise the enormity of the outer world around them and the variety and delineation of its objects. They also have to cope with the pleasure, frustration, immersion and distraction that are involved in these encounters. The integrity and coherence of the outer world is not laid out in a preselected manner for the child, and playing is the main activity through which their inner psychic reality is brought to bear on the outer world. Winnicott posited playing as a transitional phenomenon, an experience that occurs in an ambiguous intermediate area between inner self and outer reality. Playing, to quote Winnicott, is

> not inside by any use of the word. Nor is it outside, that is to say, it is not a part of the repudiated world, the not-me, that which the individual has decided to recognise (with whatever difficulty and even pain) as truly external, which is outside magical control.
>
> (Winnicott 2005a: 55)

Play opened up a potential space between the inner world and external reality, between mother and child and between therapist and patient. Winnicott often used a simple drawing game with the children he consulted. He describes the game simply:

> First I take some paper and tear the sheets in half, giving the impression that it is not frantically important. I say, 'This game that I like playing has no rules. I just take my pencil and go like that…', and I probably screw up my eyes and do a squiggle blind. I go on and say, 'You show if that looks like anything to you or if you can make it into anything, and afterwards you do the same for me and I will see if I can make something of yours.
>
> (Winnicott 2017: 415–416).

The key aspect for Winnicott was not to rush into a clever interpretation of what the child was "actually" thinking but rather an intermediate space, one of waiting to learn from the child what they had to say, a transformative form of communication where a model of reality, explanation or "truth" is not imposed on the situation, rather the situation is waited upon so that the child's responses to a particular intervention are received with care and transforms the listener in turn. Similarly, if we have to conceive the aesthetic dimensions of our experience and the values it gives rise to – both individual and communal – as existing in a potential, intermediate space, we can open ourselves to forms of understanding that privilege the creative over the limits of the objective, allowing us to act in a manner that is less frantic about its claims to objective validity and more attuned to the responses of the other, be it a child, or even the environments we inhabit.

Play for Winnicott was not merely an infantile process of discovery and equally applied to the ways in which adults constituted their social and cultural worlds. "This intermediate area of experiencing" he states, "expands into creative living and into the whole cultural life of man" (Winnicott 2005, "The Location of Cultural Experience": 138). Winnicott advances the thesis that "the place where cultural experience is located is in the potential space between the individual and the environment (originally the object). The same can be said of playing. Cultural experience begins with creative living first manifested in play" (Winnicott 2005, "The Location of Cultural Experience": 135). Winnicott, is in a sense, advancing an ontology of creativity, a social and cultural unfolding, rather than a model determined view of social formation. If creative living was life itself, how then has local and global life come to be characterised by an unyielding obsession with abstract laws, mostly economic in nature? In a Winnicottian vein, the stakeholders of such models can be said to have found creative ways of being uncreative, of denying alternatives.

If both the domination of economics and its alternative possibilities are characterised by creativity, where does their difference lie? One aspect of this answer can be found in Winnicott's account of the "squiggle game" he played with children. He is careful about initiating the child into the game gently. A paper is torn before it is given to the child to indicate non-seriousness, so as to not pressure them into a rule-following protocol. Winnicott's attempt to include and involve the child is characterised by an ethos of waiting and curiosity rather than of predicting and fixing. If the social and cultural world exists in a potential space, then abstractions regarding the social world are, in effect, both reflecting their object and creating it. The social environment is made not just of physical objects but of social concepts as well. Given that certain economic notions dominate social life, social life in turn evolves around those concepts, our present moment thus the result of a complex of self-fulfilling notions. In such an approach, our conception of social categories ought to be created in a manner that does not capture society as an enumeration of natural laws rather we ought to conceive social categories – such as economic relations and goals – in terms of how we seek to relate to our unfolding environment. It is at such a juncture that Schumacher's emphasis on meta-economic values is particularly insightful.

Limits of certainty and horizons of awareness: Schumacher and the realm of the spiritual

From what has been cited from his work up till now, we can see that Schumacher speaks of a "generous earth", while Satish Kumar terms the former's approach as one of a "reverential economy" (Schumacher 1999: 4). In his introduction to the quadricentennial edition of *Small is Beautiful*, Paul Hawken provides an indication of Schumacher's meta-economic horizons, where nature was "both mentor and spiritual sanctuary, a concept that now encompasses movements as diverse as biomimicry' and eco-feminism" (Schumacher 1999: xv). Such attitudes involve *qualities* or an aesthetics of experience and ways of *relating* and attuning to the world rather than the misleading comforts of precision that numbers might provide. It seems to foreground a desire for a social perspective, which does not view man's capacities and the rewards thought to be due to him as the basis of evaluating worth.

It was apparent to Schumacher that the much-vaunted freedom to pursue profit that was at the heart of the liberal economic imagination was structured around a deep unfreedom. This brings to mind Franz Kafka's wry evocation, used by Arendt as an epigram to her discussion on "The *Vita Activa* and the Modern Age" that man "had found the Archimedean point, but he used it against himself; it seems that he was permitted to find it only under this condition" (Arendt 1998: 248). Kafka's aphorism poses the following paradox: How could the very same man, who came to leverage such powers as to be able to move planets, come to use this capability against himself? Schumacher recognised this paradox as operative in the modern economic preoccupation with means and efficient outcomes, which "destroys man's freedom and power to choose the ends he really favours; the development of means, as it were, dictates the choice of ends" (Schumacher 1999: 36). Considering the societal aspiration for supersonic transport and space travel as illustrative of the ironic constraint technological progress places on us, he elaborates:

> The conception of these [the pursuit of supersonic transport speeds and the immense efforts made to land men on the moon] aims was not the result of any insight into real human needs and aspirations, which technology is meant to serve, but solely of the fact that the necessary technical means appeared to be available.
>
> (Schumacher 1999: 36)

Rather than a means-centred outlook, meta-economics involves putting at the heart of social praxis the ends that can be valued in themselves. This would involve valuing the entire living framework, of which we form but a part and letting it guide our priorities, for

> [m]an has not made them, and it is irrational for him to treat things that he has not made and cannot make and cannot recreate once he has spoilt them, in the same manner and spirit as he is entitled to treat things of his own making.
>
> (Schumacher 1999: 84)

But what precisely are these "real human needs and aspirations" to which Schumacher refers? Given his use of the word "real", one might imagine he is speaking of goals that can be precisely laid out. However, they are to be better understood as horizons of awareness, modes of attunement that involve an embrace of imprecision and uncertainty. Schumacher casts suspicion on the overriding emphasis on acquiring knowledge that is valued for its certainty or indubitability. In the economic sphere, it was the certainty and clarity of method that obscured the most important considerations:

> Everything becomes crystal clear after you have reduced reality to one—one only—of its thousand aspects. You know what to do—whatever produces profits; you know what to avoid—whatever reduces them or makes a loss. And there is at the same time a perfect measuring rod for the degree of success or failure. Let no one befog the issue by asking whether a particular action is conducive to the wealth and well-being of society,

> whether it leads to moral, aesthetic, or cultural enrichment. Simply find out whether it pays; simply investigate whether there is an alternative that pays better. If there is, choose the alternative.
>
> (Schumacher 1999: 215)

As we saw earlier, it was the certainty and the narrow pursuit of measure that led to science's blind spot that had no space for the experience of time. In his final work, *A Guide for the Perplexed*, completed shortly before his death, Schumacher recalls his interest in the blind spots that result from being excessively occupied by modes of certainty. He uses a cartographic analogy in order to remark on the moment he became disenchanted with the dominant paradigm that he labels as "modern materialistic scientism" (Schumacher 1978: 13):

> It then occurred to me that this was not the first time I had been given a map that failed to show many of the things I could see right in front of my eyes. All through school and university I had been given maps of life and knowledge on which there was hardly a trace of many of the things that I most cared about and that seemed to me to be of the greatest possible importance for the conduct of my life. I remembered that for many years my perplexity was complete; and no interpreter came along to help me. It remained complete until I ceased to suspect the sanity of my perceptions and began, instead, to suspect the soundness of the maps.
>
> (Schumacher 1978: 9)

Ironically, Schumacher began to doubt these maps precisely because of their interest in certainty. If the most difficult and important questions and problems in life require our continuing engagement with, rather than an amputation of, uncertainty, Schumacher wonders why these realms of doubt are not given prominence:

> The maps of *real* knowledge, designed for *real* life, did not show anything except things that allegedly could be *proved* to exist. The first principle of the philosophical map-makers seemed to be 'If in doubt, leave it out,' or put it into a museum. It occurred to me, however, that the question of what constitutes proof was a very subtle and difficult one. Would it not be wiser to turn the principle into its opposite and say 'If in doubt, show it *prominently*'? After all, matters that are beyond doubt are, in a sense, dead; they do not constitute a challenge to the living.
>
> (Schumacher 1978: 11)

Doubt and dilemma are essential conditions of lived challenges. Schumacher pointed out that while an interest in certainty was motivated by the minimisation of risk over the reliability of a particular method or a theory, in effect, it generated another kind of risk, one where large realms of our experience would be sidelined and we will eventually have to face the consequences of this blindsiding. He explains the compromises made in the name of certainty by invoking Thomas Aquinas to make a distinction between "slender" and "certain" knowledge:

> To accept anything as true means to incur the risk of error. If I limit myself to knowledge that I consider true beyond doubt, I minimise the risk of error but I maximise, at the same time, the risk of missing out on what may be the subtlest, most important and most rewarding things in life. St Thomas Aquinas, following Aristotle, taught that 'the slenderest knowledge that may be obtained of the highest things is more desirable than the most certain knowledge obtained of lesser things'. 'Slender' knowledge is here put in opposition to 'certain' knowledge, and indicates uncertainty. Maybe it is necessarily so that the higher things cannot be known with the same degree of certainty as the lesser things can be known, in which case it would be a very great loss indeed if knowledge were limited to things beyond the possibility of doubt.
>
> (Schumacher 1978: 11)

Schumacher is of course not arguing for a total banishment of convergent problems. He is more concerned about the *total* nature of the intellectual effort being concentrated on solutions to convergent problems. To characterise the nihilism inherent in this prevailing reductionism, he quotes the psychologist Viktor Frankl's observation that "[c]ontemporary nihilism no longer brandishes the word nothingness; today nihilism is camouflaged as *nothing-but-ness*. Human phenomena are thus turned into mere epiphenomena" (Schumacher 1978: 14). Schumacher offers a few options to understanding the realm of slender knowledge, cast out as epiphenomena in our age of measurement. It seems to indicate "a process of growth through adoration, awe, wonder, admiration and imitation" (Schumacher 1978: 31) or "an effort of self-awareness [...] that almost impossible feat of thought recoiling upon itself: almost impossible but not quite" (Schumacher 1978: 55) and even an advocacy for heterodox forms of knowledge that were not shown in the philosophical maps that Schumacher began to question. As he explains, those maps

> also failed to show large 'unorthodox' sections of both theory and practice in medicine, agriculture, psychology and the social and political sciences, not to mention art and so-called occult or paranormal phenomena, the mere mention of which was considered to be a sign of mental deficiency.
>
> (Schumacher 1978: 11–12)

Schumacher approaches spiritual and aesthetic matters through "a hierarchical structure of the world" (Schumacher 1978: 23), in which the world is divided into "four great Levels of Being" or "four elements – matter, life, consciousness and self-awareness" (Schumacher 1973: 34). The dominant culture of scientism approached only the two lower levels of being, namely matter and life, while ignoring the higher levels – consciousness and awareness. Schumacher values traditional wisdom in the form of religious discourse because it values the higher levels of being. He points out:

> While traditional wisdom had considered the human mind as weak but *open-ended*, that is capable of reaching beyond itself towards higher and higher levels, the new thinking took it as axiomatic that the mind's reach had fixed and narrow limits, which could be clearly determined, while within these limits it possessed virtually unlimited powers.
>
> (Schumacher 1978: 19).

Without access to these "higher levels of being", it was "not possible to find out where everything has a proper and legitimate place. Everything, everywhere, can be understood only when its Level of Being is fully taken into account" (Schumacher 1978: 23). If we were to relate this to his economics, it would be his conviction by implication, that it is impossible to work out the relations between economic production and our care for the environment without access to these "higher levels of being".

To a contemporary reader, this attitude of divine adoration to the environment can provoke reactions of aversion and suspicion given the range of pejorative connotations that may justly be invoked when an all too religious vocabulary comes into play. It also accounts for Schumacher's own cultural situatedness and the necessity of a contemporary re-evaluation of the religious aspects of his work where one is able look beyond the theological paradigms that frame his engagement to the more basic questions and attitudes that motivate his economic and environmental concerns, concerns for which a theological frame are not strictly necessary.

However, it is also possible to observe that despite such theological inclinations, Schumacher was certainly not religiously dogmatic. His call for a Buddhist economics and his attempt to incorporate and integrate spiritual teachings from various religious traditions also demonstrates a nascent attempt to work out an economics that was centred on non-western values. Schumacher was also aware that the various religious traditions that he cited were merely place holders for truths that were by nature indefinite and open-ended. This open-endedness is defined in *A Guide for the Perplexed* as necessary for the realisation of "true" humanness itself. He writes:

> This 'open-endedness' is the wonderful result of the specifically human powers of self-awareness (*z*), which, as distinct from the powers of life and consciousness, have nothing automatic or mechanical about them. The powers of self-awareness are, essentially, a limitless potentiality rather than an actuality. They have to be developed and 'realised' by each human individual, if he is to become truly human, that is to say, a *person*.
>
> (Schumacher 1978: 32)

Schumacher was also aware of the absurdity of packing a seemingly limitless horizon into a term like "self-awareness" and emphasised that such a term was only a "label", merely "a finger pointing to the moon" (Schumacher 1978: 26–27). The "moon" of this analogy "itself remains highly mysterious and needs to be studied with the greatest patience and perseverance, if we want to understand anything about man's position in the universe" (Schumacher 1978: 27).

For Schumacher, "the marvel of the Buddhist way of life is the utter rationality of its pattern – amazingly small means leading to extraordinarily satisfactory results" (Schumacher 1999: 41) led him to call for a "Buddhist economics", a study of how to achieve our meta-economic needs "with the minimum means" (Schumacher 1999: 41). Nevertheless, a deliberate non-specificity and openness qualified even this call; as Schumacher clarified: "the choice of Buddhism for this purpose is purely incidental; the teachings of Christianity, Islam, or Judaism could have been used just as well as those of any other of the great Eastern traditions" (Schumacher 1999: 36). The use of religious horizons to signal an ethical and aesthetic investment in our economic attitudes to the environment certainly carries with it a doctrinal residue of the institutional frameworks from which these teachings emerge. Yet, the indefiniteness and the non-dogmatic nature of his appeal allowed for a flexibility, an availability to open-ended interpretations. Even a cursory glance at the contributors who provided commentaries to the quadricentennial edition of *Small Is Beautiful* testifies to the range of his appeal among an eclectic set of thinkers and activists brought together by his advocacy for de-growth. These include urban planners, ecologists, environmentalists, scientists, philanthropists, eco-feminists, activists, housing campaigners and a range of other actors who have sought to improve their local communities and build campaigns against the environmental intrusions of states and corporations.

Approaching meta-economics through aesthetics: Schumacher and the Art of Living

The longevity, range and geographical spread of Schumacher's influence is due in large part to his passionate call for enhancing decentralised, local participation. This was possible because such local initiatives freely selected and interpreted his ideas in ways that were relevant to their local environments. Schumacher's legacy of an interest in smallness remains relevant not because it's a call for a stringent asceticism, but more so because it explains that we have to expand ourselves in our relationship to our surroundings if we are to move beyond the restrictions placed on us by a profit-oriented social dynamic. For Schumacher, a meta-economic awareness would allow an exploration of the world that lies beyond the realm of measure and profit, one whose "restriction in the use of instruments of cognition has the inevitable effect of narrowing and impoverishing reality" (Schumacher 1999: 61).

So, rather than emphasising a meta-economic exploration of the "hierarchical" levels of being, it might be instructive to re-describe meta-economics through another domain that Schumacher regarded as exemplary of such horizons: art. Schumacher equated religion and philosophy with art as the "higher manifestations of life" (Schumacher 1999: 67). Art is also included among his list of domains that are missing from the philosophical maps that guide contemporary society. However, Schumacher is not talking about "art" as a separate domain composed of practitioners involved in the production of "culture". His criticism extends to the separation of art from life as a whole, especially when it is limitedly perceived as self-expression or escapism or within a framework of utility. If "the most prominent doctrines shown on the 'map' accepted the possibility of art only as self-expression or escape from reality", beauty in nature too wasn't devoid of utilitarian bias (Schumacher 1978: 12). "Even in nature", he notes, "there was nothing artistic except by chance; that is to say, even the most beautiful appearances could be fully accounted for – so we were told – by their utility for reproduction, affecting natural selection" (Schumacher 1978: 12). Uninterested in art that functioned as entertainment or propaganda, Schumacher clarifies his notion of art as the valuing and exploration of awareness and experience:

> If art aims primarily to affect our feelings we may call it entertainment; if it aims primarily to affect our will we may call it propaganda. These two, entertainment and propaganda, we can recognise as a pair of opposites, and we have no difficulty sensing that something is missing. No great artist has ever turned his back on either entertainment or propaganda, or was ever satisfied with just these two. Invariably he strove to communicate truth, the *power* of truth, by appealing to man's higher intellectual faculties, which are suprarational. Entertainment and propaganda by themselves do not give us power but exert power over us. When they are transcended by, and made subservient to, the communication of Truth, art helps us to develop our higher faculties, and this is all that matters.
>
> (Schumacher 1978: 148)

The above passage clearly points to the equivalence Schumacher is drawing between meta-economic values, art and the levels or faculties of self-awareness. He emphasises this equivalence by drawing from Dante's positioning of art in the *Divine Comedy,* alluding to the episode in which Beatrice, seeing Dante from heaven, wants to help him:

> She cannot do so herself, as he has sunk too low for religion to reach him, and so she asks Art, in the person of Virgil, to guide him out of 'this savage place.' True art is the intermediary between man's ordinary nature and his higher potentialities, and so Dante accepts Virgil.
>
> (Schumacher 1978: 150)

Schumacher understood art as a guide for the potential and intermediate space of awareness and experience. Art for him, then, was to be valued as an "art of living" (Schumacher 1978: 159), an ethics that was also an aesthetics of existence. In this sense, Schumacher's understanding of art as awareness and experience resonates with Michael Foucault's notion of "technologies of the self" – a type separate from technologies of production, signification and of power – which:

> [p]ermit individuals to effect, by their own means, a number of operations on their own bodies, their own souls, their own thoughts, their own conduct, and this in a manner so as to transform themselves, modify themselves, and attain a certain state of perfection, happiness, purity, supernatural power.
>
> (Foucault 1988: 18)

In a series of lectures given two years before his passing, Foucault came to acknowledge the shift in his interest in "the interaction between oneself and others" (Foucault 1988: 19). Echoing Schumacher, Foucault's interest in the art of life comes through in the following question posed in an interview with Paul Rabinow and Hubert Dreyfus, published as "On the Genealogy of Ethics: An Overview of Work in Progress":

> What strikes me is the fact that in our society, art has become something which is related only to objects and not to individuals, or to life. That art is something which is specialized or which is done by experts who are artists. But couldn't everyone's life become a work of art? Why should the lamp or the house be an art object, but not our life?
>
> (Rabinow 1984: 350)

Foucault's interest in self-techniques and the aesthetics of existence emerged from his reading of the French philosopher Pierre Hadot's hypothesis concerning the functions of ancient philosophy. Hadot provides a well-argued case for looking at ancient philosophical disputations and discourse as forming only one part of a much more holistic praxis, and argues that:

> [A]ll ancient philosophical schools refused to consider philosophical activity as purely intellectual, purely formal or theoretical. Rather, the ancients considered philosophy as a choice which committed a person's entire life and soul. This is why the exercise of philosophy was not solely intellectual but could also be spiritual. The philosopher did not finally form his disciples only in the sense of a knowing how to speak or to debate, but a knowing how to live in the strongest and noblest sense of the term. It is to an art of living, a way of life that the ancient philosophers invited their disciples.
>
> (Hadot 2020: 59)

Hadot's conception of philosophy as "an art of living, a way of life" evidently has much in common with Schumacher's conception of art as life. This parallel becomes especially clear in Schumacher's citation of the Sri Lankan cultural historian and philosopher Ananda Coomaraswamy's understanding of art, which bears a striking resemblance to Hadot's view of philosophy:

> Let us admit that if we are to offer an education in agreement with the innermost nature and eloquence of [these great works of art] themselves, that this will not be an education in sensibility, but an education in philosophy, in Plato's and Aristotle's sense of the word, for whom it means ontology and theology and the map of life, and a wisdom to be applied to everyday matters
>
> (Schumacher 1973: 148–149)

If Coomaraswamy was interested in pointing to the relation between "great" works of art and life as philosophy, and Hadot demonstrated that the roots of philosophy originated in a concern with the art of living, Schumacher sought to make a case for an art of living that prefigured our approach to economic production and its impact on our environments. Schumacher details the relations between the art of living and our economic and environmental relations in the following manner:

> The art of living is always to make a good thing out of a bad thing. Only if we *know* that we have actually descended into infernal regions where nothing awaits us 'but the cold death of society and the extinguishing of all civilised relations', can we summon the courage and imagination needed for a 'turning around', a *metanoia*. This then leads to seeing the world in a new light, namely as a place where the things modern man continuously talks about and always fails to accomplish can actually be done. The generosity of the Earth allows us to feed all mankind; we know enough about ecology to keep the Earth a healthy place; there is enough room on the Earth, and there are enough materials, so that everybody can have adequate shelter; we are quite competent enough to produce sufficient supplies of necessities so that no one need live in misery.
>
> (Schumacher 1978: 159)

The possibilities of prioritising the art of awareness and environmental care over profit, and the optimistic picture that Schumacher paints around the transformative capacities of meta-economic values may sound naive and simplistic, but he understood it as a necessary wager. As he wisely notes in the follow up to his optimistic vision:

> Can we rely on it that a 'turning around' will be accomplished by enough people quickly enough to save the modern world? This question is often

> asked, but whatever answer is given to it will mislead. The answer 'Yes' would lead to complacency; the answer 'No' to despair. It is desirable to leave these perplexities behind us and get down to work.
>
> (Schumacher 1978: 160)

For Schumacher, economic truths were not disputational in nature, they were living truths. Economic truths were to be made and what was at stake was nothing less than a life that reckoned with beauty in its entirety.

References

Arendt, Hannah (1998) *The Human Condition*. 1958. 2nd ed., University of Chicago Press.

Canovan, Margaret (1998) Introduction. *The Human Condition,* by Hannah Arendt, 1958, 2nd ed., University of Chicago Press, pp. vii–xx.

Deringer, William (2018) *Calculated Values: Finance, Politics, and the Quantitative Age*. Harvard University Press.

Foucault, Michel (1988) "Technologies of the Self." 1982. *Technologies of the Self: A Seminar with Michel Foucault*, edited by Luther H. Martin, Huck Guttman, Patrick H. Hutton, University of Massachusetts Press, pp. 16–49.

Frank, Adam, Marcelo Gleiser and Evan Thompson (2019) "The Blind Spot." *Aeon,* 8 Jan. 2019, https://aeon.co/essays/the-blind-spot-of-science-is-the-neglect-of-lived-experience. Accessed [8 June 2021]

Hadot, Pierre (2020) *The Selected Writings of Pierre Hadot: Philosophy as Practice,* translated by Federico Testa and Matthew Sharpe, Bloomsbury.

Lindbeck, Assar (ed.) (1992) *Nobel Lectures, Economics 1969–1980*. World Scientific.

Offer, Avner and Gabriel Söderberg (2016) *The Nobel Factor: The Prize in Economics, Social Democracy, and the Market Turn*. Princeton University Press.

Rabinow, Paul (ed.) (1984) *The Foucault Reader*. Pantheon Books.

Schumacher, E. F. (1977) *A Guide for the Perplexed*. Abacus, Sphere Books.

———. (1999) *Small Is Beautiful: A Study of Economics as if People Mattered (25 Years Later.... with Commentaries*). 1973. Hartley and Marks.

Winnicott, Donald (2005) "Playing: A Theoretical Statement." 1971. *Playing and Reality*. Routledge, pp. 51–70.

——— (2005) "The Location of Cultural Experience." (1967) Winnicott, pp. 128–139.

——— (2017) "The Squiggle Game". 1968. *The Collected Works of Donald Winnicott*. Vol. 8, edited by Lesley Caldwell and Helen Taylor Robinson, Oxford UP, pp. 413–440.

8 "Man, the Prisoner of Logic"

Toward an optics of equanimity

Michael Uebel

Introduction

In the context of the present collection, this chapter can do no more than be suggestive. By gesturing toward the imbrication of art and science, it opens up the question of how particular models of knowledge serve – or do not serve – inquiry, whether those be the methods of economics or art. The proposed model here combines perspectivism, and itself an echo of pluralism, and equanimity, a balanced way of knowing the world. Art can teach economics a thing or two, precisely because, whether they have their roots in the scientific revolution and or the romantic movement or Eastern philosophy, perspectivist approaches inform the most complete inquiries. Perspectivism, like equanimity, is about nothing other than the accumulation of different points of view in pursuit of knowledge. What this chapter tempts me to suggest is that the occasion of equanimity is the fulcrum upon which the relation of our engagement and acceptance of what we "see" and our dismissal or unavoidable ignorance of the same resolves itself in the pursuit of a more complete understanding of the world. To engage equanimously with the world means that there can be no total theory or final understanding of it. A single true description of a completely independent reality – of the kind, for example, the metaphysical realist posits – cannot exist since the world does not determine unitary answers to basic ontological questions independently of our mobile conceptual assumptions. The flexibility of our assumptions is reflected by the implicit, practical understandings we generate about the world in which we are moving around and viewing from shifting angles. The preconditions of our theoretical practices in general are, as Goethe knew, tied to the unceasing activities of skillful looking that may give us a more complete access to the world. And so scientific or economic models of how things emerge by appreciating to the extent to which any object of inquiry contains within it the possibility of multiple readings. This sort of exploration from multiple perspectives forms the ground of our equanimity.

But our ways of exploring are often limited, channeled, for example, by our socially conditioned values. A telling illustration of this emerged as the result of a 1947 study in which psychologists Brunner and Goodman found that value-laden conceptual schemes exert a profound influence on the way

DOI: 10.4324/9781003105435-12

we see things. They discovered that children of lower socioeconomic status (SES) households overestimate the size of coins to a greater degree than children from higher-SES households, with the degree of overestimation varying with the value (not the physical size) of the coin (except between the quarter and the half dollar, which the authors describe as "almost too valuable [to a child of ten] to be real!" (Bruner and Goodman 1947: 39). The researchers inferred that the visual experience of money, at least in the dimension of size perception, is significantly influenced by its importance within the system of values ordering a child's life. A kind of false consciousness inheres in this collapsing of the relation of affective and logical meanings and their objects, in this case, the value and size of a coin. To confuse size with value seems now an acutely obvious symptom of late capitalism, an illustration of the false consciousness underpinning it. Indeed, Joseph Gabel finds very suggestive parallels between the confusion of concepts and percepts that takes place in both false consciousness and schizophrenia, signifying a "morbid rationalism" inherent in each way of relating to the world.[1]

Aesthetic values clearly contribute to the shape of our representations of the world. Alberti's seminal treatise *Della Pittura* (1435), in outlining a process for the most effective painting through the use of one-point perspective, emphasizes the arbitrariness of the point itself, around which the perspectival construction is generated. Alberti's instruction to the painter is deceptively simple: locate the centric point of the work just "where it seems best" (Alberti 1966: 56). There are no criteria for choosing one point as opposed to another except those of aesthetic value and proportionality. Nietzsche, to whom we will return in a moment, similarly notes that we choose among an array of cognitive perspectives only on the basis of our values and affective attunements. Furthermore, such pragmatic criteria are never sufficiently robust to require the enactment of any one point of view over alternatives. Equanimity affords, in an entirely holistic manner, the provisional locating of the "where it seems best". Perspectives actually possess relative value – and this is Alberti's point (as well as Nietzsche's) – and thus some are "better" than others, yet none are final. There is nothing other than a range, and to this perspectival range equanimity attends. Without an equanimous manner of knowing/seeing, there could be no appreciation of the manifold conditions we may be in as knowers and how these shape and unshape the choice of one perspective arbitrarily drawn from the variety of potential ones. Knowing is like seeing since both depend upon active perspective-taking. Nietzsche recommended the employment of a variety of perspectives in the service of knowledge. A famous passage from *On the Genealogy of Morals* brings before us the idea that, since different perspectives and affective attunements disclose different aspects of things, pursuing objectivity amounts to forever broadening our perspective, endlessly multiplying our attunements:

> There is only a perspective seeing, only a perspective 'knowing'; and the more affects we allow to speak about one thing, the more eyes, different

> eyes, we can use to observe one thing, the more complete will our 'concept' of this thing, our 'objectivity,' be.
>
> (Nietzsche 1967: 119).

Objects of knowledge emerge most fully when our interests in them remain multiple and flexible.

To cultivate flexible perspectives allows us to overcome the obvious limitation that we can only occupy one perspective at a time. Approaching objectivity demands that we be capable of one more inquiry, one more view – in short, that we keep perspectively moving. Such mobility produces new knowledge beyond the idiosyncrasy of our current perspective, revealing its parochialism, certainly, and, yet most crucially, marking the way toward better, that is, more complete, ones. Perspectivism, like the equanimity that enables it, is nothing other than a methodology for attaining a more comprehensive picture of the world around us and through which we move. Here, wandering succeeds where dogmatism fails, and so Nietzschean "free spirits" are modelled after Don Quixote rather than Odysseus: "He who has attained only to some degree of freedom of mind cannot feel other than a wanderer on the earth– though not as a traveler to a final destination: for this destination does not exist" (Nietzsche 1986: 203). Final destinations mark the cessation of (further) knowledge since shifts in perspective are longer necessary. Zhuangzi was one philosopher who profoundly valued perspectival shifting, wandering, as the key to achieving what he called "greater knowledge" (*da zhi*, 大知). To illustrate the relation of perspectivism to *da zhi*, the Chinese thinker tells of the fabled Peng bird, so imposing an animal that it rises 90,000 li in the air and gazes down upon the vast sky below it. Such a view from above is inconceivable to some. So, based upon their own experiences with flight, the cicada and the dove contend that the Peng bird's feat is not possible, and they mock it. Zhuangzi demonstrates a way beyond this conflict of perspectives:

> What do these two little creatures know? A small consciousness [*xiao zhi*] cannot keep up with a vast consciousness [*da zhi*]; short duration cannot keep up with long duration. How do we know? The morning mushroom knows nothing of the noontide; the winter cicada knows nothing of the spring and autumn. This is what is meant by short duration. In southern Chu, there is a tree called Mingling, for which five hundred years is as a single spring, and another five hundred years is as a single autumn. In ancient times, there was even one massive tree whose spring and autumn were each eight thousand years long. And yet nowadays, Pengzu alone has a special reputation for longevity, and everyone tries to match him. Pathetic, isn't it?
>
> (Zhuangzi 2009: 4)[2]

Like mocking the Peng bird, imitating the legendary Pengzu is absurd precisely because it fails to account for the fact that duration (or height) is only a matter of perspective and therefore must be understood contextually. In other words, one long-lived being is short-lived in relation to other longer-lived beings. Similarly, the difference between smaller and greater knowledge means that consciousness can always be shown to be narrow or lacking from some further perspective. It is for this reason – and this is one of the great teachings of Taoism that harmonizes with the equanimous view – that we are always (somewhere) in the middle. Indeed, our occupation of the mobile middle becomes a marker of human presence, and here we may recur to Nietzsche, who refers to the fundamental "perspectival character of existence" (Nietzsche 1974: 336). We know we are present to the extent that we know the places from which we view and the perspectives they furnish us. By being multiply and fluently attuned to the world, with an equanimous mind, we better grasp the world's multiplicity and appreciate its seeming contradictions, the diverging perspectives it calls forth. William Blake, in a memorable verse, offers a felicitous summary of the power of equanimity: "To see a World in a Grain of Sand / And a Heaven in a Wild Flower / Hold Infinity in the palm of your hand / And Eternity in an hour" (Blake 1972: 431).

Goethe's delicate empiricism

In 1786, poet and author Johann Wolfgang von Goethe departed Weimar in haste, not disclosing his itinerary from fear of being called back, and journeyed to Italy in order to satisfy, he wrote, his "burning thirst for true art".[3] There was an imperative nature to this journey into the aesthetic world since Goethe hoped it would be both physically and morally restorative.[4] In Rome, he connected and stayed with the painter Wilhelm Tischbein, who resided with two other painters, and he circulated among many other artists. Goethe immersed himself in the study of landscape and figure drawing with the young Swiss painter Heinrich Meyer. Drawn to Naples by an eruption of Vesuvius, Goethe, along with Tischbein, documented the natural event in the company of other new friends, the German landscape painters Christoph Heinrich Kniep, who became Goethe's personal draftsman and close friend, and Jacob Philipp Hackert. Upon his return to Germany in 1788, armed with what Merleau-Ponty has called "the painter's question", Goethe began earnestly reading Newton's treatise on color. The painter's question, Merleau-Ponty explains:

> is not a question asked of someone who doesn't know by someone who knows – the schoolmaster's question. The question comes from one who does not know, and it is addressed to a vision, a seeing, which knows everything and which we do not make, for it makes itself in us. [...] The painter lives in fascination. The actions most proper to him – those gestures, those paths which he alone can trace and which will be revelations to others (because the others do not lack what he lacks or in the same way) –to him they seem to emanate from the things themselves, like the

patterns of the constellations. Inevitably the roles between him and the visible are reversed. That is why so many painters have said that things look at them.

(Merleau-Ponty 1964: 167)

Goethe's groundbreaking method, as we will see, is one of openness, revelation, and receptivity involving acute appreciation for the role reversals that afford an optics combining the aesthetic and the scientific through a coincidence of subjective vision and objective reality. Reacting to what Ragupathy Venkatachalam, in this volume, calls "the treachery of models", Goethe set out to question, in his view, one particularly treacherous model – Newton's theory of color. Borrowing a case of optical equipment from a friend, Goethe would begin a study of color and optics spanning 20 years until, in 1810, he published *Zur Farbenlehre* (*Toward a Theory of Colors*), which, late in his life, he considered his most important work.[5] Dismissed by many scientists of his own era, Goethe's theory of color contested the dominant paradigm found in Newton's mechanistic understanding of light.[6] Goethe was convinced that there exists a greater affinity between art and nature than between science and nature, and, in contrast to Newtonian science, nature can never be forced to answer our preconceived questions but rather it is to its own voice that we must listen in order to formulate more questions. Through what he would call a "delicate" empirical science, Goethe demonstrated that the ever-changing forms of nature could become preeminently instructive and find compelling use in art theory and beyond.

The striking differences between Newton's *Optics* and Goethe's *Farbenlehre* are immediately apparent. Newton, by his methodological premises, reduces color to the relations of primary qualities in order to elucidate it. His text concerns isolated components such as angles of refraction and paths of light, not the shifting phenomenology of color. For Goethe, however, color is approached *as given*: for example, perceived polarities of tone, of brightness and darkness, of saturation. While Newton attempts to understand color in a reductionist manner, Goethe is performing a flexible examination of immediate appearances that Edmund Husserl would, some hundred years later, term "descriptive morphology". Prior to Husserl's formulation of the epistemological principles of such a science, Goethe had already begun to practice it (in fact, it was he who coined the word "morphology"). To know something via isolated facts about it, Goethe suggests, amounts to a limited form of knowledge that offers at best a partial account of phenomena, especially natural ones.

"The totality of our so-called knowledge or beliefs", W.V. O. Quine reminds us, "is a man-made fabric which impinges on reality only along the edges" (Quine 1953: 42). Goethe's manner of seeing the universe balances the aesthetic or imaginative and the scientific by attending to the edges *and*, vitally, to the center, appreciating the inner and outer forms and movements embodying the phenomenal – in the double sense of perceptible and extraordinary – world. When Goethe studied law in Strasbourg from April 1770 to August 1771, he was struck by the city's magnificent Gothic cathedral, which from 1647 to 1847 was the world's tallest building. Despite suffering from vertigo, Goethe climbed the tower in order to observe the cathedral from yet one more possible perspective. Before leaving the university, he remarked to some friends that, in his view, the tower as it stood seemed incomplete, a departure from what he imagined to be the original architectural plan. When sketches he produced of what he envisioned a tower built to the original specifications would look like were compared to the cathedral's original plans, it turned out that Goethe's suspicions were precisely confirmed. When asked how he could possibly know the original plan, since this was not by any means common knowledge, Goethe remarked that the tower itself had revealed its secret to him.[7] To see imaginatively in this way is, as John Shotter puts it so well, to "win an insight into the inner formative movements responsible for the emergence of such forms into existence by sensing within ourselves – from within our relations to them – the differential responses such movements occasion in us" (Shotter 2005: 136). Precisely in these differential responses, and through the relations they open up, resides our capacity to see, as it were, from the inside out. Here also resides our potential, as Goethe urged, to understand our place in the dynamic whole. Without this imaginative faculty of cognition, we are liable only to see from the outside in, a kind of logical looking that imperils its subject, as Wordsworth knew so well when he wrote: "Sweet is the lore which Nature brings; / Our meddling intellect / Mis-shapes the beauteous forms of things:– / We murder to dissect" (Wordsworth 2013: ll. 25–28).

Contrary to the deadliness of intellectual dissection, which must proceed from the outside to the inside, stands Goethe's "delicate empiricism" (*zarte Empirie*), the term he favored to describe a mode of inquiry, an optics of knowledge, that "makes itself utterly identical with the object, thereby becoming true theory", and, he adds, marks an "enhancement of our mental powers belong[ing] to a highly evolved age" (Goethe 1995: 307). One way to understand the "evolved" nature of this approach to the knowable world involves appreciating Goethe's departure from any disengaged, abstract theory belonging to traditional scientific inquiry while bearing in mind the central ancient Greek meanings of theory (*theorein*: to look at) as a sort of cognitive apprehending or contemplation of the cosmos. Theory, in this sense, is predicated upon what Goethe called higher contemplation or perception (*höhere Anshauung*). To engage with the world in order to know it depends upon deep mutuality and identity:

> Man knows himself only to the extent that he knows the world; he becomes aware of himself only within the world, and aware of the world only within himself. Every new object, well contemplated, opens up a new organ of perception in us.
>
> (Goethe 1995: 39)

The emphasis here on the interiority of vision and mimesis suggests that, while primacy is given to perception, such empiricism is "delicate" to the extent that it opens itself anew to each object and, in the process, enhances the observer's direct and mobile awareness. For Goethe, such a dynamic looking is a kind of humility toward the object, an affirmation of nature as something sacred: "Natural objects should be sought and investigated as they are and not to suit observers, but respectfully as if they were divine beings".[8]

This "as if" mode of study, by suspending our preconceptions, allows for the kind of respect that characterizes the attitude informing an optics of equanimity generally. Equanimity helps us to become transparent instruments of seeing and knowing and does so most successfully in the context of preserving the reciprocity inherent in all relationships. Goethe emphasizes the geniality of balancing self and nature: "It is a pleasurable practice to examine nature and self at the same time without doing violence to the spirit of either, but rather to balance them both through a gentle exchange of their reciprocal influence".[9] This equanimous, balanced perspective, practiced in non-interfering relation to self and other, is a form of attention that corresponds to Goethe's notion of authentic theorizing. "For simply to look at a thing cannot get us any further", he writes; "rather", he continues, "every act of looking [*Ansehen*] becomes observation [*Betrachten*], every act of observing becomes contemplation [*Sinnen*], every contemplation is an act of connecting [*Verknüpfen*]; therefore, one can say that, with every attentive glance at the world, we are already theorizing".[10] The progression here from looking to observing to contemplating and, finally, to connecting is one of increasing involvement on the part of the observer, one that issues in the essential unity of observer and observed. Subject and object are not two but participate in a wider process joining them in interdependency. When the early German psychiatrist Johann Christian Heinroth (1773–1843) suggested that employing this processural and participatory thinking resulted in a new kind of concrete or "objective thinking [*gegenständliches Denken*]", Goethe was decidedly approving:

> Here he means that my thinking is not separate from the objects; that the elements of the object, the perceptions of the object, flow into my thinking and are fully permeated by it; that my perception itself is a way of thinking, and my thinking a perception.
>
> (Goethe 1988: 39)

To think "objectively" is a continual rediscovery of the object in the multiple ways that "the manifestation of a phenomenon is not detached from the observer – it is caught up and entangled in his individuality".[11]

Perception, in Goethean inquiry, flows; it is animated, resonant; it moves with rather than against, in a spirit of openness. Its imaginative dynamism distinguishes it from "the gloomy empirical-mechanical-dogmatic torture chamber" of Baconian and Newtonian science.[12] Goethe's careful studies of architecture, color and light, comparative anatomy, meteorology, geology, and botany are all marked by a kind of equanimity of vision, a balancing between Aristotelian precision and Platonic intuition. For Goethe, equanimity avoids the possibility of two extreme relations to existence, both, he suggests, inimical to inquiry: on one hand, the collapse of difference into a mystical oneness and, on the other hand, the utter fragmentation of existence into isolated monads. "Everything that exists", writes Goethe,

> is an analogy for the whole of existence; for this reason, being [*das Dasein*] strikes us at one and the same time as separate and interconnected. Pursue the analogy too far, and everything coalesces and becomes identical. Avoid the analogy, and everything degenerates into infinite particulars. In both cases, contemplation falters – on the one hand there is an excess of vitality, on the other a deadness.[13]

Equanimity makes an appearance here as a form of contemplation allowing the observer to steer between an attention to concrete particularities and a holistic imagination. Whether Goethe was contemplating the plan of the Cathedral of Our Lady of Strasbourg, the intermaxillary bones of humans compared to those of animals, the experience of color, mineral formations, or the morphology of seeds and plants, he recognized that forms of knowledge exist only in dialectical interrelation with their objects. So, the conventional ways we investigate and describe the inanimate world – counting, weighing, measuring, for example – that require things to be divided into separate, self-contained bits of reality are not appropriate for living things whose fragmentation would mean nothing less than their extinction. For Goethe, the basis of economics in credit provides a salient example of such extinction: "As soon as the ideal makes a demand on the real, it in the end consumes it and also itself. Thus credit (paper money) consumes silver and its own self" (Goethe 1998: 37).

Delicate empiricism thus amounts to a subtle balancing act where, by accepting the perceived object on its own terms, it is allowed to act upon the observer. Though it can be non-interfering, knowledge can never be a strictly passive event in the sense that a dynamic interaction with the world is instated as soon as we appreciate that nothing is ever really at rest. For this reason, our knowledge of the world must itself always be in process. Describing how our knowledge of the world takes shape, Goethe employed two key terms – *Gestalt* and *Bildung* – which he explained as follows:

> The German has the word *Gestalt* for the complex of existence of an actual being. He abstracts with this expression, from the moving, and assumes a congruous whole to be determined, completed, and fixed in its character. But if we consider *Gestalts* generally, especially organic ones, we find that independence, rest, termination nowhere appear, but everything fluctuates rather in continuous motion. Our speech is

> accustomed to use, therefore, the word *Bildung* appertaining to both what has been brought forth and the process of bringing-forth. If we would introduce a morphology, we ought not to speak of the *Gestalt* at all, or if we do use the word, should think thereby only of an abstraction – a notion of something held fast in experience but for an instant. What has been formed is immediately transformed again, and if we would succeed, to some degree, to a living view of Nature, we must attempt to remain as active and as plastic as the example she sets for us.
>
> (Goethe 1995: 63–64)

Equanimity, I wish to suggest, is another way of describing this "living view", this plasticity of knowledge that mimics its objects. However useful *Gestalten* may be for the purposes of explaining or grasping something, we realize that they give way to *Bildungen* that may turn out to be momentary *Gestalten* for the ongoing formation of more *Bildungen*. We are always in the middle of, borrowing Freud's famous phrase, an *unendliche Analyse*, an interminable analysis of the world around us.[14] The operative metaphor here is that of plant morphology: an elementary seed gives rise to a complex living organism. It unfolds from the bottom up, from the inside out or, if you will, it reverses symbolically the reductive, analytic gaze to the holistic panorama. Goethe regards nature as a living whole, always in systolic-diastolic movement, exhibiting "life and development from an unknown center toward an unknowable periphery" (Goethe 1995: 43). In Kant's *Critique of Judgment*, Goethe found philosophical precedent for paralleling art and nature since both are never required to act purposively: "Nature and art are too big to be harnessed to purposes, and they also do not need them since relations [*Bezüge*] are everywhere, and relations are life".[15]

For Goethe, the shape and appearance of plants and their seeds offered the finest image of natural transformation and vital relation requiring a plasticity of mind that equals them. Goethe's first major work on the problem of developing a descriptive morphology, his *Metamorphosis of Plants* (1790), sets out with a simple question: how is it that all plants look like plants? Goethe started arranging and comparing plants, for example their stem-leaves, using a graded series in an attempt to find the rudimentary plan for all vegetal form. What he discovered was movement, metamorphosis persisting through the whole range of plant organs such that it is impossible to declare where one organ begins and another ceases. Through a careful process of descriptive morphology, it eventually appeared that all surface vegetal forms were nothing but metamorphs of a single underlying form, a transformation of the leaf. In his meticulous study of natural form, Goethe wanted to understand nature in terms of its becoming (*Werden*), and he found that its rich complexity, striking in its singularities, required models of movement and relationality to do it real justice. Equanimity in this sense means turning attention from static singularities to the transformations leading to and from them, and further to reflections of the generative field of movement itself.

Equanimity, through special resonance with the experiential world, understands it as pure movement. The germination of a seed and its development into a plant, from an equanimous perspective, is all one movement. Anything taken to be separate is just an instant of a continual process. A seed, as one form a plant takes, harbors the shapes of the protean leaf. Goethe suggests that, attuned to movement and change,

> we will not fail to recognize the leaf form in seed vessels – regardless of their manifold formations, their particular purpose and context. Thus, for example, the pod may be viewed as a single folded leaf with its edges grown together, husks as consisting of leaves grown more over one another, and compound capsules may be understood as several leaves united round a central point with their inner sides open toward one another and their edges joined.
>
> (Goethe 1995: 88)

A seed cannot be said to be "in movement" since it is movement that constitutes the seed that appears to us. It is nothing but movement, and so, we might say, is everything else or, as the *I Ching* puts it: "Nothing is absolutely at rest; rest is merely an intermediate state of movement, or latent movement" (*I Ching or Book of Changes* 1989: 282). Our consonance with the phenomenal world requires that, as David Bohm observes, we "be sensitive to the eternally changing differences that are actually to be observed within each thing, and to the unceasing emergence of new similarities and relationships across the boundaries of various things" (Bohm 1988: 101).

Knowledge, as we have seen in the example of Goethean science, is a mode of unceasing attunement, an opening to the emergence of new appearances that would otherwise be foreclosed in the absence of mimesis or the presence of stasis. In place of the abstract *Gestalt*, Goethe sought to engage the experience of transformation itself, placing before his inner eye the metamorphic sequences he encountered in nature, running them like a film, forward and then backwards. He was so successful, Ronald Brady mentions, that at one point in his researches Goethe consulted a physician about the images he saw whenever he shut his eyes. His meditations were apparently so vivid that the moving pictures he had conjured up in his contemplations sometimes refused to fade away. Only through the fluid contemplation of forms in motion, Goethe discovered, do the static forms reveal what their stasis otherwise conceals.[16] This is the mobile optics of equanimity that is succinctly captured in *The Book of Lieh-Tzu*'s citation of the sage Kuan-yin: "If nothing within you stays rigid, / Outward things will disclose themselves. / Moving, be like water. / Still, be like a mirror. / Respond like an echo" (*The Book of Lieh-Tzu: A Classic of Tao* 1990: 90).

Equanimity frames knowing as a process of dynamic questioning, even when, following philosophers Deleuze and Guattari, the answer might otherwise appear fully satisfactory or rhetorically self-evident: "To the answer already contained in a question...one should respond with questions from another answer" (*A Thousand Plateaus* 1987: 110). The presence of equanimity denies us the sense that the answers we are inclined to hold, or content to rest in, are anything more than initial paths toward further knowledge. It is only with more ways of knowing that something truly worthwhile can be approached, as in the Sufi proverb "I ask about the sky, but the answer is about a rope" (Shah 2015: 181).

Zen understandings

There was a great Japanese master of the 15th century named Ikkyu, who spent long periods as a hermit in the mountains, while, at other times, it appears, the best place to find him might be in a sake shop or a brothel. One famous story about him is that he put up a notice, beside a very gnarled, contorted pine tree in front of his house, that read, "I, Ikkyu, will pay 100 yen to anyone who can see this tree straight". Soon people crowded around the tree, lying on the ground, balancing on their heads, craning their necks and gazing at it from multiple angles, and yet no one discovered any way of seeing the tree with a straight trunk. A young boy, however, went to see Ikkyu's friend Rosen, who was a priest of another sect, and asked him, "What about Master Ikkyu's tree?" "Oh", said Rosen, "it is perfectly simple. You go tell him that the answer to seeing the tree straight is to look straight at it". So, the boy returned to Ikkyu, and said, "I claim the award. You see the trunk straight by looking straight at it". And Ikkyu gave the boy a quizzical look, and handed over the handsome sum of 100 yen, saying, "I think you have been talking to Rosen down the street".[17] One key take-away here is that getting caught up in technique, you never see the world straight. Instead, you must *just look*, interacting with the world as non-coercive agent and receptor. Stepping out of loops of re-cognizing, and moving from automatization to an equanimous view of reality where strictly rational techniques are abandoned is to eschew the rigidity – the "prison" – of conceptual or theoretical representations and move toward a distilled, self-evident, contextual, direct knowing of the thing. Consistent with central Zen approaches to knowing, Goethe insisted again and again that scientists must learn to see directly and receptively instead of imposing their assumptions upon the world.[18]

Philosopher Hilary Putnam, in his *Realism with a Human Face*, points out that theorizing about the world depends upon the concepts we use to think about the world, and these concepts "cut the world up" in some one particular way.[19] This is the state of conceptual relativity in which we live our everyday lives. Yet, the world itself, as a reality considered independently of these concepts, never determines any *single* way of "cutting things up". There cannot be a single true description of a completely independent reality – as the metaphysical realist insists – since the world does not determine unitary answers to basic ontological questions independently of our mobile conceptual assumptions, flexible as they are due to the implicit, practical understandings we have about the world in which we are moving around. The preconditions of our theoretical practices in general are, as Goethe knew, tied to the activities of skillful looking that give us access to the world. Alva Noë contends that we find out how things are by exploring how they appear such that the same experience of an object contains within it the possibility of multiple readings.[20] Equanimity meets the world through exploration: "To explore appearance is thus to explore the environment, the world. [...] The process of perceiving, of finding out how things are, is a process of meeting the world; it is an activity of skillful exploration" (Noë 2004: 164).

Rational concepts, in their crude reductionism, are singularly inadequate to the task of presenting the world just as it is – moving, changing. Miguel de Unamuno declares man "the prisoner of logic" in these unsparing terms: "The mind seeks what is dead, for the living escapes it. It seeks to congeal the flowing stream into blocks of ice... everything rational is anti-vital" (Miguel de Unamuno 1972: 100–01). Schopenhauer, like other 19th century thinkers and artists, saw the fatal fissure, symptomatic of illusion (delusion?), at the very core of human existence: "merely to think is to be self-deceived", as Terry Eagleton sums it up (Eagleton 1990: 155). When objects and concepts are disunified, there is, however, the potential for humor, a kind of joy that arises at the expense of purely rational understanding. Perception, writes Schopenhauer, here indebted to the Buddhist tradition:

> is the medium of the present, of enjoyment and cheerfulness; moreover, it is not associated with any exertion. With thinking the opposite holds good; it is the second power of knowledge, whose exercise always requires some, often considerable, exertion; and it is the concepts of thinking that are so often opposed to the satisfaction of our immediate desires, since, as the medium of the past, of the future, and what is serious, they act as the vehicle of our fears, our regrets, and all our cares. It must therefore be delightful for us to see this strict, untiring, and most troublesome governess, our faculty of reason, for once convicted of inadequacy. Therefore, on this account the mien or appearance of laughter is very closely related to that of joy.
>
> (Schopenhauer 1969: 98)

To convict reason of inadequacy, to recognize the ways in which being immured in logic leads only to what Unamuno called the essence of tragedy – "this battle of life against reason" (Miguel de Unamuno 1972: 101) – is to hope to find, in comedy, the joyous apprehensions of our intellectual finitude. Kōshō Uchiyama (1912–1999), who taught Zen at Antaiji Temple in Kyoto, favored the phrase *atamano tebanashi,* "opening the hand of thought", to describe just this hope. To open the hand of thought is to stop granting force or effect to the incessant instrumentality of thought as grasper or grasped: "When we think of something, we grasp it with our minds. If we open the hand of thought, it drops away" (Uchiyama 2004: 141). Similarly, the Tang dynasty Zen Master Xuefeng Yicun (Hsueh-Feng, 822–908) told a monk, "empty handed I leave home, and empty handed I return" (Bunyu 1982: 422). The essence of this state of what is sometimes called "non-abiding" is explained by the 16th-century Zen Master Takuan, in *The Marvelous Record of Immovable Wisdom,* in these terms:

> From the stopping mind arises the mind of attachment.... This stopping mind forms the bonds of life and death. Looking at cherry blossoms and autumn leaves engenders the mind of looking at cherry blossoms and autumn leaves, but do not stop therein.... Whether seeing or hearing, the aim is not stopping the mind in a single place.
>
> (Bunyu 1982: 422)

The mind that stops is the mind that cannot laugh, cannot grow.

I'll close this section with a comic Zen story about growth and change, and then offer a commentary on it. The story goes like this: A priest was in charge of the garden within a well-known Zen temple. Because he loved the flowers, shrubs, and trees, he was given this particular duty. Next to the temple, there was another, smaller temple where there lived a very old Zen master. One morning, before the priest was to be visited by some special guests, he devoted extra time and care to tending the garden. He pulled the weeds, trimmed the shrubs, pruned tree branches, combed the moss, and spent a long time meticulously raking up and carefully arranging all the dry autumn leaves in neat piles. As he worked, the old master watched him with interest from across the wall that separated the two temples. When he had finished, the priest stood back to admire his work. "Isn't it beautiful now", he exclaimed to the old master. "Indeed, it is", replied the old master. "But there is something not quite right. If you'll help me over the wall, I'll put it right for you". Slightly taken aback, the priest agreed to help the old man over and set him down. Slowly, the master walked to a tree near the center of the garden, grabbed it by the trunk, and shook it hard. Leaves, orange, yellow, and brown, cascaded down over the garden. "There, that does it" said the old man, "you can put me back now".

The story turns on the old Zen master's "correction" or improvement of the priest's labor. Before describing some terms of the Zen corrective, let's look at the positive dimensions of the priest's gardening. First, the gardening is clearly a labor of love, borne of the priest's appreciation for natural elements – trees, shrubs, and flowers are specified – whose beauty can be enhanced by care and tending. Second, and relatedly, the priest's actions and his mind appear to be in sync. Indeed, he is given the temple duty of tending to the garden precisely because he loves what gardening produces. He is acting on his desires – to make things aesthetically pleasing and orderly as well as to impress his impending visitors – and in this he is apparently not blocked by such things as worry or fear; in short, he is not neurotically hampered, even if he is a bit obsessive in his raking. And, third, he is thorough and meticulous in his work. Gordon Allport noted that when Freud was once asked, "What should a normal person be able to do?" he replied, "He should be able to love and work" (Allport 1937: 275). Given the priest's industriousness and penchant for gardening, he appears patently normal. Yet, the old Zen master, looking over the wall, sees something more in the priest's activities.

Something more, rather than something other to be replaced: after observing the priest's labor and its conclusion, the master agrees that indeed something beautiful has been produced. The old master has observed another man creating order and beauty by imposing his will on nature with the activities of uprooting, trimming, pruning, combing, and raking. The question is then: what has the priest missed in his creation of beauty? The shaking of the tree, causing multi-colored leaves to cover the garden is, on one level, a reminder that nature is beautiful just as it is, in its disorder (leaves do not gather naturally into neat piles), its randomness, and its growth and decay according to its own timetable. More specifically, it is only from a certain point of view that nature appears disordered, random, or untimely. From the point of view of nature, however, everything is just as it is, and the Chinese word for nature – 自然, *zìrán* – meaning "that which happens of itself", in other words, a spontaneous happening, not under control or compulsion to be this or that, reminds us that there is inherently no necessity for things to turn out one way as opposed to another. So, on another level, the beauty the priest created was an imposition on nature, perhaps based on ideas that he held concerning perfection or what his imminent guests would consider a perfect garden to be like, and therefore the beauty, from the old master's perspective, was in effect halted or limited by the priest. By shaking the tree, and recovering the garden with leaves, the master demonstrates that efforts to shape the spontaneous growth and change of nature in one direction actually stop the whole process. The Zen master, with a good shake, simply restarted it.

So, in this sense, the priest had not gone far enough in his tending to the garden, that is, in the old master's view, he did not understand that the work of tending is never complete, since there is no final mastery over the vicissitudes of nature. The Zen master, looking over the wall to survey the miniature world of the garden, is seeing with the eyes of equanimity, rooted in an understanding that true vision of the world involves keeping pace with life's constant growth. To draw a line and declare that one has "got it all", that one has put it all aright, is to oppose the fabric and structure of existence itself. Within equanimity resides an understanding that vitality is maintained by evolving in concert with the world, as seeds, plants, and the seasons do. This then is the most interesting aspect of the story because the Zen master "puts it right" by messing it up, by ruining one image of beauty by creating another. Equanimity accommodates different perspectives toward the same object and has therefore a certain playfulness and spontaneity that often cuts against the seriousness, the work, that conventionally defines our lives. It avoids a conflict between consciousness (e. g., ideas about what beauty is) and nature, between the desire for order and the reality of flux. The Zen master sees the futility of these self-created wars since he recognizes that such conflicts are really between two parts of the same thing. Alan Watts described quite well the vicious circle that results:

> when we fail to see that our life is change, we set ourselves against ourselves and become like Ouroboros, the misguided snake, who tries to eat his own tail. Ouroboros is the perennial symbol of all vicious circles, of every attempt to split our being asunder and make one part conquer the other.
>
> (Watts 1951: 43).

In its free-floating attending to what is, equanimity never tries to make sense out of life through fixation. Putting leaves into neat piles does not make sense out of change or disorder; rather, it merely provides the kind of "momentary stay against confusion" that Robert Frost once described. The liberation from "fixing" that equanimity provides allows for the freedom to dive into the pile of leaves, like few children can resist doing. The only way to understand change is to plunge into it, to go with it, to tend in its direction at any given moment. The question is not whether the world is changing but whether the mind is moving with the change. This problem of whether the mind moves was illustrated in the well-known Zen story of the two monks who were watching a flag flapping in the wind. One monk commented that the flag is moving, while the other replied that the wind is moving. Their teacher (none other than The Sixth Patriarch, Zen Master Huineng) overheard them and intervened, observing that neither the flag nor the wind is moving but the mind is. The teacher transports the monks to a third, more capacious understanding: the mind that is moving is the one that embraces both perspectives – the wind is moving and the flag is moving – and a moving mind accommodates the inner reality of knowing without fixing, without declaring it is one thing as opposed to another. When we tend to our changing realities with an equanimous mind, we are free to respond immediately and appropriately rather than in contrived, defensive, discriminatory, or forced ways. Although such responding is never finished, as the master dramatized for the priest when he shook the tree, its roots in humility, naturalness, and spontaneity transform it from something like work into something more like play. The 14th-century Persian poet Hafiz once said that our difference from the saints is that we think we still have "a thousand serious moves" (Hafiz 2006: 127).

Conclusion: equanimity as optics

Equanimity is a dynamic and holistic way of seeing – understanding – the world. The equanimous mind always moves beyond the limits of logic. Through a flexible experience of the whole, connections between multiple objects of attention may be apprehended with a directness and freshness that more habitual modes of knowing tend to fracture. When binary and linear ways of thinking customarily split and channel our experience of the world, we forfeit the wholeness that is the essential nature of what can be seen. If naturally by looking over things, we realize that we are nothing other than the world's way of revealing itself to itself, then there is also the opportunity to understand how the world in a sense wants to reveal itself. Deeply, aesthetically engaged with the world around him, Goethe grasped that, for the world to reveal itself, to be observed in its fullness, the observer must be attuned to it to the point not just of familiarity or intimacy, but of resemblance and identity. The basic idea here, Neoplatonic in nature, is that only like can know like. Goethe, in a poetic epigram that begins "if the eye were not sun-like, it could not see the sun" (Goethe 1964: 282) alludes to a famous passage from Plotinus's *Enneads* (I.6.9): "To any vision must be brought an eye adapted to what is to be seen, and having some likeness to it. Never did an eye see the sun unless it had first become sun-like". William Blake echoes this imagery in the frontispiece of his poem "The Gates of Paradise": "The Sun's Light when he unfolds it / Depends on the Organ that beholds it" (Blake 1972: 760). If what we see depends on what we in a sense mimetically bring to it, then genuine truth and knowledge emerge only from the vital harmony between mind and world, an evenness marked above all by ways of relating and resembling engendered by equanimity (L. *aequus*, "equal" + *animus*, "mind"). Every object of knowledge, in a single moment, opens up a new possibility for its perception. And to keep pace with our objects of knowledge – knowing how to "go on" with them, as Ludwig Wittgenstein would say[21] – requires that the optics of our minds remains limpid, lithe.

Notes

1 Joseph Gabel, *False Consciousness: An Essay on Reification*, trans. Margaret A. Thompson (New York: Harper & Row, 1975), p. 79. For an excellent synopsis and contextualization of Gabel's key theoretical concepts, see Alan Sica, "Gabel's 'Micro/Macro' Bridge: The Schizophrenic Process Writ Large," *Sociological Theory* 13.1 (1995), pp. 66–99.

2 Cf. Chuang-Tzu, *The Inner Chapters*, trans. A. C. Graham (Indianapolis, IN: Hackett Publishing, 2001), p. 44.

3 Albert Bielchowsky, *The Life of Goethe* (New York: Putman, 1905), p. 413. This moment in Goethe's life is captured by Daan Hoekstra, "The Artist's Study of Nature and its Relationship to Goethean Science," *Janus Head* 10.1 (2007), pp. 329–349.

4 "The chief aim of my journey," Goethe wrote in 1788, "was to cure myself of the evils, both physical and moral in nature, which annoyed me in Germany, and to satisfy my burning thirst for true art" (Bielchowsky, *Life of Goethe*, p. 413).

5 See "Conversations with Eckermann," 1 February 1827, 19 February 1829 (J. W. von Goethe, *Gedenkausgabe der Werke, Briefe und Gesprache*, ed. Ernst Beutler [Zurich: Artemis, 1948ff.], XXIV, pp. 236, 328). On the significance of the theory of color for Goethe, see Albrecht Schöne, *Goethes Farbentheologie* (Munich: Beck, 1987). Indeed, Goethe reacted to Newton's treachery of models by pointing out that the latter, with respect to optics, had "tyrannicised the whole field in a completely anti-Baconian manner" (see "To Schiller," 10 February 1798

[*Gedenkausgabe*, XX, p. 524]). In a lecture he gave in 1932 before the Saxon Academy of Science, Werner Heisenberg framed the reaction this way:

> The renouncing of life and immediacy, which was the premise for the progress of natural science since Newton, formed the real basis for the bitter struggle which Goethe waged against the physical optics of Newton. It would be superficial to dismiss this struggle as unimportant: there is much significance in one of the most outstanding men directing all his efforts to fighting against the development of Newtonian optics

(see Ernst Lehrs, *Man or Matter* [London: Faber and Faber, 1951], p. 24). For studies of Goethe's rejection of Newton, see Frederick Burwick, *The Damnation of Newton: Goethe's Color Theory and Romantic Perception* (New York: De Gruyter, 1986); Hartmut Schönherr, *Einheit und Werden: Goethes Newton-Polemik als systematische Konsequenz seiner Naturkonzeption* (Würzburg: Königshausen und Neumann, 1993); and Dennis L. Sepper, *Goethe contra Newton: Polemics and the New Project for a Science of Color* (Cambridge: Cambridge University Press, 1988).

6 Importantly, Goethe's color theory has received much recent attention from scholars seeking, more generally, a science of qualities sensitive to human participation in the phenomenal world; see, for example, Craig Holdrege, "Doing Goethean Science," *Janus Head* 8.1 (2005), pp. 27–52; David Seamon and Arthur Zajonc (eds.), *Goethe's Way of Science* (New York: SUNY Press, 1998); and John Shotter, "Goethe and the Refiguring of Intellectual Inquiry: From 'Aboutness'-Thinking to 'Withness'-Thinking in Everyday Life," *Janus Head* 8.1 (2005), pp. 132–158.

7 For the perhaps apocryphal story, see Hans Gebert, "About Goetheanistic Science," *Journal of Anthroposophy* 29 (Spring 1979), pp. 45–46; and the stimulating discussion of the story in Gary Lachman, *Lost Knowledge of the Imagination* (Edinburgh: Floris Books, 2017), p. 60.

8 Goethe, "Cautions for the Observer," in Rupprecht Matthaei (ed.), *Goethe's Color Theory* (New York: Van Nostrand Reinhold, 1971), p. 57; my emph.

9 Goethe, *Maximen und Reflexion* [Maxims and Reflections]. In vol. 12 of *Werke* (Hamburger Ausgabe) (Munich: deutscher Taschenbuch Verlag, 1982), #500, p. 434; my trans.

10 Goethe, "Vorwort," *Zur Farbenlehre. Didaktischer Teil* (1808). In vol. 13 of *Werke* (Hamburger Ausgabe) (Munich: deutscher Taschenbuch Verlag, 1982), p. 317; my trans.

11 Goethe, *Scientific Studies*, p. 307. For a fine reading of Goethe's ecological understanding of optics, whose central thesis of the interaction of phenomena, perception, and agents accords well with the meaning and practice of equanimity, see Heather I. Sullivan, "The Ecology of Color: Goethe's Materialist Optics and Ecological

> Posthumanism," in Serenella Iovino and Serpil Oppermann (eds.), *Material Ecocriticism* (Bloomington: Indiana University Press, 2014), pp. 80–94; and her "Goethe's Colors: Revolutionary Optics and the Anthropocene," *Eighteenth-Century Studies* 51.1 (fall 2017), pp. 115–124.

12 Goethe, vol. 34 of *Sämtliche Werke: Jubiläums-Ausgabe*, ed. Eduard von der Hellen, 40 vols. (Stuttgart/Berlin: Cotta, 1902–1912), p. 64. English translation in Goethe, *Maxims and Reflections*, trans. Elisabeth Stopp, ed. Peter Hutchinson (London: Penguin, 1998), #430, p. 55. For a discussion of Bacon's vision of the interrogation and control of nature and some responses to it, including Goethe's, in the history and development of scientific methodology, see Carolyn Merchant, "The Scientific Revolution and the Death of Nature," *Isis* 97.3 (2006), pp. 513–533.

13 For the English (which I have slightly modified), see Martin Swales and Erika Swales, *Reading Goethe: A Critical Introduction to the Literary Work* (Rochester: Camden House, 2002), p. 13. See also Goethe, *Maxims and Reflections*, #554, pp. 73–74.

14 Freud's notion that analysis is *unendliche* (interminable) expresses an openness to the future, a position more consistent with Goethe's than previously acknowledged, for the idea here is all that analysis can do is to "decide" its own provisional end; it can never celebrate the discovery of a definitive truth rescued from oblivion. See Sigmund Freud, "Analysis Terminable and Interminable," *The Standard Edition* (1964) 23: 216–53; see also his "Constructions in Analysis," *The Standard Edition* (1964) 23: 257–269.

15 Goethe, Letter to Zelter, 29 January, 1830, in *Briefe, 1821–1832*, vol. 4 of *Briefe* (Hamburger Ausgabe), ed. Karl Robert Mandelkow (Munich: C. H. Beck, 2013), p. 370.

16 See Ronald Brady, "Goethe's Natural Science: Some Non-Cartesian Meditations, in *Toward a Man-Centered Medical Science*, ed. Karl E. Schaefer, Herbert Hensel, and Ronald Brady (Mt. Kisco, NY: Futura Publishing Company, 1977), pp. 137–165.

17 The story is in Alan Watts, *Zen and the Beat Way* (Boston: Tuttle Publishing, 1997), p. 71; I borrow Watts's lively dialogue in the retelling here.

18 This is the integration of what Maslow has called experiential and spectator knowledge; see Abraham Maslow, *The Psychology of Science: A Reconnaissance* (New York: Harper & Row, 1966), pp. 45–65.

19 See Hilary Putnam, *Realism with a Human Face* (Cambridge, MA: Harvard University Press, 1990). My reading of Putnam here, which I have modified in relation to the insights of Alva Noë, is indebted to R. Lanier Anderson, "Truth and Objectivity in Perspectivism," *Synthese* 115.1 (1998), pp. 1–32.

20 See Alva Noë, "Experience without the Head," in *Perceptual Experience*, ed. Tamar Szabó Gendler and John Hawthorne (Oxford: Oxford University Press), pp. 411–434.

21 See, especially, Ludwig Wittgenstein, *Remarks on the Philosophy of Psychology*, 2 vols. (Oxford: Blackwell, 1980), I, no. 875; *Philosophical Investigations* (Oxford: Blackwell, 1953), nos. 154–155.

References

Alberti, Leon Battista (1966) *On Painting*, trans. John R. Spencer, New Haven, CT, Yale University Press.

Allport, Gordon W. (1937) *Personality: A Psychological Interpretation*, New York, Holt.

Anderson, R. Lanier (1998) "Truth and Objectivity in Perspectivism," *Synthese* 115.1, pp. 1–32.

Bielchowsky, Albert (1905) *The Life of Goethe*, New York, Putman.

Blake, William (1972) *Complete Writings*, ed. Geoffrey Keynes, Oxford, Oxford University Press.

Bohm, David (1988) *On Creativity*, ed. Lee Nichol, New York, Routledge.

Brady, Ronald (1977) "Goethe's Natural Science: Some Non-Cartesian Meditations, in *Toward a Man-Centered Medical Science*, ed. Karl E. Schaefer, Herbert Hensel, and Ronald Brady, Mt. Kisco, New York, Futura Publishing Company, pp. 137–65.

Bruner, Jerome S. and Goodman, Cecile C. (1947) "Value and Need as Organizing Factors in Perception," *The Journal of Abnormal and Social Psychology* 42.1, pp. 33–44.

Bunyu, Kusumoto (1982) *Zengo Nyumon* [An Introduction to Zen Words and Phrases], trans. Michael Sōru Ruymar, Tokyo, Daihorin-kaku.

Burwick, Frederick (1986) *The Damnation of Newton: Goethe's Color Theory and Romantic Perception*, New York, De Gruyter.

Chuang-Tzu (2001) *The Inner Chapters*, trans. A. C. Graham, Indianapolis, IN, Hackett Publishing.

Deleuze, Gilles and Guattari, Félix (1987) *A Thousand Plateaus: Capitalism and Schizophrenia*, trans. Brian Massumi, Minneapolis, University of Minnesota Press.

Eagleton, Terry (1990) *The Ideology of the Aesthetic*, Oxford, Blackwell.

Freud, Sigmund (1964) "Analysis Terminable and Interminable," in vol. 23 of *The Standard Edition*, London, Hogarth, pp. 216–53.

——— (1964) "Constructions in Analysis," in vol. 23 of *The Standard Edition*, London, Hogarth, pp. 257–269.

Gabel, Joseph (1975) *False Consciousness: An Essay on Reification*, trans. Margaret A. Thompson, New York, Harper & Row.

Gebert, Hans (1902–1912) *Sämtliche Werke: Jubiläums-Ausgabe*, ed. Eduard von der Hellen, 40 vols., Stuttgart/Berlin, Cotta.

——— (1979) "About Goetheanistic Science," *Journal of Anthroposophy* 29 (spring 1979), pp. 40–49.

Goethe, J. W. von (1948) *Gedenkausgabe der Werke, Briefe und Gesprache*, ed. Ernst Beutler [Zurich: Artemis, 1948ff.].

——— (1964) *Selected Verse*, ed. David Luke, New York, Penguin.

——— (1971) "Cautions for the Observer," in Rupprecht Matthaei (ed.), *Goethe's Color Theory*, New York, Van Nostrand Reinhold.

——— (1982) *Maximen und Reflexion* [Maxims and Reflections]. In vol. 12 of *Werke* (Hamburger Ausgabe), Munich, deutscher Taschenbuch Verlag.

——— (1982) "Vorwort," Zur Farbenlehre. Didaktischer Teil (1808). In vol. 13 of *Werke* (Hamburger Ausgabe, Munich, deutscher Taschenbuch Verlag.

——— (1988) "Significant Help Given by an Ingenious Turn of Phrase," In vol. 12 of Douglas Miller (ed. & trans.), *Goethe: The Collected Works*, pp. 39–41, Princeton, Princeton University Press.

——— (1995) *Scientific Studies*, in Douglas Miller (ed. & trans.), *Goethe: The Collected Works*, vol. 12, Princeton, Princeton University Press.

——— (1998) *Maxims and Reflections*, trans. Elisabeth Stopp, ed. Peter Hutchinson, London, Penguin.

——— (2013) *Briefe, 1821–1832*, vol. 4 of *Briefe* (Hamburger Ausgabe), ed. Karl Robert Mandelkow, Munich, C. H. Beck.

Hafiz (2006) *I Heard God Laughing: Poems of Hope and Joy*, trans. Daniel Ladinsky, New York, Penguin Books.

Hoekstra, Daan (2007) "The Artist's Study of Nature and its Relationship to Goethean Science," *Janus Head* 10.1, pp. 329–349.

Holdrege, Craig (2005) "Doing Goethean Science," *Janus Head* 8.1, pp. 27–52.

I Ching or Book of Changes (1989) trans. Richard Wilhelm, London, Penguin.Lachman, Gary (2017) *Lost Knowledge of the Imagination*, Edinburgh, Floris Books.

Lehrs, Ernst (1951) *Man or Matter*, London, Faber and Faber.

Maslow, Abraham (1966) *The Psychology of Science: A Reconnaissance*, New York, Harper & Row.

Merchant, Carolyn (2006) "The Scientific Revolution and the Death of Nature," *Isis* 97.3, pp. 513–533.

Merleau-Ponty, Maurice (1964) "Eye and Mind," *The Primacy of Perception*, Evanston, IL, Northwestern University Press, pp. 159–190.

Nietzsche, Friedrich (1967) *On the Genealogy of Morals*, trans. Walter Kaufman and R. J. Hollingdale, New York, Vintage.

——— (1974) *The Gay Science, with a Prelude in Rhymes and an Appendix of Songs*, trans. Walter Kaufmann, New York, Random House.

——— (1986) *Human, All Too Human: A Book for Free Spirits*, trans. R. J. Hollingdale., Cambridge, Cambridge University Press.

Noë, Alva (2004) *Action in Perception*, Cambridge, MA, MIT Press.

——— (2006) "Experience without the Head," in *Perceptual Experience*, ed. Tamar Szabó Gendler and John Hawthorne, Oxford, Oxford University Press, pp. 411–434.

Putnam, Hilary (1990) *Realism with a Human Face*, Cambridge, MA, Harvard University Press.

Quine, W. V. O. (1953) "Two Dogmas of Empiricism," in *From a Logical Point of View*, Cambridge, Cambridge University Press, pp. 20–46

Schöne, Albrecht (1987) *Goethes Farbentheologie*, Munich, Beck.

Schönherr, Hartmut (1993) *Einheit und Werden: Goethes Newton-Polemik als systematische Konsequenz seiner Naturkonzeption*, Würzburg, Königshausen und Neumann.

Schopenhauer, Arthur (1969) vol. 2 of *The World as Will and Representation*, trans. E. F. J. Payne, New York, Dover Publications.

Seamon, David and Zajonc, Arthur (eds.) (1998) *Goethe's Way of Science*, New York, SUNY Press.

Sepper, Dennis L. (1988) *Goethe contra Newton: Polemics and the New Project for a Science of Color*, Cambridge, Cambridge University Press.

Shah, Idries (2015) *Caravan of Dreams*, London, ISF Publishing.

Shotter, John (2005) "Goethe and the Refiguring of Intellectual Inquiry: From 'Aboutness'-Thinking to 'Withness'-Thinking in Everyday Life," *Janus Head* 8.1, pp. 132–158.

Sica, Alan (1995) "Gabel's 'Micro/Macro' Bridge: The Schizophrenic Process Writ Large," *Sociological Theory* 13.1, pp. 66–99.

Sullivan, Heather I. (2014) "The Ecology of Color: Goethe's Materialist Optics and Ecological Posthumanism," in Serenella Iovino and Serpil Oppermann (eds.), *Material Ecocriticism*, Bloomington, Indiana University Press, pp. 80–94.

——— (2017) "Goethe's Colors: Revolutionary Optics and the Anthropocene," *Eighteenth-Century Studies* 51.1 (fall 2017), pp. 115–124.

Swales, Martin and Swales, Erika (2002) *Reading Goethe: A Critical Introduction to the Literary Work*, Rochester, Camden House.

The Book of Lieh-Tzu: A Classic of Tao (1990) trans. A. C. Graham, New York, Columbia University Press.

Uchiyama, Kosho (2004) *Opening the Hand of Thought: Foundations of Zen Buddhist Practice*, ed. and trans. Tom Wright, Jisho Warner, and Shohaku Okumuro, Somerville, MA, Wisdom Publications.

Unamuno, Miguel de (1972) *The Tragic Sense of Life in Men and Nations*, trans. Anthony Kerrigan, ed. Anthony Kerrigan and Martin Nozick, Princeton, Princeton University Press.

Watts, Alan W. (1951) *Zen and the Beat Way*, Boston, Tuttle Publishing.

——— (1997) *The Wisdom of Insecurity: A Message for an Age of Anxiety*, New York, Vintage Books.

Wittgenstein, Ludwig (1953) *Philosophical Investigations*, Oxford, Blackwell.

——— (1980) *Remarks on the Philosophy of Psychology*, 2 vols., Oxford, Blackwell.

Wordsworth, William and Coleridge, Samuel Taylor (2013) *Lyrical Ballads: 1798 and 1802*, Oxford, Oxford University Press.

9 Economics, the plastic arts and social transformation

Sheila Dow

Introduction

In an era where the dominant discourse in economics has emphasised the separability of economics as a quantitative science, it might seem that the arts is one of the areas from which it is separated. Yet, the interrelations between economics and the arts are many, multidimensional and organic. It is the purpose here to explore these interrelations. Economics may be understood as being itself a plastic art in the sense of being addressed to transforming society. It seeks to guide government policy, the design and conduct of institutions and individual behaviour. Both economics and the arts are thus engaged, not only in creating understanding but also in challenging and disrupting existing understandings, all with a view to transforming reality.

The most direct relationship between economics and the arts is to consider the arts as an economic activity, i.e., a subject area suitable for economic analysis. From a mainstream perspective, the arts can be regarded in the same way as any other sector that requires input of labour time and raw materials and whose outputs may be given monetary values and be traded. Each sector has its own characteristics, warranting a distinct area of study, but generic economic analytical tools are applied to each. Even the activity of economics itself is subjected to a similar kind of analysis (the field of the economics of economics). Given the importance of the arts as an economic activity, its study has grown into the substantial field of cultural economics.[1] But it is generally treated as separable from the activity of economics itself in the same way as any other economic activity (such as generating energy, the subject matter of energy economics).[2]

This separation of the arts from other sectors is open to substantial challenge. But separation is a key characteristic of the mainstream approach to economics more generally, something to be discussed more fully below. The focus here will be on challenging the separation of the arts, not only from other economic activities but even more from the activity, and thus the substance, of economics.

Just as the arts provide subject matter for economics, economics provides subject matter for the arts, illuminating understanding of economic issues.

DOI: 10.4324/9781003105435-13

Therefore, we already see the separability being eroded, since economists consume the arts and thus acquire insights which were not provided by theorising within economics itself. Once the arts are involved in the construction and communication of economic knowledge the two become inextricably intertwined.

The arts may inform our economic understanding in three main ways. First, the arts may deal directly with economic issues. Thus, literature may deal with economic issues, as explored by Claire Pignol (Chapter 1, this volume) and Foteini Lika (Chapter 2, this volume). These contributions note that literature and economics can combine to create both realistic and ironic viewpoints of the world and its problems. Second, when comparing the arts and economics, the arts may provide metaphors to illuminate economics and economic theorising. Paintings by Escher and Magritte can give ideas on the incongruences economic modelling may bring forth (Venkatachalam, Chapter 5, this volume). Or, concepts from art theory on fragmentation and re-use can act as a guide on how to approach economic texts (Repapis, Chapter 6, this volume).

Third, the art of discourse plays a part, not only in economic activity but also in persuasion among economists, which in turn influences the path of development of the discipline and the world at large. McCloskey (1985) contributed to a revival of interest in the rhetoric of economics and how economists speak between themselves and also to the wider world. The choice of terms itself can persuade to accept a line of reasoning; the terms 'rational', 'natural' and 'equilibrium', for example, carry over favourable associations from other spheres. It is interesting to consider how these projections influence the viewpoint of the artist, and concepts of 'efficiency' and 'rationality' are becoming not economic but aesthetic criteria (Alifragkis, Chapter 4, this volume).

Knowledge systems are thus intertwined with the arts, such that the interrelations between economics and the arts are epistemological as well as real. We pursue these epistemological relations between economics and the arts here in order to explore the different ways in which economics is used in efforts to transform society. In particular, a contrast is drawn between transformation designed to mould society to conform more closely to an ideal model, and transformation which builds on particular understandings of real experience.

These differences stem from longstanding differences in approach to understanding the economy, which in turn correspond to differences in understanding the relationship between economics and the arts. In the process, we explore the epistemological role of the arts in economics in terms of treatment of a series of categorisations with respect to uncertainty/certainty, artifice/reality, processes/ends, open system/closed system and ambiguity/dualism. The last of these categorisations is critical. It reflects the mainstream economics application of the idea of separability which has impeded discussion of relations between economics and the arts. But it also requires the possibility of a non-dualistic understanding of all the categorisations noted above.

In particular, the approach which has dominated economics is based on closed-system thinking, expressed in ideal-type formal mathematical modelling, whereby science/art is just one example of many dualities or separations. But there is at the same time a range of open-system approaches to economics which develop theorising according to their particular understanding of the socio-economic system. This plurality of approaches also tends to draw on a plurality of methods, the complexity of the subject matter belying categoric demonstration of the superiority of any one approach or method. Away from a logical-positivist approach to science, open-system scientific thought is non-dualistic in general, but in particular is non-dualistic with respect to the relationship between science and the arts.

We therefore start with Adam Smith, an open-system thinker who drew connections between science and aesthetics.[3] We then consider different approaches to modern economics and end with some preliminary thoughts about the relationship between economics and the plastic arts.

Art and science in the beginnings of modern economics

The concept of aesthetics is complex. Here, aesthetics will be considered in the epistemological terms employed by Adam Smith, i.e., in terms of the aesthetic characteristics of a theoretical argument which, other things being equal, make it appealing. Aesthetics may be discussed differently with respect to a painting, or the creation of a dish, for example. But, while only scratching the surface of the subject of aesthetics, the arguments developed below will show that epistemological aesthetics may not in fact be so distinct from other types. We return to the topic in the final section.

Adam Smith emphasised the role of the human faculty of imagination in everyday life, facilitating the sympathy which plays a central role in social relations, including market relations. Imagination is also central to the role of aesthetics in scientific discourse. For Smith, in the absence of the scope for demonstrable truth, it is aesthetic, more than reasoned, judgement which guides persuasion as to the worth of any theory. Smith's (1795) approach is psychological: not only does sentiment guide the practice of science and debate over theories, but it also explains the motivation for science in the first place. It is a sense of awe, or wonder, at unexpected events which triggers the search for an explanation.

While direct knowledge is gained from experience, Smith regarded reason as insufficient for organising that direct knowledge in order to theorise about it, far less establish truth. Given the organic complexity of physical and social systems, it is beyond human capacities to identify true causal mechanisms. The best that can be done is to develop a system of thought by which to organise provisional theories. These are suggested by the application of techniques such as metaphor (e.g., theories as 'imaginary machines') to organising observations.[4] Thus, for example, Smith drew out his idea of the division of labour from detailed study of historical examples; this was Newton's experimental approach adapted to the social sciences (Dow 2009a). Indeed, Smith developed the concept of the division of labour in the economy as an analogy with his analysis of the division of labour in expertise.

Since no one theory could be demonstrated to be true, a new theory could only gain support through persuasion. Smith (1762–1763) had developed early on an epistemological theory of rhetoric which contrasted with the prevailing emphasis on rhetorical style (Dow 2009b). A new theory which explains a disturbing novel development is psychologically appealing if it accords with experience (evidence). Rhetoric should thus take account of the audience at hand: a theory is more persuasive the more it accords with the experience of a particular audience. But the other key element of persuasion is aesthetic appeal. In particular, he argued that it was more aesthetically appealing for a theory to be part of a system of thought and to draw on only a few principles.[5] Smith thus shifted the focus of aesthetics from the prevalent concern with absolutes to a focus instead on psychology.

But this did not mean subjectivism in an absolute sense. Smith saw the commonality of human nature (albeit with varying manifestations depending on context) as providing an anchor for judgement as to a theory's worth (Comim 2006). Ironically, in relation to how economics subsequently developed, Smith (1759) argued that it was easier for theories in the social sciences to be kept grounded in reality than theories in the physical sciences since for natural philosophers, the evidence was assessed within the scientific community rather than within broader society.

> Natural philosophers, in their independency upon the public opinion, approach nearly to mathematicians, and, in their judgments concerning the merit of their own discoveries and observations, enjoy some degree of the same security and tranquility.
>
> Smith (1759: III.2.20)

Aesthetic considerations could thus prevail for a long time in the physical sciences but moral philosophy (from which political economy was emerging) was different:

> A system of natural philosophy may appear very plausible, and be for a long time very generally received in the world, and yet have no foundation in nature, nor any sort of resemblance to the truth... But it is otherwise with systems of moral philosophy and an author who pretends to account for the origin of our moral sentiments, cannot deceive us so grossly, nor depart so very far from all resemblance to the truth.
>
> (Smith 1759: VII.ii.4.14)

The idea of the unity of nature was a psychologically-appealing feature of the Enlightenment philosophy of science, with the heterogeneity of experience being reduced to a few principles. But there is a substantive difference between Newtonian principles which are provisional in relation to application to different contexts on the one hand and axioms (believed to be true) on the other. As an example of the latter approach, Descartes developed astronomical principles in the French rationalist tradition, using deductive logic with scant reference to evidence. His theory held sway for around a century in spite of being unsupported by evidence. It clearly appealed on other grounds: this closed-system epistemology was not only elegant but also conveyed the reassurance of the certainty provided by classical logic. '[T]ho it does not perhaps contain a word of truth', Smith (1762–1763: 146) pronounced Descartes's theory 'one of the most entertaining Romances that has ever been wrote'.

In the very different Scottish tradition, Smith understood the subject matter (physical or social) as what we would now call an open system (Chick and Dow 2005). Such a system does not allow for axioms which can be demonstrated to be true, given the scope for evolving behaviour institutions and interactions, far less creativity. As echoed in modern neo-Austrian thought, economic growth arises, not just from the division of labour but also from application of the 'arts' (or creativity) to increase productivity. Smith (along with Hume) was actively engaged in promoting these arts through membership of the Edinburgh Society for Encouraging Arts, Sciences, Manufactures, and Agriculture in Scotland. The emphasis was on processes and institutional arrangements conducive to encouraging creativity.[6] This open subject matter required an open-system epistemology; in Smith's case, this epistemology underpinned the Scottish interpretation of Newton's experimental approach. But, as Smith (1795) set out in relation to astronomy, different systems of thought can arise, the success of each depending on powers of persuasion, with aesthetic appeal playing a powerful role.

Different modern approaches to economics

Smith's emphasis on the role of psychological appeal in theory appraisal applies to any theoretical approach and not necessarily to the advantage of Smith's own approach. It is ironic that the aesthetic considerations which played a part in Smith's system of thought, but not in rationalist thought, should have led to the relative success of the latter in the subsequent development of economics. Smith has been widely (mis)interpreted in rationalist terms, expressed in formal mathematical models depicting an equilibrating market system (see e.g., Torrance 2006). As with Descartes, these models may address real problems but do so in terms of the models' internal logic.

Thus, in the standard model which has dominated mainstream economics for the last several decades, propositions are deduced from the premise (taken to be true) that individuals are atomistic, rational and fully-informed, exercising choice in their self-interest. The outcome is a closed theoretical system with aesthetic appeal in spite of a disconnect with lived experience. Indeed, some mainstream economists liken the appeal of this system to the appeal of poetry.[7] Further, the fact that fundamental uncertainty can only feature in such a system as an exogenous shock adds to the psychological appeal by providing a reassuring sense of certainty. It must of course be noted that the lived experience of the recent financial and economic crisis, and now the health crisis, is breaking through, such that the mainstream approach has been subjected to substantial challenge. The aesthetic appeal of the standard general equilibrium system is no longer persuasive enough for many.

The traditional mainstream theoretical system presents an idealised depiction of society which inevitably has normative content (even if it is unacknowledged). But in this approach, aesthetic or any other sentiment only features in individuals' preferences, for which income is usually taken as the proxy. As a closed system, any creativity can only be treated as exogenous to the system, beyond the remit of economics. Yet, creativity is central to product development, for example, and is thus potentially disruptive of market conditions; it is also potentially disruptive of understandings. But in the mainstream approach, the growth of economic knowledge itself is not seen as disruptive but rather as incrementally revealing truth. This explains the inattention to the history of economic thought, since modern thought is presumed to reflect absorption and development of the best historical ideas (see e.g., Roncaglia 1996).

Most economists profess to be motivated by the wish to improve the human condition. Yet, in terms of transforming society, there has been a longstanding issue over the purpose of the mainstream approach to economics according to whether economic theory should be positive or normative. In particular, there has been debate as to whether it is even feasible for theory to be positive. There has been debate as to whether some philosophical stance or another, such as hedonism or utilitarianism, is implicit in mainstream theory (Drakopoulos 1991). But now the mainstream presents itself as value-free, a technical, scientific discipline – a particularly pernicious form of separability. Thus, while the purpose of economics is depicted as guiding the transformation of society through government policy, it is thought to be up to policy-makers to decide on the values to be applied.

John Neville Keynes (1891) had argued that, in addition to these two categories of positive and normative economics, there was a third, intermediate category of applied economics. This type of economics employed a plurality of 'arts' by which the conclusions of pure theory combined with a separate set of values could be applied. These arts were required to take account of the politics, institutional particularities, etc., of the specific circumstances to which the theory was to be applied. The theory itself was designed to be universal, context-free. Colander (1992) has promoted J N Keynes's argument in modern times for developing expertise in these arts, given the limitations of formal mainstream theory.[8] But according to him the primacy, and separability of mainstream theory itself, is not open for debate.

Yet, the 'arts' Colander advocates are in fact what non-mainstream economists think of as economics (or, to distinguish it from mainstream economics, political economy). According to this alternative approach, theory itself should be designed specifically to address real problems in particular contexts, drawing on a range of types of argument and different cognate disciplines. General principles may arise from theorising but need to be examined for relevance and for scope for adaptation to particular circumstances. Applicability is prioritised over achieving the type of certainty and universality which closed-system formal theorising produces – even though that may, in itself, be more aesthetically appealing in an epistemic sense. In Smith's terms, evident connection between theory and lived experience can trump aesthetics.

Mainstream theory faced just such a challenge in the wake of the financial and economic crisis. The logic of the mainstream approach is that the ideal model generates the socially-optimal outcome. So, any problem almost by definition must be explained in terms of some deviation from the model. Either some adaptation to the model is needed or policy is required to correct the deviation. Since the starting point was theory focused on equilibrium, the crisis was understood in terms of deviations from equilibrium. Since free market forces were normally relied upon to ensure equilibrium, the deviations were understood in terms of impediments to free market forces. Thus, the financial crisis has been explained variously as the outcome of behaviour which was not fully rational, of incomplete information or of institutional impediments to market forces. Thus, since the crisis, policies have been introduced to nudge people into being more rational, information transparency has been encouraged, and market imperfections (such as central bank support for failing banks) challenged.

Encouraging the greater exercise of rationality is particularly significant in that the mainstream notion of rationality is very specific, in particular by its own logic ruling out fundamental uncertainty and all that that implies. In the face of evident uncertainty in real life, attention to the topic has increased within mainstream economics. But since the starting point is a model based on an understanding of the subject matter as a closed system, all elements of the system are thought to be knowable and expectations can be generated with confidence by extrapolation from existing relationships. Thus, uncertainty has been analysed as 'ambiguity', whereby future outcomes are knowable but not yet known, or 'unawareness', whereby the full range of possible future states is not yet known. This approach differs fundamentally from the non-mainstream analysis of uncertainty as the norm rather than the exception within an open system where relationships are complex and evolving, where creative behaviour by definition introduces unforeseen states, and where the past provides a very imperfect guide to the future (Dow 2016). The evolution of behaviour and institutions in turn responds in order for uncertainty not (normally) to cripple decision-making.

The basis of the mainstream approach is Classical logic, requiring axioms known to be true, from which propositions are deduced. This contrasts with the 'human logic' of the non-mainstream approach, whereby multiple strands of argument contribute to conclusions held with uncertainty. If the real world is not like the ideal world of the model where there is no uncertainty in the non-mainstream sense, then the policy application of mainstream economics may alter behaviour and institutions in a counter-productive way.

In the mainstream approach, rationality is thought to be served, for example, by better-quality information, implying greater transparency. Yet, as the crisis demonstrated, market economies rely substantially on trust in institutions and the agency of policy-makers. Thus, although the inflation rate is central to mainstream macroeconomic theory and the operation of financial markets, society in general may operate better without a focus on the precise rate of inflation – or inflation at all. Similarly, while the focus of the banking literature post-crisis has been on improved public knowledge of bank portfolios, the banking system may perform its functions better if customers trust the authorities to regulate, monitor and supervise banks effectively. Indeed, what is identified in mainstream theory as a market imperfection relative to the model (as in the case of central bank support for banks) may in reality be one of the many institutional arrangements which *facilitate* markets.

But the mainstream has been able to exercise rhetorical power on the strength of their (contestable) claims to superior science, such that the conceptual constructions associated with a particular modelling strategy were widely accepted without question, at least until the crisis. Attention has been drawn to the rhetoric of mainstream economics by the modern rhetoric literature spearheaded by McCloskey (1985), a development which coincided with the emergence of postmodernism in economics. The mainstream was presented as a modernist project; the characteristics of modernism and postmodernism were compared in dualistic fashion. Since this discourse had first arisen in the arts, notably literature, architecture and painting, Klamer (1995) drew parallels between these disciplines and economics in order to explain the conceptual framework.

But ironically, by apparently abandoning the study of methodology, the rhetoric approach, particularly in its postmodern form, carried forward a (modernist) dualism. This approach therefore differed from the Smithian approach. Where Smith had seen real experience as an anchor for subjective judgement under uncertainty about the worth of theories, postmodernism and the rhetoric approach emphasised the subjectivity of understanding of experience and thus of judgment (see e.g., Peter 2001). However, the bulk of non-mainstream analysis is realist (in the Scottish Enlightenment sense, which has much in common with critical realism; see Dow 2002). From a realist perspective, a dualistic form of postmodernism cast rhetoric adrift from reality.

While mainstream economics has maintained a science/arts duality, the universal rationalist account of economic science cannot reasonably be sustained. A discourse analysis of mainstream economics reveals the arts employed, even before policy application, to persuade that one mainstream theory is to be preferred to another. It has been documented in the modern rhetoric literature that internal classical logic is insufficient for persuasion – other than the reflexive persuasiveness of being 'scientific'. This echoes the view from neuroscience that individuals cannot function – particularly make the choices which are at the core of mainstream models – by reason alone. The apparent failure of the Hilbert programme in the first half of the 20th century demonstrates the impossibility of setting up a complete, consistent axiomatic system – some non-formal input or other is necessary.[9] Models themselves have been shown to play a non-formal role, as narrative mechanisms.

So, we have the anomalous situation where mainstream economists use discursive devices to convey the notion (which is generally asserted rather than discussed) that their theoretical approach is scientific in the sense of logical positivist, value-free, for universal application. This narrative of drawing on rhetorical devices extends to the presentation of particular theoretical arguments, e.g. in favour of fiscal austerity (Dow 2015). Much of the persuasiveness of this theory rests on the false analogy drawn between the state and the household. These devices (arts) have been extended to analysis of (individual or collective) behaviour, with some highlighting the role of narrative in the economy itself (Shiller 2019). For example, narrative is a persuasive device in financial markets, where the absence of closed-system quantifiable risk has particular force, challenging mainstream ideas of demonstrative rationality (Tuckett and Nicolic 2017).

Once we broach the possibility of creativity, and of performativity, we are inevitably beyond the bounds of the mainstream approach, and into the realms of open-system reality and thinking, and of pluralism in the sense of a variety of approaches to building knowledge. Different understandings of a fragmented reality foster different epistemologies, i.e. different ways of developing and expressing knowledge about that reality using different methods, different concepts and different language, all of which makes them incommensurate. There is a common understanding outside the mainstream that no one account can be complete. Different ideas therefore emerge about economics as a vehicle for transforming society, ranging from a neo-Austrian clearing of the ground for entrepreneurial creativity, to an institutionalist focus on the preferred direction for the evolution of institutions, to a Marxian focus on creating conditions for the emergence of socialism.

Dualism and economics and the plastic arts

The pluralism of non-mainstream economics contrasts with mainstream dualism. It is this dualistic cast of mind which encourages the dichotomisation of science/non-science, sciences/arts, objective/subjective and so on. These different modes of thought (some forms of pluralism on the one hand and dualism on the other) are evident in other fields, including the arts themselves. The mainstream form of transforming society is to intervene in order to mould behaviour to conform to a rational-individualistic-fully-informed ideal, as expressed in the closed system of mainstream theorising. This might be seen as similar to an exercise in plastic arts in the narrow sense of moulding reality (in the form of clay or stone, for example) in an 'enclosed' way. Indeed, some of the literature implies a correspondence between plastic arts and the rationalist form of Enlightenment (which differs from the Scottish Enlightenment epitomised by Smith and Hume).

But this discussion itself can fall prey to undue dualism, for example contrasting objective rationalism with subjective romanticism, or with an extreme form of constructivism. Categorisation of some sort is necessary for knowledge and communication. But there is an important difference between all-encompassing, mutually-exclusive categories with fixed meaning (dualism) and categorisation according to distinctions which are partial, porous and provisional (ambiguity or non-dualism).[10] Contrasting closed systems with open systems is dualistic from a dualistic perspective but not from an open-system perspective. According to the latter, the distinction does not involve dualism because there are multiple possibilities for open systems, depending on which of the conditions for a closed system are not satisfied (Chick and Dow 2005).

Further, non-mainstream economics does not accept an objective/subjective duality. While open-system approaches do adopt different perspectives on reality, they have in common a degree of realism. Therefore, while not adopting an objectivist logical-positivist approach, non-mainstream economics is not purely subjective, just as art cannot be detached from some real experience or other. Put another way, economics is no more a pure construction than art is a pure construction. Each starts from some understanding of some element of real experience, which is constructed only to some degree. Thus, for example, the real experience of the crisis and its fall-out broke through society's passive acceptance of mainstream constructions.

Yet, economics and the arts in turn contribute to constructions of reality – each is performative. And each challenges existing constructions, encouraging re-imaginings to address new realities. For example, the financial crisis challenged the ruling narratives in the financial sector, requiring new narratives to be constructed. Similarly, Banksy's self-destructive piece of art challenged conceptualisations in the art market.[11] Taking a broad, non-dualistic understanding of the plastic arts as applicable to open systems, non-mainstream views of transforming society may therefore also be likened to the exercise of the plastic arts. But, if similarity to the plastic arts in the mainstream approach to transforming society implies some superficiality, the grounding of non-mainstream approaches in realism suggests otherwise.

Conclusion

If the goal of economics is to transform society, then it is important to understand the role of the arts, not only in society but also in our knowledge of it. We have explored here how an open-system understanding of the real world exposes the inevitability of knowledge limitations and thus the need to develop ways of building beliefs about the real world which are sufficiently grounded in experience to justify transformative action. An organicist ontology warrants an organicist epistemology which belies the strict separabilities of closed-system mainstream thought. In particular, it belies the mainstream separation between science and the arts.

Avoiding strict separation however does not mean an end to categorisation. Indeed, knowledge and communication would be impossible without it. Even with different meanings, words themselves are an open-system form of categorisation without which communication could not begin. Yet, as Keynes argued, the element of vagueness involved in verbal categorisations actually facilitates communication between those who apply somewhat different meanings (Coates 1997). At the level of theory, some boundaries are necessary, even if, as in an open system, they are provisional and porous (Chick and Dow 2005). Indeed, the whole notion of a theoretical system is impossible without such boundaries (Potts 2000).

Which brings us back to aesthetics and their role in knowledge about the economy. The discussion, particularly of Smith, may seem to imply that aesthetics are a separable factor in persuasion, along with real experience. In order to clarify the difference from mainstream views of scientific knowledge, this separating off of aesthetics as an important factor serves a valuable purpose. But, from an open-system perspective, the boundary drawn here around epistemological aesthetics is provisional and porous. It is not absolute. What has been argued here is that the arts are integral to economic knowledge. We use categories, such as 'the arts', in order to make such an argument. But the integration of the arts within economic knowledge means that the interconnections are important.

In Smith's terms, what is it about the aesthetics of modern mainstream economic theory that has appealed to economists and to the users of economics? Is the appeal of the idea of the unity of nature and thus the feasibility of universal theory aesthetic – or is it philosophical, for example? Is it because of the aesthetic appeal of a closed axiomatic theoretical system that some form of rationality axioms still hold such influence, even if cloaked by the growth of applied economics within the mainstream? Or is the continuing dominance of this approach now primarily a matter of power relations?

But, as real experience throws up huge economic problems crying out for solutions, is the criterion of usefulness in relation to real experience gradually trumping the aesthetic appeal of closed-system theorising? But what of the aesthetic appeal of open-system theorising? Just as we differ in aesthetic taste between different styles of painting, for example, do we differ in aesthetic taste between different styles of economic reasoning? Whatever the answer as to the nature and role of aesthetics, it cannot reasonably be separated from our understanding of economics and its relations with the economy and with the arts.

Notes

1 Alan Peacock was a pioneer in the economics of the arts (see e.g., Peacock (1993). The growth of cultural economics as an area of study is evident from the reach of Towse and Navarrete Hernandez, eds (2020).

2 There are exceptions within political economy, see e.g., Bakhshi, Freeman and Desai (2010).
3 An alternative starting-point would have been Keynes, also a notably open-systems thinker for whom aesthetics were important (Dostaler 2010). Unlike Smith, he engaged substantially with artists and the arts which, among other factors, had a significant impact on his epistemology (Dostaler 2007). However, we focus instead on Smith since the connection between his aesthetics and his epistemology is more explicit.
4 See Venkatachalam (Chapter 6, this volume) on models as metaphors and analogues dealing in approximations.
5 See Skinner (1996) on Smith's systems approach to the social sciences.
6 For example, Hume's analysis of the effects of a rise in the money supply focuses on processes which ensue to enhance activity and productivity; this contrasts sharply with the mainstream representation of Hume as introducing the idea of a direct causal link between the money supply and inflation (Dow 2009c).
7 This observation is difficult to reference since it is antithetical to the official discourse of mainstream economics. It emerges rather in the unofficial discourse of private conversation with mainstream economists who express the purpose of theory in aesthetic terms rather than in terms of usefulness. On a personal note, I chose to pursue a joint first degree in pure mathematics and political economy specifically because of their differing appeals in terms of aesthetics and usefulness.
8 He has built up a substantial body of work around this argument (Colander and Huei-Chun 2018).
9 This is an interpretation of the Hilbert programme which is influenced by Godel's incompleteness theorem; see Weintraub (2002: ch. 3) for a discussion of a range of interpretations.
10 The term 'ambiguity' is itself ambiguous, having been adopted in the mainstream literature as an alternative to 'uncertainty' in the limited sense of concealed knowledge (Dow 2016).
11 https://www.smithsonianmag.com/smart-news/watch-14-million-bansky-painting-shred-itself-soon-it-sold-180970486/

References

Bakhshi, H, A Freeman and R Desai (2010) 'Not Rocket Science: A Roadmap for Arts and Cultural R&D', *MPRA Working Paper* No. 52710, University Library of Munich, https://ideas.repec.org/p/pra/mprapa/52710.html, accessed 28 July 2020.

Chick, C and S C Dow (2005) 'The Meaning of Open Systems', *Journal of Economic Methodology*, 12(3): 363–381. reprinted in S C Dow (2012) *Foundations for New Economic Thinking*. London: Palgrave Macmillan.

Coates, J (1997) 'Keynes, Vague Concepts and Fuzzy Logic', in G C Harcourt and P A Riach (eds), *A 'Second Edition' of the General Theory*, vol. 2. London: Routledge.

Colander, D C (1992) 'The Lost Art of Economics', *Journal of Economic Perspectives*, 6(3): 191–198.

Colander, D C and Huei-Chun, S (2018) *How Economics Should Be Done: Essays on the Art and Craft of Economics*. Cheltenham: Edward Elgar.

Comim, F (2006) 'Adam Smith: Common Sense and Aesthetics in the Age of Experiments', in A Dow and S Dow (eds), *The History of Scottish Economic Thought*. London: Routledge, pp. 123–145.

Dostaler, G (2007) *Keynes and His Battles*. Cheltenham: Edward Elgar.

Dostaler, G (2010) 'Keynes, Art and Aesthetics', in R W Dimand, R A Mundell and A Vercelli (eds), *Keynes's General Theory After Seventy Years*. International Economic Association Series. London: Palgrave Macmillan.
Dow, S C (2002) 'Historical Reference: Hume and Critical Realism', *Cambridge Journal of Economics*, 26(6): 683–697.
Dow, S C (2009a) 'Smith's Philosophy and Economic Methodology', in J T eYoung (ed.), *The Elgar Companion to Adam Smith*. Cheltenham: Edward Elgar, pp. 100–111.
Dow, S C (2009b) 'Knowledge, Communication and the Scottish Enlightenment', *Revue de Philosophie Economique/Review of Philosophical Economics*, 10(2): 3–23.
Dow, S C (2009c) 'David Hume and Modern Economics', *Capitalism and Society*, 4(1), Article 1.
Dow, S C (2015) 'The Role of Belief in the Case for Austerity Policies', *Economic and Labour Relations Review* 26(March) 2015: 29–42.
Dow, S C (2016) 'Uncertainty: A Diagrammatic Treatment', *Economics: The Open-Access, Open-Assessment E-Journal*, 10(2016–3): 1–25.
Drakopoulos, S A (1991) *Values and Economic Theory*. Aldershot: Avebury.
Keynes, J N ([1891] 1955) *The Scope and Method of Political Economy*, 4th edition. New York: Kelley and Millman, Inc.
Klamer, A (1995) in S C Dow and J Hillard (eds), *Keynes, Knowledge and Uncertainty*. Cheltenham: Edward Elgar.
McCloskey, D N (1985) *The Rhetoric of Economics*. Madison: University of Wisconsin Press
Peacock, A. (1993). *Paying the Piper: Culture, Music, Money*. Edinburgh: Edinburgh University Press.
Peter, F (2001) 'Rhetoric vs Realism in Economic Methodology: A Critical Assessment of Recent Contributions', *Cambridge Journal of Economics*, 25(5): 571–589.
Potts, J (2000) *The New Evolutionary Microeconomics: Complexity, Competence and Adaptive Behaviour*. Cheltenham: Edward Elgar.
Roncaglia, A (1996) Why Should Economists Study the History of Economic Thought?. *European Journal of the History of Economic Thought*, 3: 296–309.
Shiller, R (2019) *Narrative Economics*. Princeton: Princeton University Press.
Skinner, A. S. (1996) *A System of Social Science: Papers Relating to Adam Smith*. Oxford: Oxford University Press.
Smith, A (1759, 1976) *The Theory of Moral Sentiments*, Glasgow edition, ed. by D D Raphael and A Macfie. Oxford: Oxford University Press.
Smith, A ([1762–1763] 1983) *Lectures on Rhetoric and Belles Lettres*, ed. by J C Bryce. Oxford: Oxford University Press
Smith, A ([1795] 1980) 'The History of Astronomy', in W L D Wightman (ed.), *Essays on Philosophical Subjects*. Oxford: Oxford University Press.
Torrance, T (2006) 'James Mill as Economist: Theory Dominated by Deductive Method', in A Dow and S Dow (eds), *The History of Scottish Economic Thought*. London: Routledge, pp. 146–162.
Towse, R and T Navarrete Hernandez (eds) (2020) *Handbook of Cultural Economics* (3rd edition) Cheltenham: Edward Elgar.
Tuckett, D and M Nicolic (2017) 'The Role of Conviction and Narrative in Decision-Making Under Radical Uncertainty', *Theory and Psychology*, 27(4): 501–523.
Weintraub, E R (2002) *How Economics Became a Mathematical Science*. Durham, NC: Duke University Press.

Index

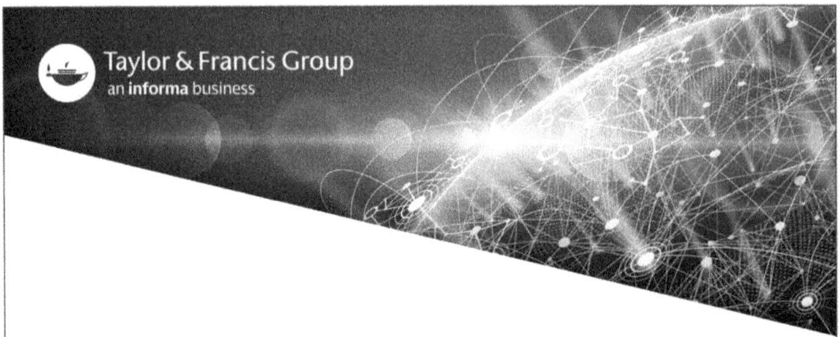
Taylor & Francis Group
an informa business

For Product Safety Concerns and Information please contact our EU representative GPSR@taylorandfrancis.com
Taylor & Francis Verlag GmbH, Kaufingerstraße 24, 80331 München, Germany

www.ingramcontent.com/pod-product-compliance
Ingram Content Group UK Ltd.
Pitfield, Milton Keynes, MK11 3LW, UK
UKHW020007200926
475702UK00015B/2526
* 9 7 8 0 3 6 7 6 1 5 4 1 3 *